John Muir

John Muir

The Scotsman who saved America's wild places

MARY COLWELL

LION

Published by Lion Books
an imprint of
Lion Hudson plc
Wilkinson House, Jordan Hill Road,
Oxford OX2 8DR, England
www.lionhudson.com/lion

ISBN 978 0 7459 5666 4
e-ISBN 978 0 7459 5667 1

First edition 2014

A catalogue record for this book is available from the
British Library

Printed and bound in the UK, October 2014, LH26

*For my wonderful dad who treasured the
ordinary and marvelled at the spectacular,
22 October 1932 – 20 March 2013.*

Contents

Acknowledgments

Thanks are due to my husband and sons for putting up with my writing when I could have been sailing and cycling, to Chris Boles who shares my passion for John Muir, and to Peter France, my encourager, critic, and friend for many years.

Foreword

John Muir's name is rarely included in the pantheon of "greats" as far as most environmentalists are concerned. Unlike Rachel Carson, often top of the list, especially in the USA, or Fritz Schumacher, always in there somewhere. Despite being seen by many as "the founding father of conservation", name-checking John Muir here in the UK would excite little interest, let alone enthusiasm among those in today's loosely-defined green movement, let alone those outside it.

As a relatively new admirer (having stumbled across the Muir Woods National Monument on a visit to San Francisco a decade or so ago), Mary Colwell sets out to explore that conundrum. And there's absolutely no doubt that John Muir was indeed a quite extraordinary man. Equally, there's no doubt that the author eloquently captures what it was that made him so special "as a naturalist, pioneering explorer, botanist, glaciologist, mystic, writer and activist."

And part of this extraordinary life is that he lived through extraordinary times. Arriving in the USA in 1849 (after 11 years growing up in Dunbar in Scotland), he died there 65 years later in 1914 – a period of unparalleled growth in the US in terms of population, industrialisation, growth, and environmental devastation.

Muir's response to that growth and destruction was fascinating. It wasn't until the 1890s that he took on the campaigning role for which this "founding father" is now revered. In that role, he was one of the founders (in 1892) and the first President of the Sierra

Club, still one of America's most admired and influential NGOs today. Before that, for 30 years, he was a traveller (early in his life, as the author puts it, "he was more like a cork bobbing on an ocean rather than a man with a mission to fulfil"), a reveller in and devotee of nature ("wilderness pumped through John's veins"), a farmer (though more out of family duty than out of any natural calling) and, above all, a writer.

It took him a while to realise that this was his real calling – there were many points in his life where it was his friends and mentors that had to urge him to focus more purposefully on his writing. His style was lyrical and deeply spiritual ("he wrote like a preacher, but his congregation was as yet undefined"). His description of the sequoia forests of California as "God's first temples" is indicative of the kind of panentheism that sustained him throughout his life – not so much worshipping nature in itself as worshipping God in every nook and cranny of nature. And no other author had quite the impact on gathering environmental sensibilities than he did.

> He had the ability to reach through the page, take the reader by the hand, and guide them to singing streams, towering trees, intimate conversations with wildlife, and ranges of mountains so beautiful they made him fall on his knees in prayer. He was the voice of the wild, and the tip of his quill glowed with divine love.

One of Mary Colwell's recurring questions is this: "Who has taken up that baton?" On the literary side of things, that's a hard question to answer, not least because that kind of Wordsworthian lyricism (in poetry or prose) is so deeply out of fashion. For instance, the writer Alastair McIntosh (brought up on the Isle of Lewis) would undoubtedly be counted as one of today's most influential writers on the relationship between humankind and the natural world, but his style is so much more economic, so much terser.

It's no accident that Alastair McIntosh draws so heavily on the residual fragments of wilderness to be found in Scotland. You won't find such wilderness elsewhere in the UK, and it's disappearing fast

. . literally every corner of the world. Contemporary campaigners may still romanticise about the wild, but it has less and less authentic resonance these days, let alone the kind of real, emotional power that it did in the nineteenth century.

Which is why John Muir will be seen by many as an improbable role model for today's environmental battles, let alone as "the hero the world is searching for to help guide us into the future". Though most environmentalists will wholeheartedly endorse Muir's belief that today's environmental destruction can only be stopped if people "learn to love and respect the land", and would share his sorrow that people's souls are being filled with the crass trappings of consumerism rather than with beauty and truth, the unattainable purity of his "Earth first" credo has not aged well.

As is borne out by the fact that the philosophical approach of his constant antagonist and personal nemesis – Gifford Pinchot – has fared much better. Pinchot's "Wise Use movement" – the forerunner of concepts like "sustainable yield management" and sustainable development more broadly – is the dominant leitmotif in today's environmental debates.

Just compare Gifford Pinchot and John Muir as they fought it out hammer and tongs, between 1908 and 1913, over the campaign to stop the Hetch Hetchy Valley being turned into a vast reservoir to provide the burgeoning population of San Francisco with the water it so badly needed even then. Pinchot first:

> The object of our forest policy is not to preserve the forests because they're beautiful or wild or the habitat of wild animals; it is to ensure a steady supply of timber for human prosperity. Every other consideration is secondary.

And then John Muir:

> These temple destroyers, devotees of raging commercialism, seem to have a perfect contempt for Nature, and, instead of lifting their eyes to the God of the mountains, lift them to the Almighty Dollar. Dam

Hetch Hetchy! As well dam for water-tanks the people's cathedrals and churches, for no holier temple has ever been consecrated by the heart of man.

Muir lost; Pinchot won. The pristine wilderness of Hetch Hetchy was duly and irreversibly "desecrated". One hundred years on, the fact that Hetch Hetchy's water still sustains San Francisco through the duration of the current – and ever-worsening – drought across the state of California reveals just how far beyond "nature's limits" our industrialised, consumptive way of life has taken us.

And that's Mary Colwell's most profound challenge to her readers. Could it be that decades of diligently seeking some accommodation, between, on the one hand, humankind's boundless needs and aspirations, and, on the other, nature's bounded resources and fragile integrity, should now be seen as a worthy but ultimately forlorn failure? Should we be giving up on today's dominant pragmatism – and reinventing instead Muir's uncompromising defence of (what's still left of) the natural world?

For me, personally, that's never likely to be the conclusion I'll come to. But John Muir's life and work have been important to me for a long time. At different points, they've provided both a "reality check" on the compromises I make every day in the name of sustainable development, and at other times a licence to allow his kind of panentheistic spirituality to keep my heart and soul anchored in a different kind of reality.

Jonathon Porritt
August 2014

Jonathon Porritt is Founder Director of Forum for the Future www.forumforthefuture.org.

His latest book, *The World We Made* (£24.95, Phaidon) is available from www.phaidon.com/store

Introduction

"To live in hearts we leave behind is not to die."

Thomas Campbell, "Hallowed Ground"

The best way to think of John Muir is to imagine a Scottish combination of the wildlife broadcaster Sir David Attenborough, the wilderness explorer Bear Grylls, the environmental theologian Pierre Teilhard de Chardin, and the animation characters Wallace and Gromit. To this eclectic mix add a very large dose of good humour and simple, honest kindliness, and John Muir begins to emerge – a giant of the past and perhaps the hero the world is searching for to help guide us into the future.

In his lifetime, John Muir inspired millions to cherish nature, much as Sir David does today. He was similar to Bear Grylls in that he was a hard-muscled, rugged wilderness man who survived alone for weeks on end on iron rations – in his case a loaf of bread, a packet of tea, and a copy of the poetry of Robert Burns. John Muir's intensely spiritual relationship with the natural world aligns him to Fr Pierre Teilhard de Chardin, a mystic who saw the universe as an ever-evolving expression of God. His similarity to Wallace and Gromit is not physical but due to his extraordinary handmade inventions that astonished those who saw them in action.

I first came across John Muir in the early 2000s on a work trip to California. Driving down Highway 1, just a few miles outside San Francisco, I saw a sign pointing to Muir Woods National Monument. With a few hours to spare, I pulled off on a whim and found myself lifted out of the sunshine busyness of modern American life into a cathedral of giant trees. At the entrance a plaque quoted Muir:

"In every walk with nature, one receives far more than one seeks."[1] I had never heard of John Muir, but I liked the sentiment. As I wandered the over-manicured walkways, the air gently quivered with birdsong and the breeze was calm and respectful.

The same quote is repeated at the beginning of a section of the park called Cathedral Grove. It also asks visitors to "Enter Quietly", and goes on to say:

> Cathedral Grove was set aside as a quiet refuge to protect its natural soundscape in an increasingly noisy world... By walking quietly, we experience the natural sounds of a living, ancient forest. We hope you enjoy the beauty of Muir Woods through both sight and sound.

As I explored Cathedral Grove and marvelled at the magnificence of the trees, I felt I was not alone. Drifting among the giant redwoods like an invisible mist was the ghost of John Muir. This forest is dedicated to him in recognition of his extraordinary contribution to nature and his passion for all wild places. After returning to the car I bought every book about him that I could afford, and my journey with Muir began.

This visit to Muir Woods was a tame introduction to the founding father of conservation – one of the most rugged, exciting, and humane champions of the natural world that has ever lived. For me, it was the start of a journey of discovery that was, and still is, exhilarating and emotional. Muir has now been dead for a century yet his words are fresh and personal. It is as though I am walking a mountain trail and John Muir has left his journals by the wayside for me to read, and he is just ahead out of sight. They could have been written last week, as their message of passion, fun, and forgiveness soothes the anxiety of living in today's broken world as much as it helped those troubled by the destruction of nature 150 years ago.

> Walk away quietly in any direction and taste the freedom of the mountaineer. Camp out among the grass and gentians of glacier

meadows, in craggy garden nooks full of Nature's darlings. Climb the mountains and get their good tidings. Nature's peace will flow into you as sunshine flows into trees. The winds will blow their own freshness into you, and the storms their energy, while cares will drop off like autumn leaves.[2]

His words are infused with joy, bringing wildlife and wilderness together in a disarmingly simple way. I was enchanted by his essay "The Water Ouzel" (or American Dipper, as it is known today). Now recognized as a seminal piece of nature writing, it captures the spark that ignited his whole life – his love of all things wild.

Here is the mountain streams' little darling, the hummingbird of the blooming waters, loving rocky-ripple slopes and sheets of foam as a bee loves flowers, as a lark loves sunshine and meadows. Among all the mountain birds none has cheered me so much in my lonely wanderings – none so unfailingly. For both in winter and summer he sings sweetly, cheerily, independent alike of sunshine and love, requiring no other inspiration than the stream on which he dwells.[3]

John Muir's writings do more than describe wildlife, though; they make us all friends. Landscapes too, either bathed in sunshine or softened by snow, beckon us to explore. This earth is our home, says Muir, there to be loved by all and open to all. It is hard for us today to appreciate the impact of these sentiments. In his time the natural world was something to be either feared or conquered. He smashed apart that notion and presented his readers with a vision of nature that was warm and irresistible. It was revolutionary.

He felt, however, that no words could ever capture the essence of wilderness, any more than a description of a glass of water will relieve a raging thirst. He knew that the solution to the ills of America was reconnecting people with nature. At the end of the Water Ouzel article he urges:

And so might I go on writing words, words, words, but to what purpose? Go see him and love him, and through him as through a window look into Nature's warm heart.[4]

It is undeniably true that in the nineteenth century others wrote beautifully about nature, climbed mountains, and urged for environmental protection. For me, though, John Muir's unique gift was to effortlessly intertwine a deep and personal spirituality without ever straying into preaching. He didn't place humanity in a separate box and apart from the natural world, but held a more contemporary view that all of life is interrelated. "One fancies a heart like our own must be beating in every crystal and cell,"[5] he wrote. "No wonder when we all have the same Father and Mother."[6] John Muir's spirituality was earthed and this added dimension seasoned his life and writings with gladness.

It is therefore hard to sum up John Muir. He defies categories and seems to inhabit many different spaces with equal integrity. He was both a solitary wilderness man and a dinner-party raconteur. He was a man's man yet his closest friends and confidantes were women. He was as rugged as they come yet unashamed of his emotions. He was a man of God but not of the traditional Church. In a way that only the truly authentic can, he touched many people's lives and his personal and direct approach still resonates today.

John Muir is little known outside America; he is Britain's best-kept secret. Whenever I meet someone who has never heard of him I admit to feelings of envy. Ahead lies a wealth of beautiful and inspiring literature. To discover John Muir is to discover a wise, fun-loving friend. We should treasure him, rediscover his wisdom, and carry on the work he began in the nineteenth century, bringing his passion for wildlife and wild places into the twenty-first century and beyond. As we search for today's inspirational environmental leader, perhaps we could do no better than look back to John Muir.

All the wild world is beautiful, and it matters but little where we go, to highlands or lowlands, woods or plains, on the sea or land or down among the crystals of waves or high in a balloon in the sky; through all the climates, hot or cold, storms and calms, everywhere and always we are in God's eternal beauty and love. So universally true is this, the spot where we chance to be always seems the best.[7]

Chapter 1

Dunbar Boy

*"All nature has a feeling: woods, fields, brooks
Are life eternal: and in silence they
Speak happiness beyond the reach of books."*

John Clare, "All Nature has a Feeling"

Standing at the top of Dunbar High Street is a statue of a boy, one arm leaning on a crooked walking stick, the other stretching upwards towards three birds that are flying away on the wind. His trousers and coat are ragged, as though torn by scrambling over rocks and brambles. The birds form a streamer above the boy's head; they fly up towards freedom, to live their wild lives over the fields and shores of eastern Scotland. It is hard to read the look on the boy's face; it seems wise beyond his years. He is not whooping with joy, or laughing out loud: his expression is more restrained as though his thoughts run deep as he savours this contact with nature.

On the plinth of the statue is a quote, written by the boy years later in a journal:

As long as I live, I'll hear waterfalls and birds and winds sing. I'll interpret the rocks, learn the language of flood, storm, and the avalanche. I'll acquaint myself with the glaciers and wild gardens, and get as near the heart of the world as I can.[1]

Indeed he will do just that. This is John Muir, naturalist, pioneering explorer, botanist, glaciologist, mystic, writer, and activist. He will grow up to inspire the president of America to protect large areas of wilderness and leave a legacy of national parks, forest reserves, and wildlife refuges that remain sanctuaries to this day. He will forge a new paradigm for humanity's relationship with the natural world and express it in a new genre of nature writing. He will contribute to science by journeying to the tops of the tallest mountains and into the very heart of glaciers to change the understanding of ice ages. He will found one of the oldest and most successful conservation organizations in the United States, the Sierra Club. Most of all he will be the people's nature prophet, kindling a fire for the protection for all wild things, animate and inanimate. But all that is to come. For now the statue depicts a typical boy growing up in the first half of the nineteenth century in an industrious part of lowland Scotland.

It would be tempting to imagine a wilderness pioneer emerging from the Highlands of Scotland, soaked in the mist of legend and heather clad mountain, but the truth is more prosaic. Although he was to become the embodiment of the wilderness, John Muir's first eleven years were lived amid trade and agriculture. Dunbar was then an important coastal market town with one of the most strategic and sheltered ports in Scotland. It lies twenty-eight miles east of Edinburgh, where the fertile plains meet the sea. It was respectable, hard-working, and a perfect example of commercial endeavour underpinned by a strong Christian ethic. The brooding remains of a medieval castle, which still towers above the harbour walls, served as a constant reminder of the sacrifices of the citizens of Dunbar who were part of the fierce and proud history of Scotland.

The streets of the main town were orderly and wide, the solidly built houses were modest. Butchers, bakers, milliners, shoemakers, and furniture manufacturers sold local and imported goods. The local churches dominated the culture, reminding residents of the requirement to lead sober lives underpinned by hard work. Down by the water, however, the fishermen and visiting sailors created a more cluttered, seedier atmosphere, with plenty of pubs.

The North Sea brought an abundance of fish. When herring ran down the coastline in their millions in late summer they attracted boats from far and wide and a good living for the fishing community. The gutted herring were packed in barrels of brine to be sent off to the West Indies, Ireland, and the main ports of Europe. In the winter the fishermen went after cod, whiting, crabs, and lobsters. When John was not fighting imaginary battles between the Scots and the English with his schoolfriends on the seashore, no doubt inspired by the castle, he might have watched the small boats being hauled up the beach laden with fish.

The early nineteenth century saw the fastest growth in the fishing industry along the east coast of Scotland. In 1842 Dunbar received a grant to build a large new port, Victoria Harbour, which was opened with great expectations. The town could now safely shelter up to 800 vessels and fish could be loaded straight onto the dock rather than the beach. John was just four years old when the Masonic procession led the way to the laying of the foundation stone. Perhaps he was taken to see the pomp and ceremony, witnessing first-hand the relentless growth of Victorian Scotland.

It must have been constantly busy down by the old Cromwell Harbour in early days. The sharp smell of sea air mingled with the odour of fish, giving a tangy and vital scent to the air. The harsh cries of gulls soaring overhead or squabbling over discards competed with the busyness of harbour life. The chattering of fishwives, shouts of fishermen, clattering of boats, haggling of traders, and exotic languages of foreign sailors produced a loud and at times fractious underscore to daily life. This intoxicating blend was carried on the blustery wind and it filled John's young senses. Many years later these memories would suddenly resurface, brought to life by the smell of the ocean, amid the stifling heat and humidity of Florida. They brought a yearning for Scotland's air: cold, fresh, invigorating.

The Muir's fortunes, however, were not tied to the vagaries of the sea but rested on the less wild, more predictable grain trade. The fertile fields of south-east Scotland were the country's grain basket. The soil was formed from clay-rich, glacial earth left behind after the last ice age ended 10,000 years earlier. It is fitting to think that the mind of a prominent glaciologist was nurtured on what remained of the work of ice, a subject he would be fascinated by for most of his life, but which would pitch him into ideological battles with his father.

The coastal location of Dunbar provides relatively warm, wet winters and sunny summers. This happy combination of soils and climate produces a large tonnage of crops. The wheat, barley, and oats were stored in granaries and then shipped to the world. The railway was built in 1846, and, as steam power replaced muscle and wind, trade boomed even more. The traders and merchants reaped the benefits. Fish and grain were the bedrock of the town, and as both were in high demand in the burgeoning economies of Europe and North America, this small East Lothian town of just a few thousand souls was well placed to bring prosperity to many. In the early nineteenth century Dunbar was riding the crest of a commercial wave.

It was into this booming yet restrictive Victorian environment that the inspirational father of the conservation movement and lover of the wilderness was born on 21 April 1838. John Muir was the third of eight children of Daniel Muir and Ann Gilrye and their home was on the High Street, away from the more raucous influences of the fisherfolk.

Daniel Muir was a fascinating Dickensian character. He had been born in Manchester in 1804 but orphaned in his first year of life. He and his sister, Mary, were brought up by relatives in Lanarkshire and worked on the land. His education was minimal and he was mainly self-taught. By all accounts he was handsome and lively, a boy who loved sport, carving wood and playing the fiddle. In fact, his musical and woodworking skills allowed him to design and construct his own violin. A popular story tells of his running ten miles in the dark to the nearest village to buy strings. He was also a fine singer, and John was to comment later, "My first conscious memory is of the singing of ballads, and I doubt not they will be ringing in my ears when I am dying."[2]

Daniel left the countryside as a teenager to head for Glasgow with just a few shillings in his pocket. He joined many others looking for work but the desperate conditions of the poor in the deprived Glaswegian streets, combined with loneliness and hunger, drove him into the army. There he rose through the ranks to become a recruiting officer and he eventually found himself scouting for soldiers in Dunbar. Here love won out over adventure and he married a wealthy woman, Helen Kennedy, who bought out his discharge in 1829. Married bliss was short-lived. In a story all too common at the time, his wife and baby were dead by 1832 and Daniel found himself alone yet again. By this time he had undergone a profound religious experience, dedicating himself to Christ and determining to live a virtuous life. Who or what converted him, and exactly when, remains unknown, but it was to be a lifelong commitment that increased in zeal as he grew older.

In 1833 he remarried, this time to Ann Gilrye, the daughter of David and Margaret Gilrye who owned the butcher's shop in Dunbar High Street. David was nervous about giving his precious daughter to a man who appeared to be a religious fanatic who burned with a passion for God and strict righteous living. As a respectable member of the Church of Scotland David Gilrye was content with worship in its traditional form; those who wanted to dismiss all authority and ritual worried him. Perhaps he sensed an increasingly austere approach to life, which would condemn his daughter to servitude.

His concern was well founded. Daniel became more extreme, leaving one church for another, constantly dissatisfied with their respect for hierarchy and lack of rigour. The two men openly disagreed over religion and their relationship became strained. David was right though, Ann's life was to shrink over the years to little more than domestic drudgery. Music, poetry, embroidery, and literature were systematically banned in the house as Daniel's beliefs became more extreme. With so little colour or laughter, their marriage would eventually end in separation.

Seen in the context of the time, Daniel's conversion to hard-line, evangelical Presbyterianism was not uncommon. The dreary lives of the working classes in Victorian Britain were given hope by

23

a doctrine that preached an ultimate glorious existence away from the sweat and tears of daily life. Through manual labour and living a God-fearing life, people could place their hope in better things to come. The egalitarian heart of the message also rang true for a nation that saw itself as oppressed by the English and was longing for equality, political as well as financial. This fundamentalist branch of the church did away with authority figures, another welcome concept at a time of immense social inequality.

All these aspects appealed to Daniel, a young man forging his way by his own inner strength and with dreams of lifting himself and his family's souls out of the darkness. His developing faith gave him purpose and convinced him to organize his life around strict biblical teachings and to reap the reward of the virtuous. He set about making his money in Dunbar with vigour, first of all as a shopkeeper and then as a grain trader. He was known as a tough but scrupulously honest businessman. When he and Ann, with their growing family in tow, moved into a large house on the main street, the family seemed set for a prosperous life in lowland Scotland.

Whether it was Daniel's zealous interpretation of his faith or simply his personality that made him a strict father it is hard to know, but even by the norms of the day he was extreme. He truly believed that any relaxation could allow the devil access to the soul. The best way to protect himself and his family was through hard work and a thorough knowledge of the Bible. These conditions were applied ruthlessly. He regularly whipped his children for nothing more than innocent pranks or making mistakes when reciting the Bible from memory.

John's young life was full of the threat of corporal punishment at home and at school. He wrote in *The Story of My Boyhood and Youth*, that "much warlike thrashing", at home and in Mungo Siddons's Infant School helped him commit "the whole of the French, Latin and English grammars to memory", and, as if this wasn't enough for a primary-school child, "Father made me learn so many Bible verses every day that by the time I was eleven years old I had about three-fourths of the Old Testament and all of the New by heart and by sore flesh. I could recite from the beginning of Matthew to the end of Revelation without a single stop."[3] When John's writing career took off many years later, biblical imagery and phrases would lace his text in creative, imaginative ways, so ingrained were they in his heart and mind.

With no paternal role model to influence his ideas, Daniel took on an almost God-the-father-type character for himself. He became a stereotypical Old Testament authoritarian, an omnipotent head whose word was law. It was a strange contrast with the egalitarian message of his faith. In his writings, however, John never gave the impression that he was unloved, just strictly treated for the good of his soul and for the improvement of his mind. Behind the sternness He recalls affection and at times even playfulness. In the early days, when music was still allowed, Daniel sang old Scottish ballads and played his fiddle. He got down on his knees to show the children how to carve toys from vegetables. Many years later John wrote, "Naturally, his heart was far from hard, though he devoutly believed in eternal punishment for bad boys both here and hereafter."[4] In the obituary he wrote for Daniel when he died in 1885, the words were infused with forgiveness. "He loved little children and beneath a stern face, rigid with principles, he carried a warm and tender heart."[5]

He was, however, to remain highly sensitive to harshness towards children for the rest of his life. He believed there was nothing more tragic, and no sound more able to tear the heart than to listen to a child crying itself to sleep after being subjected to severe and overpowering punishment.

It was from this successful merchant, a stalwart of Dunbar's respectable classes and a fundamentalist Christian, that John Muir inherited many of the traits that carried him through his extraordinary later life. Daniel passed on to his son passion, resilience, single-mindedness, manual skills, and the ability to endure hardship, all of which saw John through testing times. What he rejected about Daniel was his rigid religion and severity, but there is no doubt that they were similar in many ways.

Ann, his mother, is a much more shadowy figure. She is remembered as a gentle, poetic soul who appreciated nature and was skilled at embroidery. She had a far kinder disposition than Daniel, although she was a devoted and obedient wife. Up until her death, at the age of eighty-three, she wrote kind and loving letters to John, often sending him pressed flowers from the meadows and woods around the home. He remembers being hurried to bed before his father got home, fearful of his temper. It is from his mother and the grandparents Gilrye that all the Muir children experienced compassion and kindness; a tenderness that instilled itself into John's personality and was never to be suppressed. When Ann passed away in 1896, his grief was profound. She was, he said, "as beautiful in life as in death".[6] Whatever character Ann possessed, however, barely registers against the iron presence of her husband, who ran his family with a military discipline that increasingly worried and alienated her parents.

Margaret and David Gilrye lived across the street and they seem to have been the perfect grandparents. It is from Grandfather Gilrye that John learned the letters of the alphabet by reading shop signs. They enjoyed country walks together, holding hands as they chatted in the lanes by the fields or explored rock pools on the shore. He recalls sitting down to rest on a haystack with his grandfather when he was barely three, and hearing "a sharp, prickly, stinging cry".

Digging down into the hay they found a mother field mouse feeding her young: "No hunter could have been more excited on discovering a bear and her cubs in a wilderness den."[7] Grandfather Gilrye is a mysterious, faceless character; a featureless influence who nurtured John's innate curiosity and introduced him to the many wonders of nature.

All the Muir children, must have been a source of great joy for the grandparents Gilrye. Out of the ten children they had produced, only three survived to adulthood, with the others probably dying from tuberculosis. With so much grief to bear they transferred their affection to Ann's brood of healthy, bright sprites who lived ran in and out of their house, filling it with fun and optimism. After so much tragedy, the young Muirs brightened their grandparents' lives, and many evenings were spent at their fireside learning school lessons.

John's memories of these cosy family times are sharp, but it is interesting that he gives very few descriptions of his relatives and friends or of the wildlife that filled his world back then. He focused on events and personal experience. The everyday nature such as robins, gulls, and skylarks are assumed friends that need no description. What we get more of in these early recollections is a picture of a rough-and-tumble boyhood full of secret and wild adventures, usually on a Saturday.

With "red-blooded playmates", the young Muir could be found running for miles through fields or exploring the black coastline with its cliffs and tidal pools. On the crumbling walls of old Dunbar Castle he learned how to climb, and, "took chances that no cautious mountaineer would try".[8] He pinched fruit and flowers and grew his own in a small patch of garden that Daniel set aside for him. He marvelled at his aunt's lilies, never daring to touch them, wondering if one day he would be rich enough to grow his own. He collected birds' eggs and hunted for sea monsters along the shore. He waged warrior battles in gangs of boys and fought with his fists, inflicting and receiving many black eyes – for which he was always punished. He played endurance games that involved long-distance races over fields, or the boys tested each other's ability to bear pain without flinching. None of these Saturday adventures were actually allowed: outside the house it was too easy to fall into bad company or heard bad words.

There were, however, no threats that could keep him imprisoned at home when fun was to be had. "No punishment, however sore and severe, was of any avail against the attraction of the fields and the woods," he wrote, and so as often as he could he slipped away from the confines of the yard and headed for freedom with his friends. "Oh the blessed enchantment of those Saturday runaways in the prime of the Spring!... Every particle of us thrilling and tingling with the bees and glad birds and glad streams!"[9]

But always in the background was the certainty of "sore punishments that followed like shadows", from a home that valued discipline, religion, and education above all else. Whippings were useful for focusing the mind, but useless when it came to taming a wild spirit. If Daniel Muir wanted a pious and demure boy, he didn't make one of John, no matter how often he administered a "skelping".

This freely administered discipline however did have its uses. Throughout his adventurous life, John Muir would need all the grit and endurance he could muster. "All of these thrashings," he wrote, "were admirably influential in developing memory but fortitude as well."[10]

Daniel didn't realize it but he was helping to create a tough wilderness pioneer. The restrictive diet that he had imposed to counteract the sin of gluttony meant that John not only was able to withstand long periods of hunger but lost his basic interest in food. Daniel Muir was convinced that overeating was a direct route to hell, and so everyone ate sparingly. Porridge, barley cakes, boiled potatoes, and milk mixed with water and sugar formed the mainstay of the family's diet. Meat is never mentioned, but with a butcher for a grandfather it is unlikely they never had cheap off-cuts. For a growing, energetic boy this was a restrictive regime and he remembers always being hungry, as hungry after a meal as before. All his life he ate very little, preferring bread and tea to rich food. It was good training, as more than once he would teeter on the edge of starvation and still be required to walk for miles to find civilization. John always longed to be free from the requirement to eat. Later he would write, "Just bread and water and delightful toil is all I need."[11]

Throughout these early years we see a vigorous young boy learning the physical skills he would need in later life. Alongside this, emotional traits were developing that would shine through his writing and endear him to millions.

John Muir's writings overflow with empathy and a sense of justice for all of life, not just human. Remembering when he first began to read at only three years old, with the patient help of his grandfather, he recalls a story that "deeply interested and touched me". It was a classic Welsh tale of a faithful dog, Gelert, who was mistakenly slain by his owner, Prince Llewelyn, who thought he had attacked his young son. Llewelyn found the dog dripping with blood and immediately assumed he had mauled and killed the baby. In fact the brave dog had been defending the child against a wolf. When Llewelyn found the smiling baby safe with the dead wolf by his side, he was distraught and sank to his knees, wailing with remorse. That story was read over and over again as John imagined he was there, seeing everything first-hand. He believed he witnessed Llewelyn despairing over his son and that despair turning to anger, which he vented on poor Gelert. Oh the injustice that raged in John's heart! And then the terrible realization that what the prince had done was actually to slaughter his most faithful friend. In John's mind he knelt down with Llewelyn and wept beside the body of the dog: "…how great maybe the capacity for a child's heart for sorrow and sympathy for animals as well as human friends," he wrote.[12]

The realization that people were capable of terrible crimes against non-human life was also evident outside the pages of a book. One spring afternoon he watched a soldier, who was lodging in the town, raid a robin's nest in an elm tree. As the soldier collected his horse to leave, he climbed up and took the nestlings to sell as caged song birds, which were popular then to brighten town houses. He describes watching the soldier gather up the panicked chicks that had fallen to the ground while the distraught parents tried to protect their young. It was a painful memory: "I remember as if it happened this day, how my heart fairly ached and choked me." His mother tried to comfort him, assuring him that the birds would have a happy life in a fancy parlour, but he cried himself to sleep. Later he heard her explaining to Daniel "a' the brairn's hearts were broken over the robbing of the nest in the elm."[13]

John was no angel, however. This budding naturalist could just as easily be a cold ruffian who was capable of committing crimes similar to the ones he despised so much. "Boys," he remarked, "are often at once cruel and merciful, thoughtlessly hard-hearted and tender-hearted, sympathetic, pitiful and kind in ever changing contrasts."[14] As much as he was capable of weeping over robin chicks he was also able to delight in dog fights, drop cats from top-storey windows to see if they would land on their feet, and scale walls to see a butcher slaughter a squealing pig and then beg for the bladder for a football. He also took nestlings from skylark nests he found in the fields and kept them in cages. He carefully constructed a miniature moorland of turf and fed his captives for up to two years. Come the spring the trapped lark would try to soar above its small patch of wildness: "Again and again it would try to hover over the miniature meadow from its miniature sky just underneath the top of the cage."[15] Compassion and hard-heartedness sat side by side in the young John Muir; he was not yet ready to draw threads together and bind a coherent, whole view of the earth and his place in it.

Wild adventures were experienced alongside driven learning. Although sorely administered, John's education was thorough: he was literate, mathematical, and well versed in classics, and knew about geography. It also introduced him to the giants of natural history upon whose shoulders he would later stand to become the father of modern conservation. His wild ramblings among the fields and shoreline of Dunbar brought him into physical contact with nature but Maccoulough's Course of Reading, his school set book, introduced him to the natural wonders of America and the titanic figures who wrote so evocatively about them.

To a boy from a land that had already been cut down, ploughed, planted, and tamed, the images presented by this schoolbook were astonishing. Scottish wildlife was mainly small and confiding – robins, skylarks, and rabbits – but in Maccoulough's Course there were tales of gigantic trees, ferocious sky battles between huge birds of prey, and rivers running with gold. This was Harry Potter country, but real.

It was in this book that John encountered one of his first heroes. Although the ornithologist Alexander Wilson had been dead since 1814, his tales of the birds of America embedded themselves deeply in his heart. Wilson's life and character were in some ways similar to John's. Wilson was a Scot who emigrated to America as a young man and travelled the vast continent in search of its bird life. He taught himself to be a poet, writer, and painter and, like John, he used his talents to interest the public in the richness of the natural world. He wrote of Wilson that "he had the good fortune to wander for years in the American woods while the country was yet mostly wild".[16] Wilson had an engaging turn of phrase and he enticed the reader to travel with him, "from the shores of St Lawrence to the mouths of the Mississippi and from the Atlantic Ocean to the interior of Louisiana".[17] In the days before binoculars he always carried a gun to shoot birds in order to paint and study them (including two ivory-billed woodpeckers, which became extinct in the twentieth century), and he collected a vast array of specimens and discovered many new species. He also sincerely believed the natural world was akin to a vast book full of lessons to be learned and wonders to behold, rather than something to be feared and subdued. And, like John, he saw the face of God in nature.

Wilson's description of an epic battle between an osprey and a bald eagle, over a fish the osprey had caught in the sea was awe-inspiring prose. Although ospreys were still to be found in many places in Scotland when John was a boy it is unlikely he would have seen one in Dunbar, as heavy persecution kept them restricted to more remote areas. (The last breeding record before recent times was in 1899, although single birds were occasionally seen until 1916. They recolonized Scotland from Scandinavia in 1959 and are now established once again, though in small numbers.)

The osprey, "the long winged hawk circling over the heaving waves", plunged into the water to catch a fish but all the while a bald eagle was watching from a tree, "with kindling eye spreading his wings ready for instant flight". The osprey grasped the struggling fish tightly in its talons and tried to fly higher and higher, "with wonderful wing work in the sky". The eagle soared above, however, and at last the osprey was compelled, "with a cry of despair to drop his hard-won prey". The eagle was triumphant and, "descending swift as a lightning bolt",[18] seized the falling fish before it reached the sea. This writing was dynamite and it fired the young Muir's imagination filling him with awe at this country where people could watch giant birds fighting battles above their heads.

Wilson's lively poetry brought the osprey closer to life in Dunbar. The idea of using a hawk to guide fishermen to shoals of fish was pure wonder:

THE OSPREY sails above the sound,
The geese are gone, the gulls are flying;
The herring shoals swarm thick around,
The nets are launched, the boats are plying;
Yo ho, my hearts! Let's seek the deep,
Raise high the song and cheerily wish her,
Still as the bending net we sweep,
"God bless the fish-hawk and the fisher!"
Alexander Wilson[19]

John James Audubon, the giant of American ornithology, provided what was perhaps the most important piece of natural history writing at this time in John's life – the migration of the passenger pigeon. This was one of the greatest spectacles on earth and Audubon's story celebrated the abundance of nature, but it also details one of the most shameful episodes of European colonization, the elimination of the most numerous bird on the planet. It is a tale that struck deep into John's soul and he was to ponder on this many times in the years to come.

Audubon lived in America at the beginning of the nineteenth century, only ahead of the Muirs by a few decades, yet his writings and paintings were already well known by the time John was at school. His description of the sheer numbers of passenger pigeons was gripping. "The multitudes of Wild Pigeons in our woods are astonishing," he wrote in his seminal work *The Birds of America* (1827–39). "Indeed, after having viewed them so often, and under so many circumstances, I even now feel inclined to pause, and assure myself that what I am going to relate is fact. Yet I have seen it all, and that too in the company of persons who, like myself, were struck with amazement."[20] Audubon watched a flock fly overhead for three days and estimated that 300 million pigeons passed him each hour.

Passenger pigeons migrated across the continent in an endless search for food and in such huge numbers that they formed a constant river of birds in the air, many miles wide and long. It was often said that they blocked out the sun. "The air was literally filled with Pigeons;" wrote Audubon, "the light of noon-day was obscured as by an eclipse, the dung fell in spots, not unlike melting flakes of snow; and the continued buzz of wings had a tendency to lull my senses to repose." They were also enchanting on the ground, where they "walk with ease, as well as on the branches, frequently jerking their beautiful tail, and moving the neck backwards and forwards in the most graceful manner… When an individual is seen gliding through the woods and close to the observer, it passes like a thought, and on trying to see it again, the eye searches in vain; the bird is gone."

Audubon watched them flying, roosting, and feeding, but he also witnessed them being slaughtered in their millions. He describes vividly what it was like to observe at first hand local farmers awaiting the arrival of the pigeons in nearby woods, sticks and guns at the ready:

Suddenly there burst forth a general cry of 'Here they come!' The noise which they made, though yet distant, reminded me of a hard gale at sea, passing through the rigging of a close-reefed vessel. As the birds arrived and passed over me, I felt a current of air that surprised me. Thousands were soon knocked down by the pole-men. The birds continued to pour in. The fires were lighted, and a magnificent, as well as wonderful and almost terrifying, sight presented itself… It was a scene of uproar and confusion. I found it quite useless to speak, or even to shout to those persons who were nearest to me. Even the reports of the guns were seldom heard, and I was made aware of the firing only by seeing the shooters

reloading. No one dared venture within the line of devastation...
The uproar continued the whole night... Towards the approach of
day... all that were able to fly had disappeared... the howlings of the
wolves now reached our ears, and the foxes, lynxes, cougars, bears,
racoons, opossums and pole-cats were seen sneaking off, whilst
eagles and hawks of different species, accompanied by a crowd of
vultures, came to supplant them, and enjoy their share of the spoil...
The Pigeons were picked up and piled in heaps, until each had as
many as he could possibly dispose of, when the hogs were let loose
to feed on the remainder.[21]

The cruel, thoughtless eradication of these birds hangs like a pall
of shame over the actions of immigrants into America. Even
Audubon, a hunter himself, describes humanity as "the tyrant
of creation". But as the pigeon spectacle didn't succumb to this
slaughter until the late 1880s it was still to be observed when John
read this account; and what an image it must have presented to his
imagination. What was this land full of fighting eagles and billions
of pigeons? The passenger pigeon joined the eagles, hawks, sugar
maples, and gold nuggets as inhabitants of a magical land far across
the sea.

Other countries entered the wish-list of places to see through
the writings of Alexander von Humboldt, who was still alive when
John was at school. Humboldt was a polymath, explorer, naturalist,
and mountaineer with a particular interest in plants. He was
acclaimed in his lifetime and Charles Darwin described him as "the
greatest scientific traveller who ever lived". Nature must be viewed
holistically, declared Humboldt:

The most important aim of all physical science is this: to recognize
unity in diversity, to comprehend all the single aspects as revealed
by the discoveries of the last epochs, to judge single phenomena
separately without surrendering their bulk, and to grasp Nature's
essence under the cover of outer appearances.[22]

He travelled the world collecting precise data and describing species, puzzling over how everything fitted together. His descriptions of his travels in the Amazon were so exotic that John was determined to follow him.

These hugely influential naturalists seeped into this wild Scottish boy's very being and he yearned to have adventures of his own. But as a child he was content with the tamed fields of lowland Scotland, seeking out their pockets of wildness: "Nature saw to it that besides school lessons and church lessons some of her own lessons should be learned, perhaps with a view to the time when we should be called to wander in wildness to our heart's content."[23]

In 1847 a dramatic public meeting in Dunbar provided the first giant step towards realizing these dreams. When Daniel went to hear a visiting preacher from America, Thomas Campbell, he was so shaken by his message that he began to lay plans that would wrench the Gilryes from the Muirs and the Muirs from Scotland. Campbell was a Scot who had been brought up in Northern Ireland and then went to found a frontier family in Pennsylvania. He had a powerful intellect and a persuasive manner. He was an outstanding public speaker who seemed to burn with the fire of the Holy Spirit. In other words, he was irresistible to the searching, dissatisfied Daniel Muir.

What Campbell proclaimed was a community of pure Christians unsullied by worn-out traditions and the arrogance, as he saw it, of clergy. In this collection of believers only the true meaning of the New Testament would be found, simply lived, and humbly obeyed. Ordinary lay folk would be their own ministers and take authority from the Bible alone. This was egalitarianism in the form Daniel longed for. He had been searching for such purity in Dunbar's churches, but they were fogged by church politics and social norms. Only in the New World, fresh and open, could one truly find the freedom to live a holy life. His mind was made up. He immediately joined the Campbellite group establishing itself in Dunbar, the Disciples of Christ, and began to make plans which would bring to a close the Scottish phase of John Muir's life.

The Story of My Boyhood and Youth is the sole source of information on these early years. It was however one of the last books written, in 1908, towards the end of his life. It was dictated to a scribe who followed him around, noting down as many memories as he could draw out of the ageing Goliath of the wild. The picture we are given is therefore filtered through years of changing thoughts and ideas, and might not represent what he truly felt at the time. There are no photographs of the young John or his family and we can only surmise that he was an irrepressible imp, fun-loving, bright and energetic.

> When I was a boy in Scotland I was fond of everything that was
> wild, and all my life I've been growing fonder and fonder of wild
> places and wild creatures… I loved to wander in the fields to hear the
> birds sing, and along the seashore to gaze and wonder at the shells
> and seaweeds, eels and crabs in the pools among the rocks when
> the tide was low; and best of all to watch the waves in awful storms
> thundering on the black headlands and craggy ruins of old Dunbar
> Castle when the sea and the sky, the waves and the clouds, were
> mingled as one.[24]

The Scottish years held precious memories. What Dunbar offered was the first selection of colours for the palette from which he would eventually paint a universe of many hues. In these early days, however, that picture was far from complete. What we see is a typical childlike drawing with John large in frame and the birds, flowers, and sea life dotted around him as entertainment. As he grew in maturity and experience, he would eventually create a landscape made up of all the colours of the rainbow, accompanied by the textures, shapes, sounds, and songs of the earth. This transition began in Scotland but did not find its completion there. Scotland was not destined to be his home. With characteristic dominance, Daniel swiftly and cruelly severed the children's ties with their grandparents and with no warning John found himself heading for the land of giant trees, eagles, and gold.

Chapter 2

Early American Days

"Come forth into the light of things, let nature be your teacher."

William Wordsworth, "The Tables Turned"

The moment the Muir children found out they were to emigrate to America is a heart-rending story. It was in the evening on 18 February 1849, two months before John's eleventh birthday:

> One night, when David and I were at grandfather's fireside solemnly learning our lessons as usual, my father came in with the news, the most wonderful, most glorious, that wild boys ever heard. "Bairns," he said, "you needna learn your lessons the night, for we're gan to America the morn!" No more grammar, but boundless woods full of mysterious good things; trees full of sugar, growing in ground full of gold; hawks, eagles, pigeons, filling the sky; millions of birds' nests, and no game keepers to stop us in all the wild, happy land. We were utterly blindly glorious.[1]

The excitement of John, David (nine) and Sarah (thirteen), the ones chosen to go in the vanguard party with Daniel, was shadowed by the bitter sadness of Grandfather Gilrye. This gentle, loving man, who had taught his grandchildren so much, was grief-stricken. "Poor grandfather, about to be forsaken, looked with downcast eyes on the floor and said in a low, trembling, troubled voice, 'Ah poor laddies, poor laddies, you'll find something else ower the sea forbye gold and sugar, birds' nests and freedom fra lessons and school. You'll find plenty hard, hard work.'" With hindsight John knew that his grandfather was devastated, but at the time he was too overcome with delight at what was in store: "Nor could we in the midst of such measureless excitement see or feel the shadows and sorrows of his darkening old age."[2]

It isn't hard to imagine how difficult this must have been for Margaret and David Gilrye. They had loved and nurtured their grandchildren and proved to be a refuge of gentleness from the strictness of Daniel. Now they were about to lose their treasured family when they needed them most, in their last few years. David managed to persuade Daniel to leave behind, at least for a short while, Ann, John's eldest sister, Margaret, and the three youngest children, Daniel, Mary, and Anna, until a house had been built for them. He knew though that it was only a temporary respite. Daniel had won the battle and removed his family from the softness of Scottish religion to found his own spiritual microcosm thousands of miles away.

At the age of forty-five it was a brave move. Although he had grown up working on the land, most of Daniel's adult life had been spent in trade, yet he was setting out to wrest a living on foreign soil with no help but his young children. He had no thought for family ties, or for the future of his business; his focus was solely on leading his family to purity. He knew he would join other hard-working, God-fearing Disciples of Christ who wanted no truck with the worldliness of Europe. A life revolving around the commands of the Bible was what Daniel was seeking; anything less and he could risk losing himself and his family to the devil. With such high stakes, business and family relations were insignificant. Whatever Ann thought about the move is not recorded.

Now, in the twilight of life and after having endured the death of so many of their own children, David and Margaret were yet again to be alone. They would lose their daughter and grandchildren to an unknown future in a faraway land, and were full of fear for the type of life they would lead. After Ann left Dunbar to join Daniel just six months later, the grandparents would never see any of them again. Within four years both had died and were laid to rest beside their children.

Single-mindedness, abstinence, and hard work were traits that many settlers took to the New World and they paved the way for America's future success, but life for the pioneers was often unrelentingly harsh. Optimistic, enthusiastic young hearts though are not easily subdued: "Even the natural heart-pain of parting from grandfather and grandmother Gilrye, who loved us so well, and from mother and sisters and brother was quickly quenched in young joy."[3]

Daniel was not the only Scot heading for a new life. Three hundred thousand would make a similar journey that year, the Carnegies of Dunfermline had left just months before. Andrew Carnegie, three years older than John, went on to lead the expansion of the American steel industry and become one of the richest men in the world. As worker unrest disrupted British industry, many decided to find a life of political equality away from the class-ridden system based in Westminster.

A draining of people across the Atlantic was also occurring across the Irish Sea. In 1845 a devastating potato blight caused widespread crop failure and starvation for the poor tenant farmers who relied on potatoes as a main source of food. One million died from hunger; another million Irish left their homes, many to go to America and Canada. For many people, therefore, America offered a new life, the possibility of wealth, and a break from the binds of British and Irish working-class drudgery. Daniel had no financial reason to leave Scotland; his driving aim was to enhance his spiritual wealth.

The journey across the sea on the *Warren* took six weeks and three days and began on 3 March 1849. It was done under sail and John, with the other boys who seemed immune to seasickness, played on deck and watched the "big, curly topped waves", and no doubt got in the way of the sailors as they hauled the ropes and climbed the rigging. His father joined many other passengers who spent most of their time below deck. The "auld rockin' creel" challenged their stomachs and left their unruly offspring with free rein above. The long sea voyages were not undertaken lightly; they were expensive and dangerous, and many of the adults rued the day they had decided to make this hellish, nausea-inducing journey. In 1834 seventeen ships were lost at sea and, in 1853, 10 per cent of Irish emigrants died from cholera on the voyage. Disease ripped through the cramped and unhygienic conditions and there was no help for those who were ill.[4]

None of that bothered John; he was having too good a time exploring the ship. He doesn't describe any ocean wildlife until they neared the coast of America, but, as they approached New York, the family stood on deck and watched with wonder the whales, seabirds, and leaping dolphins. The air must have been filled with the cries of birds gathering to breed. It was a fine introduction to the land of opportunity with its wealth of resources that lay beyond the harbour walls.

The United States as a political entity was only sixty years old when the ship docked on 10 April 1849. They couldn't have known what tumultuous years lay ahead, both politically and philosophically. This vast land of contrasts and opportunities was sliding relentlessly towards civil war. Slavery for many, particularly in the southern states, sat uneasily with the more liberal north. Three million slaves lived in America, out of a total population of just over 23 million.[5] The cotton industry was expanding, requiring cheap labour on a grand scale, and many saw the abolition of slavery as a threat to its survival. It was a fundamental disagreement that would lead to a bloodbath in just over a decade. On the other hand, gold had just been found in the Californian hills, enticing thousands of hopefuls, known as Forty-Niners after the year they arrived to dig for the huggets, to make the long and often treacherous journey across the interior. Neither cotton nor gold interested Daniel, however.

Tension of a different, more philosophical form was just over the horizon over the publication of a book. In 1859 Charles Darwin would publish his incendiary *On the Origin of Species*, which would change the way the world was viewed by scientists and clerics alike. It also rocked the world of traditionalist God-fearing Christians like Daniel. Before its ideas became known, man was the centre point of creation. Afterwards, humanity was seen as living in a vast, inhospitable universe driven by forces beyond our control. People were not the pinnacle, at the top of a chain of being, but merely part of a process. It challenged many to their core and shook faith to its foundations.

Science as a whole was gradually leaving behind its attachment to religion and becoming more secular, allowing for greater freedom of thought. Pure and applied sciences were undergoing growth as never before, changing the way people lived and worked. It wasn't just the Muir family who were starting out on a new path of self-discovery: the whole Western world was undergoing a profound change.

On arrival there was no time to take in the wonder of New York. The Muirs immediately boarded a ferry, which sailed up the Hudson River to Albany, and they then took a train to Buffalo, where Daniel had arranged to meet a former Campbellite neighbour for on-the-ground advice. This neighbour, William Gray, had attended the meeting in Dunbar with Daniel to hear Thomas Campbell preach. He was a trusted source and had been in America for a few months, setting up his own grain-trading business. Daniel's original plan had been to head for Canada, but he was persuaded that life there would be extremely hard. The ground was much more difficult to clear and the climate harsh, although many Campbellites had taken up the challenge.

After much discussion and mind-changing about where the new family home should be built, Daniel decided on Wisconsin. Here was a new state that was actively seeking immigrants to fill its prairies and increase its wealth. It produced what Daniel knew well – wheat. As the repeal of the Corn Laws had allowed American grain to flood British markets, the future looked secure. Agricultural fields and the price of grain were things Daniel understood, and growing grain was more closely allied to his idea of an honest life than making good in a sinful city. The large, cast-iron weighing scales and measures he had hauled over from Scotland could be put to work once more. The decision was made and Wisconsin was marked on the map.

More boat and wagon rides lay ahead to get them over the Great Lakes to Milwaukee. Daniel did not believe in travelling light. He took ample food, "enough provisions for a long siege", along with the beam scales, cast-iron weights, cast-iron stove, and carpentry tools. In the town he bought more heavy goods; iron pots and pans, a stove, and a cradle for harvesting wheat. The roads were rough and muddy, difficult enough to travel with an ordinary load, but with this vast tonnage of freight it was a slow, sorry journey; which John described as a "cruel, heart-breaking, wagon-breaking, horse-killing load",[6] but eventually they arrived in the small town of Kingston. Daniel left the children in a rented room and went in search of a suitable plot for a farm. John describes how he and David immediately found the local boys and challenged them to a fight. In the meantime Daniel laid claim to a fine location in an area of open woodland with flower meadows leading down to a lake. The final stage of the journey was made with a team of oxen pulling their load to the newly named Fountain Lake Farm.

In many ways Daniel had chosen well. Like the south-eastern plains of Scotland, Wisconsin had been shaped by ice. In fact, few states show the effects of the last ice age as clearly as Wisconsin. Huge continental glaciers had advanced and retreated several times across most of the state. As they moved, the glaciers had ground down hills and scoured out basins for lakes, and, as they retreated, they had deposited vast amounts of debris from large rocks to soil. These glacial deposits were quickly colonized by plants of many types. When John arrived, much of the state (almost 85 per cent)[7] was still forested and teemed with birds, insects, frogs, and mammals of every size and temperament. Here was an endless, vibrant playground. Woodlands of oak, pine, and sugar maple sat amid an understorey of violets and wild geraniums. The meadows sported colourful flowers such as the delicate white arrowhead and pink swamp milkweed. He knew the deliciously perfumed and delicate lady's slipper, the scarlet painted cup, and the nodding trillium. Every step was a journey of discovery, bathed in sunshine.

Daniel hadn't completely grasped that the thin, sandy soils would become quickly depleted once the land had been ploughed, meaning crop yields would be less year on year. He had also failed to factor in the difficulty of coping with the extremes of the climate. He arrived in the spring and a long, hot summer stretched ahead. The winter would be very different, with temperatures plummeting to well below zero for months on end and thick snow, up to five feet deep, lying for long periods without melting. It must have been tough for Ann to arrive in such freezing, Spartan conditions.

As the first summer in Wisconsin got under way, Daniel and his neighbours made a cabin to live in while a larger house was built, leaving the children mainly free to explore. John didn't realize it, but these early days were the last taste of freedom he would experience for years to come. He raced over hilltops, searched for birds' nests, and "began an acquaintance with the frogs, snakes and turtles in the creeks and springs". "This sudden plash into pure wildness – baptism in Nature's warm heart – how utterly happy it made us! Nature streaming into us, wooingly teaching her wonderful glowing lessons." This is John Muir in his element, a young spirit who was literally overcome with the bounties of nature. This unbounded joy would be his hallmark all his life and would never be dimmed.

> Oh that glorious Wisconsin wilderness! Everything new and pure and in the very prime of spring when Nature's pulses were beating highest and mysteriously keeping time with our own! Young hearts, young leaves, flowers, animals, the winds and the streams and the sparkling lake, all widely, gladly rejoicing together![8]

Time was ticking by, though, and before long everyone's heart would beat strongly for another reason. The "hard, hard work" his Grandfather Gilrye had foreseen was soon to begin, but for a short while John, David, and Sarah could immerse themselves in the abundance of the New World.

How humdrum a blue tit must have seemed in comparison with a blue jay, the stunningly coloured, bold, and aggressive passerine that would have created a flash of azure blue as it collected acorns, seeds, berries, and insects. The blue jay was his first experience of the wild. As soon as the wagon carrying their goods arrived, John and David leapt down, raced towards a tree and found a nest. They were amazed by how noisily and angrily it tried to chase them away – far braver and more aggressive than the robins that had fluttered uselessly around the thieving soldier. Blue jays are thieves, avian predators that eat other bird's eggs and chicks. Perhaps it thought it was about to get a taste of its own medicine.

Pugnacity was a common trait among the wildlife that revealed itself around the new home. What an impressive fighter the kingbird was, and fighting was a skill John admired very much. Brought up waging street battles against schoolmates and listening to tales of valiant Scottish warriors at school, he considered that this plucky flycatcher "whips all the other birds", and it fast became a favourite. He would no doubt have seen flycatchers at home, but here they were confrontational, in-your-face little critters that even took on "hen hawks", a red-tailed hawk, one of the most common birds of prey in North America and often seen in both agricultural and urban areas. He describes with glee how a kingbird he was watching became so infuriated with a hawk that was in its territory that it chased it away by constantly flying over it and dive-bombing it to peck its head, even settling on its shoulders to carry on with the attack when it was too tired to fly. Now that was a bird worth its salt in John's eyes.

The blue jays, hawks, and flycatchers were joined on John's list of wonderful playmates by the red-headed woodpecker. This boldly striped bird of red, white, and black, also called the "flying checkerboard", so inspired Alexander Wilson when he first saw one in Delaware that it set him off on his ornithological trail through America in the late 1700s. Wilson declared it to be the most beautiful bird he had ever seen. It also appears in North American Indian folklore as the bird that made the first flute and as the protector of children, presumably because it so cleverly hides its own young from danger. John marvelled at their beautifully circular nest holes, which he doubted any human could make, even with the finest tools. Such a stunning bird, and here they were flitting about the farm as common as you like. So common, in fact, that many were shot by farmers to protect their fruit trees. Audubon records that 100 were shot in 1840 on a single cherry tree.[9]

The sight of so many birds was matched by the cacophony of their calls. For sure, back in Scotland a skylark had a voice of liquid silver and a blackbird one of liquid gold, but the variety and sheer power of American birdsong must have been overpowering. Daylight hours were filled with cackles, piping, shrill squeaks, drumming, and other tuneful flurries of sound. Some less than attractive singing joined these: the beauty of the blue jay is not matched by its call, which sounds like the handle of a creaking rusty pump.

Dotted around the trees, the bluebird was a long-awaited spring arrival. A common description says that they wear the blue of heaven on their backs and the rich brown of the freshly turned earth on their chest. Their call is evocative and pensive and would forever herald, for John, the start of a fresh year of growth and vitality:

With the first hints of spring came the brave little bluebirds, darling singers as blue as the best sky, and of course we all loved them. Their rich, crispy warbling is perfectly delightful, soothing and cheering, sweet and wistfully low, Nature's fine love touches, every note going straight into one's heart.[10]

Over in the Catskill Mountains another boy, just a year older than John, was also destined to grow into a titanic literary figure, bringing nature into the lives of millions of Americans. John Burroughs was listening to the bluebird in his own oak woodlands, allowing its beautiful song to inform his heart:

A wistful note from out the sky,
"Pure, pure, pure," in plaintive tone,
As if the wand'rer were alone,
And hardly knew to sing or cry.

But now a flash of eager wing,
Flitting, twinkling by the wall,
And pleadings sweet and am'rous call,
Ah, now I know his heart doth sing!

O bluebird, welcome back again,
Thy azure coat and ruddy vest
Are hues that April loveth best,
Warm skies above the furrowed plain.
John Burroughs, "The Bluebird"[11]

John Burroughs and John Muir would one day be great friends, spearheading a new genre of nature writing, but for now they wandered their own woods and listened intently to, as Burroughs wrote, "all the soft, wooing influences of spring on the one hand, and the retreating footsteps of winter on the other".[12]

All the birds on the farm appear in *The Story of My Boyhood and Youth* in a chapter called "A Paradise for Birds". The bluebird was joined by the robin, which nested around the house and called "Fear not, fear not, cheer up, cheer up." It was loved by the settlers, "for they reminded us of the robin redbreast of Scotland". The brown thrush or thrasher appeared at the top of trees after thunderstorms, "when the winds have died away and the steaming ground and leaves and flowers fill the air with fragrance". Its song was loud and fruity. The bobolink, a species of blackbird, then arrived, "singing as if its whole body, feathers and all, were made up of music, flowing, glowing, bubbling melody, interpenetrated here and there with small scintillating prickles and spicules". It was a cause of great sadness that when the bobolinks left the farm in the autumn to feast on the rice fields of the southern states; they were "slaughtered in countless numbers for food. Sad fate for singers so purely divine."

Of all the many birds described with great love, one seems to stand out: "But no singer of them all got further into our hearts than the little speckle-breasted sparrow, one of the first to arrive and begin nest building and singing. The richness, sweetness and pathos of this small darling's song as he sat on a low bush often brought tears to our eyes."

Intriguingly, he wrote that the "modest chickadee midget" was loved by all, "every innocent boy and girl, man and woman, and by many not altogether innocent".

Ducks, swans, prairie chickens, and owls were also loved, chased, and observed. But the bird life was only one part of the wildlife of Fountain Lake Farm. There were snakes, racoons, American badgers, flying squirrels, chipmunks, and gophers. It was treasure beyond John's dreams. The Maccoulough's Reader he had absorbed so avidly in his primary school in Scotland had only touched the surface of this land of riches.

Once the sun began to set on the long summer days and the calm of the evening settled over the Muir household, the night creatures began their hours of calling, hunting, and feeding. A whip-poor-will, a once very common nightjar, sat outside the Muirs' cabin at dusk endlessly calling its name, whip-poor-will, "with loud, emphatic earnestness". It is an incessant, mournful sound and Native Indian myths connected it to death. It can call over 1,000 times during the night (the scientific term "vociferous" means "given to insistent outcry"). It was enchanting and he wrote, "What a wild, strong, bold voice he had, unlike any other we had ever heard on sea or land!" It is easy to imagine him as the family gathered for evening prayer, one ear on his father, the other captivated by this low, constant call just a few yards from the door.

Another nightjar, commonly called "the bull bat", added its strange, piercing calls to the whip-poor-will's monotone. It flys strong and low, emitting, "keen, squeaky cries" as it swoops to catch insects. Its wings then made, "a loud, ripping, bellowing sound, like a bull roaring".

The calling of numerous frogs contributed to the natural orchestra of the Muir farm, "varying from sweet, tranquil, soothing peeping to the purring of the hylas to the awfully deep low-bass blunt bellowing of the bull frogs". The smaller frogs amusingly called their biblical names, "Isaac, Isaac, Yacob, Yacob; Israel, Israel... as if they had been to school and severely drilled in elocution". The hylas or tree frogs were particularly enchanting. In classic John Muir style he meshes the physical with the spiritual when describing their calls as "a sort of soothing immortal melody filling the air like light".[13]

Night-time also saw the emergence of the lightning bugs: flying, glowing insects that drifted over the meadows as though fairies had come out to dance. Lyrical as the sight was, it reminded John of the stars that floated before his eyes after a bruising fight. Mesmerized, he went with a farmhand to collect some in a jar and watched them throbbing like a glowing heart as they bumped around the glass. Years later he visited the Himalayas and saw "a splendid display of glow-worms", but he thought them "far less impressive than the extravagant, abounding, quivering, dancing fire on our Wisconsin meadow".[14]

Surrounded by so much natural beauty, even Daniel couldn't fail to look up from the pages of the family Bible. One bright winter's night he called the family outside to see the aurora filling the sky:

> Come! Come! Mother! Come bairns! And see the glory of God. All the sky is clad in a robe of red light. Look straight up to the crown where the folds are gathered. Hush and wonder and adore, for surely this is the clothing of the Lord Himself, and perhaps He will now appear looking down from his high heaven.[15]

Daniel, like Thomas Campbell, saw the hand of God in creation, but it could be viewed only through strict biblical eyes. Nature could inspire men to ponder on God's mystery but could also lead them astray, setting up false idols or impressions. Always be wary, cautioned Daniel; men, women, and children are easily corrupted by sights, sounds, and words in this sinful world. The only sure truth is written on the pages of the Good Book. To that end, nothing other than the Bible was allowed in the house, and no music.

John therefore had to be content with stories and melodies of nature. From singing trees to starry, fire-filled nights, "Everything about us was so novel and wonderful," he wrote, "that we could hardly believe our senses except when hungry or when father was thrashing us."[16]

It is a pity that, for Daniel, the God who created such splendour also inspired such harshness. "The old Scotch fashion of whipping for every act of disobedience or of simple, playful forgetfulness was still kept up in the wilderness," he wrote, not without a tinge of bitterness. "Most of them were outrageously severe and utterly barren of fun."[17] Daniel used every opportunity to instil hard, fear-inducing lessons on the retribution that awaited bad boys. Even the burning of brush created theological horrors; fires that burned boys for eternity if they ever failed to live righteously.

How John didn't cave in under such brutality and scaremongering is a testament to the spirit that bubbled within him and refused to be cowed. No matter what harshness he endured, it seemed to have little effect on his ability to love and see joy everywhere, "for no fire can be hotter than the heavenly fire of faith and hope that burns in every healthy boy's heart".[18] Perhaps, in the absence of his grandparents' comfort, the perceived softness of nature counterbalanced the hard-line approach to life imposed by his father.

John loved the lake most of all. It was surrounded by the most beautiful flowers and its edges were fringed with lilies and rushes. Many creatures came out of the woods to drink and an old Native Indian trail skirted its edge.

Our beautiful lake, named Fountain Lake by father, but Muir's Lake by the neighbours, is one of the many small glacier lakes that adorn the Wisconsin landscapes. It is fed by twenty or thirty meadow springs about half a mile long, half as wide, and surrounded by low finely-modelled hills dotted with oak and hickory, and meadows full of grasses and sedges and many beautiful orchids and ferns. First there is a zone of green, shining rushes, and just beyond the rushes a zone of white and orange water-lilies fifty or sixty feet wide forming a magnificent border. On bright days, when the lake was rippled by a breeze, the lilies and sun-spangles danced together in radiant beauty, and it became difficult to discriminate between them.[19]

The frogs were intriguing, and Daniel decided they would make perfect teachers for the children, who, he declared, needed to learn how to swim. Whether he could swim himself is not known. "Go to the frogs," he said, "and they will give you all the lessons you need." It was an irresistible suggestion, and as it did not involve ploughing or digging it was taken up enthusiastically. It was not easy, though. The frogs seemed to glide around the lake effortlessly, but when the children tried to imitate them they ended up sinking, panicking, and gasping for breath.

Eventually John learned to swim underwater without taking a breath, and decided it was time to cross the lake to a small skiff floating in the middle. When he reached the boat he was too small to reach the gunwale and so began to sink. He was terrified, and sank and surfaced many times before he managed to get back ashore underwater, where he was hauled out by his friends, faint and gasping. It was a small, but potentially lethal adventure, but what followed presaged the man he was to become.

I was very much ashamed of myself, and at night, after calmly reviewing the affair, concluded that there had been no reasonable cause for the accident, and that I ought to punish myself for so nearly losing my life from unmanly fear. Accordingly at the very first opportunity, I stole away to the lake by myself, got into my boat, and

... rowed directly out to the middle of the lake, stripped, stood on the seat in the stern, and with a grim deliberation took a header and dove straight down thirty or forty feet... I then swam around the boat, glorying in my sudden acquired confidence and victory over myself.[20]

Many years later he would "punish himself" in a similar way. Returning to the mountains after a trip to the city he slipped and fell, hitting his head so badly he was knocked out. When he came round he found he had tumbled down a slope and to his horror saw that it was only bushes that had broken his fall. If he had gone a little further he would have slipped over the edge of a cliff and into a canyon far below. His reaction was to be angry at his carelessness. "'There,' said I, addressing my feet, to whose separate skill I had learned to trust night and day on any mountain, 'that is what you get by intercourse with stupid town stairs, and dead pavements.' I felt degraded and worthless." Others would have been thankful to be alive, but in a Muiresque response he decided, "No plushy boughs did my ill-behaved bones enjoy that night, nor did my bumped head get a spicy cedar plumed pillow mixed with flowers. I slept on a naked boulder and when I awoke all my nervous trembling was gone."[21]

Such intolerance of any failing was the result of his upbringing and marked his personality throughout his life: "Like Scotch children in general we were taught grim self-denial, in and out of season, to mortify the flesh, keep our bodies in subjection to Bible laws, and mercilessly punish ourselves for every fault and failing imagined or committed."[22]

Yet the same God-fearing farmers who instilled humility and virtue in themselves and their children could also engage in truly horrific cruelty towards the very nature they ascribed to God. It was a dichotomy that troubled John. How, he wondered, could the beautiful natural world, sculpted with such loving care by the hands of the divine, be subject to unbridled torture and bloodlust by those who longed for peace on earth? Passenger pigeons still flew onto the farm in the early Wisconsin days, bringing to mind the passages he had read by Audubon at his primary school in Scotland.

John wrote, "I have seen flocks streaming south in the autumn so large that they were flowing over from horizon to horizon in an almost continuous stream all day long, at the rate of forty or fifty an hour, like a mighty river in the sky."[23] He describes holding one in his hand, tenderly feeling the bird's beating heart and marvelling at the rosy breast feathers. They were beautiful birds and a few neighbours shared his wonder, though most simply lifted their guns and fired. "Every shot gun was aimed at them and everyone feasted on pigeon pie," he wrote.

When John expressed to his neighbours his sorrow at the indiscriminate slaughtering of such lovely birds, "some smug, practical old sinner would remark, 'Aye it's a peety, as you say, to kill the bonnie things, but they were made to be killed, and sent for us to eat, as the quails were sent to God's chosen people, the Israelites, when they were starving in the desert ayont the Red Sea. And I must confess that meat was never put up in neater packages.'"

All the boys were encouraged to shoot and he describes, with palpable contempt, the hunting parties of boys who went into the woods in rival gangs to kill anything they could find in a gruesome game of bloody point scoring. Different creatures were assigned different tallies: the head of a grey squirrel counted for four points, the head of a red only two. A whip-poor-will's head counted for two and all the wonderful songbirds John loved to listen to scored only one point each. The boys went systematically through the woods, spreading out to give each team a maximum chance of bagging as many as possible. The heads were torn off the bodies and stuffed into sacks, the torsos left on the forest floor. Red bags, dripping with bloodied heads, were waved aloft with great excitement, and the team of boys with the most heads won a large supper.

John called them "abominable head hunts", and did not join in. He did, however, do his share of more orderly hunting, shooting hawks, muskrats, gophers, and woodpeckers, but it troubled him then and haunted his conscience in later years, when he wrote a heartfelt plea for compassion: "Surely a better time must be drawing nigh when godlike human beings will become truly humane, and learn to put their animal fellow mortals in their hearts instead of on their backs or in their dinners."[24] He yearned for a "divine, uplifting, transfiguring charity", to replace the mere bloodlust that he saw as a child and which he continued to observe in adult life. For the most part, however, his pleas went unheard.

These early Wisconsin experiences were crucial to John Muir the naturalist. He gazed upon nature with a pure heart that saw only wonder, not opportunity, danger or profit. As he grew older other ideas came into play, adding complexity to his view of the world, but for now he revelled in nature, pure and simple. Everywhere was intriguing life: strange, beautiful, bizarre, and fascinating.

The abundance that he witnessed on the farm is hard for us to comprehend today because so much of the natural world has been thinned out. When John Muir was a boy, the sight, sound, and smell of nature were still rich and vibrant, despite the march of the Industrial Revolution. Large parts of America remained mostly untamed by European acquisitiveness and it still presented a wild face. Even so, 23 million people can inflict an awful lot of damage. During that century half of the forest cover of America was eliminated to feed a burgeoning timber trade and as the trees disappeared so too did the wildlife that depended on them. Even as early as 1820 the British artist and writer Basil Hall described fields with "numerous ugly stumps of old trees; others allowed to lie in the grass guarded, as it were, by a set of gigantic black monsters, the girdled, scorched and withered remains of the ancient woods".[25]

In one short century America saw the populating of the Great Plains and the West, the decimation of Native Indian tribes, the growth of national transportation and communication networks, and the rise of major cities. It also witnessed battles for land and water, and inevitably it was nature that was vanquished. With the rise of large-scale agriculture came vast clearances of forest, wetland, and meadow. This was a century of unprecedented transformation of the landscape to support the growing economy. So although Wisconsin was full of life in the mid-nineteenth century, it was not to last. John's creature-filled home would be transformed into farmland and much of its natural splendour consigned to descriptions in the journals of naturalists.

It is an irony that John Muir, the renowned naturalist and father of conservation, took part in that transformation. His was a frontier family that cleared the woods and ploughed the land, shot the pigeons and eradicated the carnivores. It is as though he tasted wilderness only to subdue it, along with all his God-fearing neighbours. It did, however, raise serious questions in his young mind that stayed with him throughout his life. Torment would be too strong a word, but certainly it produced a friction that he would forever try to soothe. The tension between what religion taught and how it was lived, between what people wanted and what they had to destroy to get it, and between keeping wilderness wild yet inviting all to partake of its pleasures – all these dichotomies tore at his mind and heart. He would spend the rest of his life trying to find solutions that pleased both God and man.

It was important, however, that this abundance of wildlife, with its joys and mystery, was laid down so early in his consciousness. As he grew up it was a constant source of comfort and inspiration, and would lead him to fight for what remained.

The next stratum to be added to this bedrock of formative experience was a deeper understanding of the relationship between people and farmland. As John's life was transformed from joyful exploration into the hard, physical reality of making a homestead, he began to gain more insight into our relationship with nature, both wild and domesticated. As he pitched himself into the gritty business of burning, digging, and wrenching a living from the earth, he began to question what it was to be a human being on a living planet. The vision that emerged is just as fresh and inspiring today as it was then, but it would take many years of back-breaking, spirit-sapping toil to develop.

Chapter 3

The Years of Labour

"If people knew how hard I had to work to gain my mastery, it would not seem so wonderful at all."

Michelangelo

From the age of eleven to twenty-two, John Muir was one of the many thousands of immigrants who imposed a settled, European way of life on a landscape already honed by Native Indian tribes. Even in the fifteenth century, when Columbus stepped ashore, it was a land that was lived in and manipulated, but by people with a very different mindset from the inhabitants of the countries across the ocean. For generations, native people had made use of the abundance of this vast continent, reaping the rich harvest of creatures and plant life in its many different habitats. From mountains to woodlands to plains and the coast, they understood the life that thrived there and survived by hunting, fishing, and, when suitable, growing crops. To increase the number of game, they developed management techniques such as periodic burning and fertilizing the soil. One major difference however between the Europeans and the Native Indians is that the tribes lived and moved in rhythm with the seasons. They followed the migrations of herds and flocks, retreated from cold or intense heat, and returned again when the time was right for profusion. The ebb and flow of the Indian way of life certainly left its mark across the continent, but it was a mark that went with the grain of nature, not against it.

Contrast that with the arrival of people with a very different view of what life was about and how to live it. Ownership of land was paramount and wealth creation a virtue, and that wealth came directly from nature. The earth was something to possess and Europeans marked their territories with stakes and built fences. What was once a route along which generations of native people had travelled was now locked off and protected. The new settlers controlled and subdued nature ruthlessly so that every last drop of produce could be wrought from the soil, and they proclaimed a Christian right to fill this land and subdue it. The seasons were to be overcome and the birds, mammals, and fish were a resource to be utilized for food or entertainment without much thought for the future.

Any wildlife that threatened this sedentary, agricultural way of life was exterminated, and the wolf was particularly badly persecuted. Not only was it a predator of livestock but it carried the burden of prejudice. Common sayings showed a deeply ingrained bias that was brought over from Europe: "keep the wolf from the door" and beware of "a wolf in sheep's clothing", for example (the latter referring to the Bible story of Christ sending his followers out to be like sheep in the midst of wolves). Here was a creature that was the embodiment of the devil. In the nineteenth century alone, up to 2 million wolves were slaughtered and large bounties were put on their heads.[1] Hunting, trapping, and poisoning virtually eradicated them from large parts of America, mirroring their persecution throughout Europe.

In contrast, to many Native Indian tribes the wolf was a symbol of courage, strength, loyalty, and good hunting skills. Wolves, and bears, which were also persecuted by the settlers, were thought to be closely related to humans, and some tribes tell of their first ancestors being transformed from wolves into men.[2]

The attitude to wolves is just one example of an immigrant mentality that could not have been more different from that of the native tribes, who were powerless to stop the destruction. Indeed, they were almost wiped out themselves, not only by having their lands and thus their livelihoods stolen, but also by the diseases introduced by the settlers. Colds, flu, smallpox, and many other common viruses carried by the Europeans met no resistance in the New World and whole tribes disappeared in a handful of years.

Europeans, however, had no memory of any other way of living. They and their ancestors were settled farmers and had been so for thousands of years. Attitudes towards the land had been developed by generations of families farming on a continent that runs mainly east to west, giving it broadly similar ecological zones and a more or less uniform terrain. It is possible to travel from Eastern Europe to Britain without being hindered by vast mountain ranges or dramatic changes in climate, and thus domesticated animals as well as ideas moved freely from east to west. But the New World stretched from the Arctic to the tropics encompassing huge topographical and climatic variation. With no other model, however, the same farming rules were applied everywhere. Such was the perceived supremacy of the European mind that they believed the Indians were "savages" and could teach them nothing about how to live. What they saw were impoverished wretches who had failed to make their continent fruitful and who lived as though destitute. They didn't see the reality, which was a continent of diverse peoples who were part of the weft and weave of nature and living full, complex, and rich lives.

By the time the Muir family arrived in the mid-nineteenth century, much of this saga had already been played out and America was well on the way to becoming a huge clone of Europe. Already, generations of gritty, determined incomers had dismantled ecosystems, introduced foreign animals, drained wetlands, clear-felled forests, slaughtered migrating creatures, and imposed boundaries irrespective of natural movement. The Muirs settled on a land that was in the process of changing hue from a brilliance of colour of unimaginable brightness to one more toned down and restrained.

European settlers, though, were too concerned with survival to worry about the state of nature. Land had to be tamed and money made. John's days were filled with digging out stumps of felled trees, erecting fences to create fields, ploughing, planting, and looking after the farm animals. "I was put to the plough at the age of twelve years, when my head reached little above the handles, and for many years I had to do the greater part of the ploughing."[3] He was so short that he used the mane of the horse to guide him along a straight line.

Planting was more enjoyable and relatively light work, soothed by the awakening of spring and the song of birds, but harvesting was sheer drudgery, requiring long, sweat-filled hours: "We were called in the morning at four o'clock and seldom got to bed before nine, making a broiling, seething day seventeen hours long, loaded with heavy work, while I was only a small, stunted boy... In the harvest dog-days and dog-nights and dog-mornings, when we arose from our clammy beds, our cotton shirts clung to our backs as wet with sweat as the bathing suits of swimmers, and remained so all the long, sweltering days."[4]

In the winter the day started at six o'clock with feeding the livestock, followed by grinding axes, collecting wood, shelling corn, making yokes, and many other tasks that never seemed to end. If the weather was particularly harsh they worked in barns in temperatures well below freezing. There was always hard work and seldom any break. The only time off was Sunday afternoon after long church services. Some aspects of farm labour could be made into fun, particularly if Daniel was away on business, but other tasks were simply a daily grind that almost drove John into the ground. He believed his small stature was due to overwork and the poor food imposed on him by a father who viewed comfort as sin. "Think of that, ye blessed eight-hour-day labourers!"[5]

Even in the depths of winter a small kitchen stove, barely big enough to hold more than a few sticks, struggled to raise the temperature of the room above zero and the frozen boots and socks could not defrost overnight. Forcing chilblained feet into cold boots was very painful. What was galling for John was that this hardship was self-imposed austerity. Great trunks of hardwood lay rotting in the fields and could have been used to stoke large fires to warm the homestead thoroughly, but that was not the puritan way. John wrote bitterly, "Instead of hauling great heart-cheering loads of it for wide, open, all-welcoming, climate changing, beauty making, Godlike ingle-fires, it was hauled with weary heart-breaking industry into fences and waste places to get it out of the way of the plough, and out of the way of doing good."[6]

John's notebooks are full of resentment at the drudgery he and his siblings were made to endure, for precious little benefit. They were allowed no rest under the shade of trees. Even in the fiercest heat, they dared not even go to the streams to drink in case Daniel saw them and punished them as shirkers. It created anxiety and stress that wore away at everyone's temperament. It is hard to imagine today that such child labour was commonplace and even encouraged. Such was the drive to live a holy life on the land that Daniel stopped any more education. In Scotland he had been fierce about lessons and had made the children commit vast tracts of information to memory. In Wisconsin, none of the children went to school.

Not even illness deterred Daniel from his drive to wrestle a farm from the land with as little comfort or ease as possible. John describes one harvest when he had mumps and could only swallow milk: "I staggered with weakness and sometimes fell headlong among the sheaves."[7] It was to no avail; he was made to carry on working. Only when he contracted pneumonia was he allowed to retreat to bed. For weeks he lay gasping for breath, but, as Daniel believed that all that was needed for a healthy body and soul was hard work and the benevolence of God, a doctor was deemed unnecessary. He would recover, if the Almighty willed it, declared Daniel. When John did pull through he was left with a weakness in his lungs that troubled him all his life.

Daniel was by no means alone in his attitude to work, but he was considered extreme. "We were all made slaves through the vice of over-industry," wrote John, as he saw the neighbouring farmers struggling alongside his own. But for what end, he wondered? This was pure madness in his eyes; work for work's sake took the bloom out of young cheeks and the joy out of life. Many of the settlers had not owned land back home; here it was available in unimaginable proportions. God would consider it sinful to waste productive land and therefore work became a religious duty.

Yet to John it was counterproductive. The exhaustion of mind and body brought about by endless toil dimmed any spirituality: "Many of our neighbours toiled and sweated and grubbed themselves into their graves years before their natural dying days, in getting a living on a quarter-section of land and vaguely trying to get rich, while bread and raiment might have been serenely won on less than a fourth of this land and time gained to get better acquainted with God."[8]

When first ploughed and planted, the sandy soils produced a good-sized crop, but they were quickly depleted. "At first, wheat, corn, and potatoes were the principal crops we raised; wheat especially. But in four or five years the soil was so exhausted that only five or six bushels an acre, even in the better fields, was obtained, although when first ploughed twenty and twenty-five bushels was about the ordinary yield."[9] Eventually the farmers learned to plant clover to replenish the soils, realizing that the earth could not give year on year without rest. The fields were given time to recover; the people were not.

The Native Indians, on the other hand, did not toil themselves into an early grave, fuelling the notion held by the settlers that they were lazy. They lived differently, resting in times of plenty and hunting when the need arose. John marvelled at their ability to know where creatures were in the forest, seemingly by instinct. He was impressed by their lack of wastefulness and never saw a hint of triumphalism in killing wildlife. He had a complex relationship with the Indians he came across, and was not always so complimentary, but he had a lifelong respect for their innate understanding of animals, plants, and seasons.

Every so often throughout his life a chance encounter or conversation embedded itself in his soul, feeding him wisdom as he grew and helping form his own philosophy. One exchange with a fellow farmer stood out from these early farm days. It was between his father and a Scottish neighbour, Mr Mair, who seemed to demonstrate rare compassion towards the few Native Indians who were still to be found around the farms. Mr Mair suggested that the European treatment of the Indian tribes was questionable at best, and that these poor "children of Nature" were being thrown off their land and made to scrape a living off smaller and smaller areas while alien races took over, often depriving them of their livelihoods.

Daniel Muir could not agree. God could never have intended such a feeble use of land, he argued. An Indian family might require thousands of acres to keep them alive, whereas God-fearing Christians could make unproductive wilderness yield great fruit, exactly as the Bible intended. Mr Mair argued back that European farming was clumsy, full of mistakes, and unskilled on many levels, and if one day superior farmers came along with scientific methods and were able to take five or ten times more from the land than the pioneering Europeans, then the same argument would have to be used to remove them, making way for the more efficient producers.

It was an attitude that John had not heard before. He does not record Daniel's reply, but this obviously struck a chord. He came down firmly on the side of Mr Mair, agreeing that what they were witnessing was the mighty (as regards technology and force) ruling over the weaker race, with no thought for their rights or welfare.

Many other famers arrived in Wisconsin soon after the Muirs had settled, not put off by the life of labour.

Although in the spring of 1849 there was no other settler within a radius of four miles of our Fountain Lake Farm, in three or four years almost every quarter-section of government land was taken up, mostly by enthusiastic home-seekers from Great Britain... The axe and plough were kept very busy; cattle, horses, sheep, and pigs multiplied; barns and corncribs were filled up, and man and beast were well fed; a schoolhouse was built, which was used also for a church; and in a very short time the new country began to look like an old one.[10]

After eight years of back-breaking labour, Fountain Lake Farm was in good working order. In 1856 John's eldest sister, Sarah Muir, married David Galloway and the couple bought the farm from Daniel, along with its now-imposing homestead. Sarah became mistress of the original house and Daniel moved his remaining brood four miles to the south-east. Here, on a ridge dotted with old hickory trees, he bought another plot of land, 320 acres, "doubling all the stunting, heart-breaking, chopping, grubbing, stump digging, rail-splitting, fence building, barn-building and so forth".[11] This property was named Hickory Hill Farm. Beautiful as it was, it was dry. There was no stream or lake and the only way to get water was to excavate a shaft through ninety feet of rock. The first ten feet was shale and relatively easy to dig out, then they hit fine-grained sandstone. Daniel tried blasting but it was inaccurate and slow work. The best way, he decided, was to set John to the task.

John was already marked out for his precise work with the plough and in making fences. He was now given a hammer and chisel: "I had to sit cramped in a space about three feet in diameter, and wearily chip, chip, with a heavy hammer and chisels from early morning until dark day after day, for weeks and months." As the well got deeper John was lowered in a bucket, and the chippings hauled up to the surface. "Constant dropping wears away stone. So does constant chipping, while at the same time wearing away the chipper." It was hard, soul-destroying work and the well had to have perfectly straight walls, which he achieved with the most rudimentary tools, but it was an awful and almost deadly experience.

One morning, when the well had reached eighty feet, John nearly died from breathing poisonous carbon dioxide gas which had seeped into the cavity and lay heavily at the bottom. As his basket was lowered he was quickly overcome. As he got out he collapsed against the wall of the well: "I swayed back and forth and began to sink under the poison." Daniel realized he had gone silent, panicked, and yelled for him to get back in. "Somehow I managed to get into the bucket, and that is all I remembered until I was dragged out, violently gasping for breath." It was a very lucky escape. A neighbour taught Daniel to throw water and hay down the well before work to stir up the gas and absorb it. After two days off for recovery from shock John was lowered down again, chipping away as normal until a gush of pure water was struck. A well that still produces water today. By now he was nineteen years old. He had endured seven years of hard labour on two farms and there seemed no end in sight. He rightly saw himself as little more than slave labour, and the slave driver was his father. In a rare show of bitterness he wrote, "Father never spent an hour down that well."[12]

Life on a frontier farm did, however, produce food for thought as well as for the table. Through his intimate dealings with cows, pigs, horses, dogs, and cats John peered closely into the heart of the animal world and saw reflected back a soul very similar to his own. He realized that all of life is capable of nuanced behaviour – of courage, fear, sadness, pleasure, love, and faithfulness – in ways that chime directly with our own experience. Some of John's farm stories are sad; others show how people and animals shared life's joys as well as its trials. It is interesting that he gives us a more detailed picture of the characters of the farm animals than of his own family, whose personalities mostly remain a mystery.

Far from being unintelligent, cattle were remarkably astute, and "we soon learned that each ox and cow and calf had individual character".[13] An ox, Old Buck, seemed to know by instinct how to break open a pumpkin without having to wait for someone with an axe. He lumbered over to a pile, picked one out as though he were choosing the best on offer, rolled it between his front legs, knelt down, and smashed it with his head. John had never seen another animal do this and was impressed by his inventiveness. Two other oxen, Tom and Jerry, showed an instinct for the lie of the land even though they were in new territory. Late one night, Daniel was driving back to the farm and left the usual track to find a short cut. The oxen stopped still after a while and refused to move. It was pitch black. Daniel eventually unhitched them and held on to their tails and they led him straight home by another route, but he had to abandon the cart until the morning. Only in the light of day did he find how close he had come to disaster, as they had stopped on the edge of a ridge that fell away into a swamp.

These patient and forgiving beasts did all the hard work of hauling and much of the ploughing day after day. "The humanity we found in them came partly through the expression of their eyes when tired, their tones of voice when hungry and calling for food, their patient plodding and pulling in hot weather, their long drawn out sighing breath when exhausted and suffering like ourselves, and their enjoyment of rest with the same grateful look as ours... their love of play; the attachments they made; and their mourning long continued when a companion was killed."[14]

Horses and ponies were an integral part of the Muir farm, both as beasts of burden and as pets. Nob was a female pony and greatly loved for her playfulness, and she followed the children whenever she could. One day an Indian crept into her field and stole her. John believed that he must have treated her very badly for the few months he held her captive, because when at last she was found and returned to the farm by a neighbour she would always stop in terror at the place where she had been taken, obviously frightened that the man would appear again.

Her end was untimely and cruel. Daniel rode her to Portage and back – a long, twenty-four-mile round trip on a hot summer's day. He drove her hard to get home in time for a religious meeting and John was charged with putting her in the stable. "I shall never forget how tired and wilted she looked that evening when I unhitched her; how she drooped in her stall, too tired to eat or even lie down."

That night she developed pneumonia and John recognized the same symptoms that he had endured. Nothing could be done and she wandered slowly about the farm, "in the weary suffering and loneliness of the shadow of death". She tried to stay with the children and they did their best to comfort her, but on her last day, after a severe haemorrhage, "she came to me trembling, with beseeching, heart-breaking looks, and after I had bathed her head and tried to soothe and pet her, she lay down and gasped and died. All the family gathered around her, weeping, with aching hearts."[15]

The way a sow cared for her piglets also moved John, and he delighted in the "queer, funny animal children" who rushed about, raising false alarms with their squeals and constantly demanding to be suckled. The mother protected them as though she would gladly die to keep them safe and as they grew she took them further and further afield into the farmland to show them how to grub up roots and snuffle out acorns. One day an ominous shot was heard from the old path by the lake. Not long afterwards the sow and piglets came rushing back to the farm, "out of breath and terror stricken". One piglet was missing and when John went there later he found blood on the track. "The solemn awe and fear in the eye of that old mother and those little pigs I never can forget; it was an unmistakable and deadly a fear as I ever saw expressed by a human eye, and corroborates in no uncertain way the oneness of all of us."[16]

These stories of life on the farm show a young John Muir trying to piece together what he saw with his own eyes, what he felt in his soul, and what he was taught was the truth. It was a testing time not just physically but spiritually as he constantly wrestled with contradiction. The evidence of his eyes seemed at odds with the unwavering view of life his father presented every evening at family prayers, and what he heard from the pulpit during the long hours spent in church on Sunday. The beliefs that everything on earth was there to serve man, and that only human beings had souls and therefore able to reflect God, seemed to be a gross misunderstanding of the evidence observed every day. The wide range of emotions that the farm animals expressed bore such a close resemblance to his own experience of joy, pain, and toil that he began to question whether they were simply beasts of burden put on earth to provide us with what we need. "Of the many advantages of farm life for boys one of the greatest is the gaining a real knowledge of animals as fellow-mortals, learning to respect them and love them, and even to win some of their love."

He later reflected that getting close to animal life in a day-to-day way, including domesticated animals, was one of the greatest gifts he gained from his hard farm years: "Thus godlike sympathy grows and thrives and spreads far beyond the teachings of churches and schools, where too often the mean, blinding, loveless doctrine is taught that animals have neither mind nor soul, have no rights that we are bound to respect, and were made only for man, to be petted, spoiled, slaughtered or enslaved."[17] In this he was closely in tune with the emerging animal rights movement in Europe. Acclaimed thinkers such as the German philosopher Arthur Schopenhauer and Charles Darwin urged compassion for animals, which were increasingly being shown to be similar to ourselves. Schopenhauer wrote that Europeans were "awakening more and more to a sense that beasts have rights, in proportion as the strange notion is being gradually overcome and outgrown, that the animal kingdom came into existence solely for the benefit and pleasure of man".[18] He was directly targeting and challenging the dominant Christian notion at the time that animals were "mere things, mere means to an end". Darwin compared the treatment of animals with the treatment of slaves, something he abhorred: "Animals whom we have made our slaves we do not like to consider our equals. Do not slave holders wish to make the black man other kind?"[19] Animals, he said, experience affection, sorrow for the dead, pain, fear, and respect. Why then should they not be treated with kindness and compassion?

John also began to understand that humans were capable of what he deemed to be gross hypocrisy. Watch was the family dog, a curious animal with a great sense of smell, and "a good judge of character". When he was young he was playful enough but as he grew older he became "cross and … fell on evil ways". Neighbours started to complain that Watch was catching and eating whole broods of chickens and had to be destroyed. No one wanted to believe it but eventually Daniel shot him, despite the "tearful protests". When Watch's stomach was examined it was found to contain the heads of eight chickens.

> So poor Watch was killed simply because his taste for chickens was much like our own. Think of the millions of squabs that preaching, praying men and women kill and eat, with all sorts of other animals great and small, young and old, while eloquently discoursing on the coming of the blessed, peaceful, bloodless millennium! Think of the passenger pigeons that fifty or sixty years ago filled the woods and sky over half the continent, now exterminated by beating down the young from the nests together with the brooding parents... None of our fellow mortals is safe who eats what we eat, who in any ways interferes with our pleasures, or who may be used for work or food, clothing or ornament, or mere cruel, sportish amusement... it is a great comfort to learn that vast multitudes of creatures, great and small and infinite in number, lived and had a good time in God's love before man was created.[20]

These hard farm years were formative in so many ways. They created a steely inner strength honed from hard, physical labour sustained on only a little food and scant comfort, a strength that would prove invaluable in the years to come as John wandered mountains, swamps, and glaciers alone and with few supplies. He wrote, "Without hard work and suffering there could be no pleasure worth having", and he also believed work was essential for spiritual development: "It is through suffering that... saints are developed and made perfect."[21]

Farm labour taught John practical skills of which he was proud and which he would later use to pay his way and to fund his travels. In the years to come he would work as a carpenter and shepherd, allowing him long spells in the mountains. Farm life also pitched him directly into the outdoors whatever the season, so that cold, heat, rain or snow never deterred him. On the contrary: he often sought out storms and revelled in severe weather.

Perhaps most importantly, it allowed him close contact with animal life, both wild and domesticated, and he drew great wisdom from watching them closely, learning lessons from their behaviour and identifying with their emotions. He never held the mechanistic view of animals as creatures purely driven by instinct and with no individual characteristics, and throughout his life in the wilds he looked for those traits in all the creatures he came across. He believed that wild animals have personalities, an unpopular view in the growing scientific milieu. He also began to draw away from the blinkered religious views of his father (although those links would take many more years to fully sever) and began to form his own judgments about what it is to be human surrounded by a vast array of other forms of life on a planet imbued with the spirit of God. And, although he still had to endure beatings and harshness, he found that his own warm, generous spirit always triumphed.

Maybe it was because John also watched how his own family and neighbours squared up to the challenge of farming this land of plenty and hardship that he never lost his love of humanity. He saw their spirit of community and their support for one another, especially for the weaker people who found it hard to cope. He admired them for their steadfastness, devoutness, and faithfulness to what they believed was true, and throughout his life he treasured people as well as wilderness and yearned for civilization to share in his love of nature: "I care to live only to entice people to look at Nature's loveliness."[22] Far from his experiences clamping his spirit into a harsh and critical adult, they seem to have remoulded it, producing a joyous, far-reaching love for all of life.

John Muir is renowned for his understanding of nature, his work for conservation, and his spiritual insights, but it his sense of fun that always comes across as a strong and enduring characteristic right from his earliest days. Whether it was childish tomfoolery such as clamping a snapping turtle onto a dog's ear or tying a stick to a sow's tail, or more adult student mischiefs, his sense of humour never failed him. Many years later, a college friend described him as "bubbling over with fun, and a keen participant in frolics and college pranks".[23] Fun is infectious and it may be this characteristic that drew so many people to see him as a friend rather than as a remote, wilderness pioneer. "All God's people, however serious or savage, great or small, like to play. Whales and elephants, dancing humming gnats and invisibly small mischievous microbes – all are warm with divine radium and must have lots of fun in them."[24]

Whatever he did in his eventful life, John found something to make him smile, and his personality endeared him to everyone he spent time with. He seemed able to take criticism without resentment and to separate the goodness he believed dwelt in all people from their often foolish (as he saw it) actions.

One other side of John Muir emerged in these important years, a surprising and intriguing side which showed an unusual mind that was able to see offbeat solutions to problems. This side allowed him to find his own creative life in this highly controlled environment. John Muir the inventor emerged out of the darkness of a freezing cellar and set him apart from the other young farmhands toiling away on the land. His bizarre inventions, sometimes playful, often strange or comical, yet all meticulously conceived, were about to pave the way to freedom.

Chapter 4

Learning and Inventing

"I believe that dreams - day dreams, you know, with your eyes wide open and your brain-machinery whizzing - are likely to lead to the betterment of the world. The imaginative child will become the imaginative man or woman most apt to create, to invent, and therefore to foster civilization."

L. Frank Baum, *The Lost Princess of Oz*

This quote from the author of *The Wizard of Oz* could have been written for John Muir. From the age of fifteen, he began to flower into a rare and extraordinary young man.. Just as a wildflower meadow can bloom into a myriad of beautiful and diverse plants only if the soil is kept low in nutrients, so the mind of John Muir blossomed into a landscape full of surprise and creativity. Physical graft, simple and limited food, an austere, unwavering regime, and an atmosphere dominated by stifling religious beliefs proved to be the perfect soil for growth.

He was already insatiably curious about life, but as there was no one to answer his questions he set about discovering answers for himself. One of the first puzzles he solved was how honey bees find their way around. Although they were first introduced into America in the 1600s, European honey bees didn't buzz around the farm until ten years after the family arrived, and formal beekeeping was in its infancy. The bees were feral, building nests in the hollowed-out trunks of trees or other cavities. The only way for John to find a treasure trove of sweetness was to learn how to track a bee back to its wild nest. He would have to be precise and quick, though. The Native Indians (who called the honeybee the "white man's fly") were fine observers of wildlife and known to track bees as soon as they arrived.

John trapped a bee in a wooden box containing honey and, after it had eaten its fill, he let it go and watched as it flew around the box, taking bearings and noting features in the landscape. It then shot off in its zig-zagging flight back to its nest. Ten minutes later the bee returned to the exact same spot to get more honey, but John found that if he moved his box to even just a few yards away the "cunning little honey gleaner... whirled round and round as if confused and lost".[1] He raced after the bee once it was on its way home to find the nest, which was in an old log, but alas someone had been there beforehand and the honey was gone. He was saddened, however, that the nest had virtually been destroyed and all the honey taken, leaving none for the workers who had spent so long gathering their resources for the winter.

This was John the curious naturalist at work, a puzzle-solver who used science and logic to explain what he saw around him. But he wanted more; he wanted to understand the world outside the farm too, and his teenage years were dominated by an almost desperate attempt to quench a raging thirst for knowledge.

One summer he persuaded his father to buy him books on mathematics, deemed suitable by Daniel as he judged they couldn't interfere with the teachings of the Bible. The same could not be said, however, of books on literature, which were banned in the house as works of the ungodly. "The Bible is the only book human beings can possibly require throughout the whole journey from earth to heaven," he pronounced.[2] Fortunately, some neighbours were not as extreme and lent him their books, which he read in secret.

By selling grain from a small plot of land he had set aside, he slowly saved up some money to buy a few more for himself, such as some of the works of Scott, Shakespeare, Milton, Cowper, Henry Kirk White, Campbell, and Akenside. These and other authors began to introduce different lives and realities into John's blotting-paper mind and he "began to relish good literature with enthusiasm and smack my lips over favourite lines".[3]

Interestingly, many of the authors whose work he chose to buy were both Scottish and religious. John remained fiercely proud of being Scottish and never lost his accent. In a letter to a friend years later he wrote, "... there is heather in me, and tinctures of bog juices ... oozing through all my veins".[4] His belief in God also never wavered, though it was to change form many times. Perhaps some of the "lip-smacking lines" he refers to touched his life in comforting ways. When the days seemed long and hard the words of Mark Akenside, an eighteenth-century Scottish poet, in "To Sleep" must have affirmed that his weariness was part of the lot of man through the ages, experienced even by those whose lives were lived through the pen rather than the plough:

> Thou silent power, whose welcome sway
> Charms every anxious thought away;
> In whose divine oblivion drown'd,
> Sore pain and weary toil grow mild[5]

Or perhaps the pertinent words of another Scottish poet, Thomas Campbell (1777–1844), in the tragic lover's tale "Lord Ullin's Daughter" helped him express his difficult relationship with Daniel:

> I'll meet the raging of the skies, but not an angry father.[6]

Although from a past age, these Scottish poets seemed excitingly courageous to a sheltered boy. They fired his patriotic blood with yearnings for gallant deeds, anti-English sentiment, and inspiring visions of wild lands. These literary heavyweights were also steeped in religion, but they were different. Here faith was expressed through imagery and not confined to Bible verses. Their Christianity was romantic and gutsy; it spoke of the oppressed and the pain of lost love. It appeared in the darkened skies above the moor and burned in the fires of crofts. It even spoke of the divine in nature and its ineffable mystery. John knew the Bible off by heart, but here were new slants on deep truths. He had no desire to shake God off as a bad experience – a sense of the divine would always guide his path – but, as with natural history, he wanted to think for himself and take what he knew and test it against the reality of his own experience.

By now, thanks to the combination of the writers housed on the bookshelves of neighbours, his own collection, and his reading from school days, John was gaining some knowledge of the rich interpretations of all aspects of life that literature offered. The likes of Robert Burns, William Wordsworth, and John Clare had shaped the landscape of nature writing in Britain and they formed a fresh, thoughtful, spiritual view of the rolling hills and downy heathland of the British Isles. Drawing from the experience of mountains, fells, and fields, these leviathans of literature broke new ground: like ploughs through untilled earth, they smashed opened dry clods and allowed new growth to flourish.

Underneath the confident and familiar Scottish brogue of Burns, John found a kindred spirit who was fiercely patriotic and also viewed nature as kith and kin, both sentiments very close to John's heart. Burns often wrote with a deep empathy about the suffering of the animals that populated his daily life, from an injured hare "crying like a child" to the fate of a field mouse whose nest was wrecked. Burns' words evoked grief and pain for mere animals. In "A Winter Night" he aches for a poor bird outside in a snowstorm, wondering where it will find warmth and protection:

> Ilk happening bird, – wee, helpless thing!
> That, in the merry months o' spring,
> Delighted me to hear thee sing,
> What comes o' thee?
> Whare wilt thou cow'r thy chittering wing,
> An' close thy e'e?[7]

John had often sympathized with the birds that stayed on the farm throughout the freezing Wisconsin winter. As he lay shivering under a few blankets he marvelled at "the brave, frost-defying chickadees and nuthatches".

Burns would always hold a special place in his heart. In an article in 1907 John described him as "one of the greatest men", and said, "His lessons of divine love and sympathy to humanity, which he preached in his poems and sent forth white-hot from his heart, have gone ringing and singing around the globe, stirring the heart of every nation and race."

In some ways their lives followed similar paths. John Muir and Robert Burns both knew hard, physical toil; they both worked the land and were taught their religion at their father's knee. They both knew the sapping heat of summer and the disabling cold of winter, and they both saw the glory of divine creativity in the world around the fields. In a eulogy to Burns he wrote, "The eye of the Poet, the Seer, never closes on the kinship of all God's creatures, and his heart ever beats in sympathy with great and small alike as 'earth-born companions and fellow mortals' equally dependent on Heaven's eternal love." Throughout his life John referred to Burns' phrase "fellow mortals" many times.

Burns, however, never escaped grinding poverty making his all-embracing, sympathetic, and love-filled words even more remarkable. "On my lonely walks I have often thought how fine it would be to have the company of Burns. And indeed he was always with me, for I had him in my heart."[8]

Wordsworth, who was also inspired by Burns, put away traditional church sentiment and presented the reader with an individual understanding of God that could not be captured by strait-laced religious tracts. Through the glories of the Lake District, from the shining daffodils to the snowy ridges, the divine became a shape-shifter. At times God reached out a hand of friendship to mere mortals, as sunshine warms the earth, but at others he remained hidden behind a dark, rain-filled cloud. God and nature were inseparable, and mountains, Wordsworth wrote, "haunted me like a passion, that the colours and forms of nature, were then to me, an appetite; a feeling of love…" But nature also echoed the deepest sorrow of man, reflecting "the still, sad music of humanity…"[9] Therefore God was not a constant powerful presence; more of an ungraspable yearning that revealed itself in birdsong or flowers, and then shrank to despair. Nature was imbued with a shifting holiness that had to be experienced first hand; God could not be found purely between the covers of one book. This view of the world was far removed from John's father's teachings of God as an unchanging taskmaster who was easily roused to anger and retribution. In "The Tables Turned", Wordsworth subversively wrote:

One impulse from a vernal wood
May teach you more of man,
Of moral evil and of good,
Than all the sages can.[10]

This must, quite simply, have blown John Muir's mind wide open.

He also gained access to Lord Byron and Edgar Allan Poe, as well as to the travels of Mungo Park and more of Alexander von Humboldt. These books were far more than collections of clever words; they were windows through which he gazed with a longing heart.

This heady mix of travel, nature, and religion began to stir yearnings to know more. In a few years' time he would experience the joy of discovering the revolutionary writings of Ralph Waldo Emerson, Henry David Thoreau, and Walt Whitman, the writers who were already at work redefining nature and its place in literature. But in the intellectually confined world of his farm they were a bridge too far and he would have to wait for the dangerously liberal city of Madison before such subversion was freely on offer.

John kept trying to persuade Daniel to buy at least some books other than holy works, and his accounts of their exchanges are amusing and revealing. We begin to get a glimpse of his unusual and quick mind, which often drove Daniel mad with annoyance. On one occasion John proposed that it was important to read books other than the Bible because how else would people gain the knowledge to make spectacles to enable old people like Daniel to read the holy book? That was no argument, retorted Daniel, as there would always be sinners to make spectacles. Not so, came the reply, for all will eventually come to the light, we are told, so then who will make the spectacles we all will need? Daniel was not amused, refused to let books into the house and called him a "contumacious quibbler too fond of disputation".[11]

On another day, John managed to stop Daniel enforcing a vegetarian diet by pointing out that God had sent ravens to feed Elijah when he was hiding from the enemy. As surely Daniel knew, ravens would not have brought vegetables to the great prophet, but meat. Meat therefore could not be frowned upon by the Almighty if a man as blessed as Elijah ate it. Daniel was promptly persuaded and meat was re-established.

John was a superb "quibbler" and it was a skill that he would use many times in the future. Mostly he used his wit to get what he needed, such as a meal or a bed for the night, but at other times he exasperated his companions and they gave up even trying to engage with him.

These exchanges with his father show that in his teenage years a more independent John was emerging. He was still held fast by an iron grip, but, like Houdini in a straitjacket, he was using skill to wriggle free and prepare for his escape.

John had found ways of gaining access to books but his greatest problem was finding time on his own to read and study. His daily life was highly regulated and the hours long and tiring. He grabbed minutes here and there between jobs, but any serious stretch of time for thought and concentration was denied him. Daniel insisted that everyone went to bed after evening prayers – "I will have no irregularity in the family" – and in the winter months that could be as early as eight o'clock. John always tried to slip into a corner with a candle to catch just five minutes before Daniel noticed and ordered him upstairs, an order he had to keep. He plaintively wrote, "How keenly precious those few minutes were, few nowadays can know… father failed perhaps two or three times in a whole winter to notice my light for nearly ten minutes, magnificent, golden blocks of time long to be remembered like holidays or geologic periods."[12]

Daniel eventually lost his temper and told John he had to go to bed with the others without having to be told separately. Perhaps on that one evening Daniel felt some sympathy – after all, John was reading a book on church history – and so he added the fateful edict, "If you will read, get up in the morning and read. You may get up in the morning as early as you like." And with those few precious words John Muir now had the key to unlock the door and fly. Daniel could not have known that his last sentence would set John on a path of self-discovery and creative blossoming that would eventually lead to his leaving the farm and begin to prepare the way for vast tracts of the United States to be protected in perpetuity. It was a special winter's night.

John went to bed, "wishing with all my heart and soul that somebody or something would call me out of sleep", which it did. He sprang out of bed "as if called by a trumpet blast", and rushed downstairs in the dark. When he held a candle to the clock he found to his unbridled delight that it was only one o'clock. His happiness could not have been more complete. "Five hours to myself! Five huge solid hours! I can hardly think of any other event in my life, any discovery I ever made that gave birth to joy so transportingly glorious as the possession of those five frosty hours." Reading was out of the question. It was so cold that he would have needed to light a fire, which he knew Daniel would not allow. He therefore took his candle, went into the cellar, and began to make machines out of wood.

It was as though his fertile mind had long been planning for these precious hours of darkness. Already he had many blueprints filed away, stored in his memory like designs in a filing cabinet, ready to be laid out and followed. His first machine was a self-setting sawmill. With only the light of a tallow candle, and no heating despite the temperature that night being below freezing, John hammered and banged and sawed through the early hours.

There were very few tools to work with and many of the things he needed he had to make for himself, such as a fine-toothed saw from the metal out of an old corset: "I also made my own bradawls, punches, and a pair of compasses, out of wire and old files."

Throughout the night this astonishing young man worked with precision and intensity. Daniel's bedroom was directly above all this activity but, as he had told John he could get up when he liked, and he was a man of his word, there was little to be done. The work went gloriously on night after night. He was driven by adrenalin, the creative impulse, and a sense of freedom that enabled him to work without a break and to feel no ill effects during the day.

After the sawmill, John made "water-wheels, curious door locks and latches, hygrometers, pyrometers, clocks, a barometer, an automatic contrivance for feeding horses at any required hour, a lamp-lighter and a fire-lighter, an early or late rising machine and so forth". The latter was a curious clock that could tell the day of the week and the day of the month as well as strike the hour and, if an attachment was fitted, could tip a sleeper out of bed in the mornings. It was this particular construction that John hid behind a bed in a spare room.

So far the work went officially unacknowledged, although everyone knew something was going bump in the night. John kept his designs secret and hoped Daniel would not ask what he was doing. This worked for just two weeks until Daniel found the curious bed-tipping device.

Shortly afterwards, during the evening meal, Daniel spoke up, demanding to know what the contraption was and why it was being made. John made a feeble attempt to justify his "early rising machine" but Daniel was unimpressed: "If only you were half as zealous in studying religion as you are in contriving and whittling these useless, nonsensical things, it would be infinitely better for you." John "feared the doom of martyrdom was about to be pronounced on my grand clock". But, perhaps because it was so extraordinarily well made, so unusual and accomplished, Daniel spared it from being put on the fire. A few days later, in fact, he was seen studying it on his hands and knees, trying to work out how it worked.

With the need for secrecy at an end, ever-more-ingenious devices emerged from the cellar like creatures out of a swamp. These were beautiful, precise pieces of work that astonished anyone who saw them. In these few intense teenage years John blossomed into an inventor of extraordinary and remarkable creativity. The lack of sleep didn't seem to affect him. The joy he gained from being allowed to create in peace seemed to spur him on to ever-greater things.

The inventions suggest two things about John Muir. First, he was at ease with science and technology, and could envisage how to harness forces of nature such as gravity, sun, wind, and water. Second, he showed a unique creativity that took the ordinary and made it extraordinary. Everyday objects were transformed into creations that delighted and amazed, as well as looking good. In some ways it is surprising that someone who worked so hard used his ingenuity to encourage people to do more work by making them get up early, read more books, make more things, keep precise time, and so on, and it shows just how steeped in the Protestant work ethic he had become. Newtonian mechanics and a God of retribution dominated John's world and those strictures were impossible to shake off – yet.

The making of machines would also later feed in to his desire to fit together the pieces that make up the natural world. John's mechanical mind saw interconnectedness, the very essence of ecology. The great web of life weaves and meanders throughout the earth, binding us altogether. In 1911 he came to the conclusion that "[w]hen we try to pick out anything by itself, we find it hitched to everything else in the Universe".[13] In some ways life is a highly complex machine, one huge, glorious set of parts, interrelated and interdependent. The removal of even a tiny cog may affect the smooth running of the whole. Studying the great machine of life gives the explorer a glimpse of the mind of God. The candlelit hours in the cellar laid the foundations for a lifetime of immersion in God's extraordinary creation.

Even though John lived away from the intensity of industrial expansion in the cities, he slotted into the prevailing milieu of industrial inventiveness. At this time the sewing machine, typewriters, the internal combustion engine, and washing machines were entering public life as mechanization spread and people became fired up by the challenge of saving time and making money. He had been given a golden ticket to create by his father, and he could not be accused of letting the opportunity slip away. As John Muir the teenager was hammering in the cellar of Fountain Lake Farm, Thomas Edison, then just a pre-teen destined to become America's most famous inventor, was devouring knowledge in Ohio, and preparing himself for his extraordinary life. Edison famously once said, "Opportunity is missed by most people because it is dressed in overalls and looks like work."[14] John Muir was not one of those people. Hard work and overalls were his natural attire, and invention flowed easily from his young, quirky mind and out through his skilled hands.

Although so many things bound him to a blinkered view of the world, this creative outburst was freeform in its own way. His mind managed to be at once constrained by his cultural environment, but also uninhibited and experimental. This combination allowed unusual connections to be made between humanity and machines. In this he was a product of his time, particularly in America, where the land was changing daily from nature to utility. The technological and scientific exhibitions that were springing up all around the developing world showed off to the public the ingenuity of the modern industrial age and were full of remarkable fantasies of what humanity could now achieve. In his own backwoods kind of way, John was right there contributing to this explosion of ideas.

Some of his inventions, however, never made it into reality but remained as lines on paper. They show a more hidden side, a dark, anxious young man who saw the world as full of forces that controlled rather than liberated. His own experience of being treated like a machine to do farm labour played out in his subconscious as images of angst. One particularly nightmarish image is of a doll attached to a machine that made its arms move up and down, something more at home in a nursery scene in a horror movie than in the bright, life-filled meadows of Fountain Lake Farm. Others show straight lines, arrows, wheels, and cogs hovering above deforested landscapes, and people are seen as tiny pawns that obey the relentless laws of mechanics, driving them to act.

One invention that did make it into physical reality was displayed proudly on the farm. It was a clock made from a large wooden scythe, which hung in a tree. A Bible quote from Isaiah, "All flesh is grass", was inscribed on the wooden handle. It was designed to be displayed outside, to act as a warning to the viewer that they are as transitory as the grass growing in the fields. One day all will be cut down to return to dust. It was a disturbing design for a young man. Daniel, however, was very pleased with this piece of embellishment, as were the rest of the family and their neighbours, but for a boy with so much life ahead of him it speaks of a bowed spirit. Perhaps it is not surprising Daniel had taught all his children to view themselves as worthless sinners not deserving of praise, and so a scythe that cut through time and sheared away life was a natural manifestation of his philosophy.

How much John was aware of the horrors of the slums of industrial cities, where people were simply cogs in an enormous machine producing wealth for the wealthy, is not clear, but his inventions showed him to be of the mindset that industry, not idleness, was the destiny for all good people. This sentiment was never totally abandoned, even after years of immersion in wilderness. John was forever to hold two contradictory aspects of his personality in tension; one that welcomed the changes brought by industrialization and technology and the other that of a nature mystic who looked with increasing dismay at the changing world he had helped design. These two different men walked in one body, presenting a mystery that no one ever completely understood or unravelled.

Much later, when the early memories of his life were actually written down, John reflected that his machines were doing what

Ralph Waldo Emerson had celebrated as a great achievement for mankind: allowing nature to work for you. Emerson was no Luddite; he too welcomed the enhancement of human society by utilizing nature in a thoughtful and respectful way. He wrote:

> I admire still more than the saw-mill the skill which, on the sea-shore, makes the tides drive the wheels and grind the corn and which this embraces the assistance of the moon, like a hired band, to grind, and wind and pump, and saw, and split stone, and roll iron.
>
> Now that is the wisdom of a man, in every instance of his labor, to hitch his wagon to a star and see his chores done by the gods themselves. That is the way we are strong, by borrowing the might of the elements. The forces of steam, gravity, galvanism, light, magnets, wind, fire, serve us day by day, and cost us nothing.[15]

In the late 1850s, John had not yet immersed himself in the acclaimed natural vision of Emerson, but this sentiment went to the heart of his creations. His machines used only natural power to ease the burden of the labourer. In Emerson's world that was a fine achievement, and he would later call John "one of my men". It was not until 1871, over a decade later, that the two soulmates at last came face to face.

By now the inventions were something of a talking point among the neighbours, as some of them were so large they could be seen from a distance away. One such was a thermometer that was bracketed to the wall of the homestead. This was so sensitive that it could even detect the warmth of a human body passing within five feet, causing the great needle to spin around. Even Daniel, "my own all-Bible father", considered it a wonder. But how was he to turn all this into the means to venture into the world?

That was the question that vexed him. John had no income and no idea how to get one. Given free rein, he thought he might like to become a physician; his mother wondered if he would travel the world like Mungo Park, but hoped he would turn to the church and become a minister. His sisters were so impressed by his "whittlings" that they wanted him to be a famous inventor. John doesn't say what Daniel wanted for him – no doubt to stay and work on the farm.

It was a chance conversation with a local farmer that set him on a one-way track. This wise neighbour advised him to take his inventions to the State Fair in Madison, where his genius would surely be recognized and job offers would flow like wine at a banquet: "Just as soon as they are seen they will open the door of any shop in the country to you… There's nothing else like them in the world. That is what will attract attention, and besides they're mighty handsome things anyway to come from the backwoods."[16]

Praise though was not easy to accept, as "Father carefully taught us to consider ourselves very poor worms of the dust, conceived in sin",[17] but it was a lifeline he held onto. He made the decision to leave home, packed his bags, and began his goodbyes. He had a gold sovereign that Grandfather Gilrye had given him and a small amount of his own savings from selling his wheat. All in all only about $15. Daniel refused to give him money, saying he should rely only on himself, and offered no words of encouragement. John, in a rare instance of resentment, recorded the only advice Daniel imparted: "I would soon learn that although I might have thought him a hard task master at times, strangers were far harder." Hardly uplifting words for a shy, socially isolated young man who had worked very hard for many years.

Perhaps Daniel was trying to keep him at home, or maybe he genuinely believed that the world was full of cruelty and indifference; either way, it was a heartless and unnecessary send-off. Tellingly, John describes only the parting from his mother and sisters as "aching", although he was grateful that Daniel did allow his brother David to drive him to the station at Pardeeville. It was only nine miles from Hickory Hill Farm, but somewhere John had never been to before. We can only imagine what it was like for him to leave the safety of home with only some inventions bundled together, one of which (a thermometer) was made of an old washboard. He must have struck a lonely, almost hobo figure standing on an empty platform, dressed in rough work clothes and hovering nervously between two worlds.

Chapter 5

The Transition Years

*"The mind is not a vessel that needs filling but wood
that needs igniting."*

Attributed to Plutarch

It was late summer in 1860 when John Muir, aged twenty-two, stood on Pardeeville platform as a group of admirers gathered round him asking questions about the curious bundle he carried on his back. Someone wondered if it was a machine to remove the bones from fish, and all were mightily impressed. They were eager to know what a phrenologist would discover if his skull were to be examined: "I wish I could see that boy's head, he must have a tremendous bump in invention!"[1] This gawky young inventor so impressed the conductor of the train that he persuaded the engine driver to let John ride on the cowcatcher. For a boy used only to horses and carts that must have been an exhilarating experience, and a hopeful start. Madison lay forty miles to the south. The power of the engine, the speed, and the rushing scenery must have helped blow away some of his anxiety, racing him towards a new future.

His overwhelming experience of his first few days of freedom did not support Daniel's gloomy prediction that the world was harsh, on the contrary he found people kind and supportive. At the Fair he was welcomed as a phenomenon from the back-country and his odd-looking but beautifully made inventions were given pride of place in the main exhibition hall. They were the star attraction and appeared in the local papers, which then forwarded them to the eastern press, describing his inventions as "prodigies in the art of whittling" and "executed by genuine genius".[2]

His bed-tipping device was a crowd-puller, especially when John persuaded two young boys to pretend to sleep in it until they were unceremoniously dumped on their feet to the sound of cheers and enthusiastic applause. The mother of one of the boys looked on admiringly; she was there by invitation from the Fair officials to come and see the "meritorious inventions". This lady was Jeanne Carr, arguably the most influential person in John's adult life. Their meeting at the Fair was brief, and neither realized at the time that they were destined to be the closest of friends for the next forty years. Jeanne recommended that he be given a special award, and then she moved on.

News of John's success even reached Hickory Hill Farm and Daniel was concerned. Adulation and praise sprang from the Devil himself and would tempt his son to the sin of vanity, but John reassured him that "he had refrained from reading the newspaper praise lest it go to his head".[3]

A Mrs Johnson, the wife of a local judge and newspaper editor, was also present at the exhibition and recalled him as 'a rather clumsy looking boy",[4] but she, along with Jeanne and many others, was struck by his peculiar scythe clock and its pious engraving. He was given a special cash prize and much encouragement to take his obvious talents out into the world, proving that John's old neighbour was right. Exactly who would take on this budding genius, though? The inventions delighted and impressed, and as the exhibition hall thronged with entrepreneurs, businessmen, manufacturers, and investors it was just a matter of time before John the farm boy was on his way to being a man of the Industrial Revolution.

An entrepreneur called Mr Wiard did take him on, and they went to his workshop in the small town of Prairie du Chien on the banks of the Mississippi, 100 miles east of Madison. Wiard was himself an inventor and had designed an ice boat which he hoped would open up the frozen upper parts of the river in winter, when ordinary boats could not travel. Wiard, however, was neglectful and disinterested and he spent long periods away, leaving John wondering what he should be doing. After scooping him up, Wiard then ignored his backwoods protégé and, as his ice boat idea failed to gain ground, John left his employment.

John decided to stay on in the town as an odd-job man in a boarding house run by the Pelton family. The Peltons were good, kind people and they became lifelong friends. The same Mrs Johnson who had seen him at the Fair was also staying there, and in a newspaper article after John's death she recalled him as being a conscientious worker and student. Every evening after work he carried on studying science in his room. She did have a criticism, though: he was overwhelmingly priggish when it came to the guests having fun with parlour games. In fact, he was so "disgusted" one Thanksgiving evening by the frivolity and flirting that, as he left the room, he "freely expressed his opinion of the whole performance",[5] which must have put a dampener on the party. Next day the guests apologized. Outside the security of the farm there was much to tempt the devout young John Muir from his righteous ways, but he held fast to his upbringing, writing reassuring letters home that his moral stature was intact.

By the time winter arrived John was back in Madison and making a meagre living off commissions for a few of his inventions and by doing odd jobs. He was lonely and unsure about where he wanted to be, but he wrote a reassuring letter to Mrs Pelton, "For a week or two after leaving you all I often felt rather lonely perhaps gloomy though always happy in the centre".[6] No dream job offers arrived, however, and nothing tempting was on the horizon, apart from the University. This beautifully situated monument to learning was all he desired, but he had no idea how to become a student.

The University of Wisconsin was only fifteen years old when John arrived in town, and the main building, sporting its impressive dome and grand pillars, was completed only in 1859. After his handmade, homespun world it must have been an awesome sight. He recalls being "charmed with its fine lawns and trees and beautiful lakes", but even more mesmerized by the sheer knowledge contained within its stately walls. It spoke of an optimism for the future of this land that seemed to know no bounds. Lack of confidence kept him in the shadows but he looked on with envy at the students he saw wandering around the grounds carrying their precious books. His thirst for education was stronger than ever and he was "willing to endure anything to get it", but with so little money he was convinced a university education would remain forever a dream.

Once again, a chance conversation changed the course of his life. A casual exchange with a student he had met at the Fair must have felt like meeting an angel with great tidings. Of course John could join the freshman class, the student told him, if he could find a few tens of dollars to pay the fees for a term, was prepared to live on a simple diet of bread and milk, and could put up with cheap board. Little did the student know he was talking to the master of simple living. No more encouragement needed, apart from some cash. Probably owing to his mother's intervention, an unexpected gift of money arrived from his father. In a seeming change of heart about education, Daniel sent him enough for half a year and, surprisingly, sent his blessing, albeit with an admonition to be temperate, love God more than machines, and pray for the poor heathen. This was a timely and welcome gift, and John shored up his nerves and applied.

> With fear and trembling, overladen with ignorance, I called upon
> Professor Sterling, the dean of the faculty, who was then acting
> president, presented my case, and told him how far I had got on with
> my studies at home, and that I hadn't been to school since leaving
> Scotland at the age of eleven years, excepting one short term of a
> couple of months at a district school, because I could not be spared
> from the farm work. After hearing my story, the kind professor
> welcomed me to the glorious University – next, it seemed to me,
> to the Kingdom of Heaven. After a few weeks in the preparatory
> department I entered the freshman class.[7]

John's life at university was a combination of hard work, intellectual revelation, and fun. Sometimes his allowance was reduced to half a dollar per week for food, when he had to buy his own equipment for experiments. He studied hard during term time and worked long hours in the holidays, harvesting fields to help pay his way. Every evening he returned to his books, but rather than taking complete courses he chose those subjects that fascinated him most, "particularly chemistry, which opened a new world, and mathematics and physics, a little Greek and Latin, botany and geology".

To supplement his poor income, one winter he taught at a school ten miles away. The schoolrooms were perishingly cold during the harsh, bitter months and it was difficult for the children to concentrate until the fires had got going. Ever the inventor, he saw a way round the problem. He searched out an old hickory clock and modified it into a bespoke fire-lighting machine. "I had only to place a teaspoonful of powdered chlorate of potash and sugar on the stove-hearth near a few shavings and kindlings, and at the required time make the clock, through a simple arrangement, touch the inflammable mixture with a drop of sulphuric acid... All winter long that faithful clock never failed, and by the time I got to the school house the stove was usually red hot."[8]

Back on campus he also carried on manufacturing more of his bizarre ideas, whittling them out of wood and anything else he could find, carrying on his cellar-night frenzy away from home. Some of his creations were simply odd and nothing more than pure entertainment. One extraordinary invention was a "loafer's chair" that fired a pistol when the unsuspecting slouch leant on the backrest. It was said that the leaps of unwary victims were quite impressive. Others had a more serious side to them, such as a useful invention that measured the growth of plants by attaching a single hair from the head of a female student wrapped around a seedling and fixed to a clock.

One of his most famous creations appeared at this time, a desk that controlled his study time:

I invented a desk in which the books I had to study were arranged in order at the beginning of each term. I also made a bed which set me on my feet every morning at the hour determined on, and in dark winter mornings just as the bed set me on the floor it lighted a lamp. Then, after the minutes allowed for dressing had elapsed, a click was heard and the first book to be studied was pushed up from a rack below the top of the desk, thrown open, and allowed to remain there the number of minutes required. Then the machinery closed the book and allowed it to drop back into its stall, then moved the rack forward and threw up the next in order, and so on, all the day being divided according to the times of recitation, and time required and allotted to each study.[9]

Clearly his desire to be controlled and to fight laziness was still deep-seated. In the absence of Daniel, a machine was created to take his place.

To complement his inventions he cultivated an unusual look, with long hair, straggly beard and rustic clothes. He was still a backwater boy, innocent and religious, but he was brilliant with it. All the machines, specimens, rocks, and curiosities ended up in his room, drawing admirers at all times of the day and night. Even the groundsman pointed out John's window to visitors, telling them of the wonders that lay behind the glass. A roommate described John as "gentle and loving – a high-minded Christian gentleman, clean in thought and action… he was in no respect austere or lacking in humour but bubbling over with fun".[10] He was also acclaimed as the best chemistry student.

It was an exciting time to be learning the sciences. The late nineteenth century was an era of revolution when old ideas were in the process of being replaced, especially in the enticing subjects of geology and biology. The great creakings and grindings of a change of order were already being felt in the halls of learning throughout Europe, and increasingly in America,

Long-held and sacred paradigms were toppling as new ideas gained ground. The study of science was also becoming more secular and God was slowly being removed from the corridors of scientific departments. The divine's direct role in shaping the form of species and the layout of the land was under intense scrutiny and subject to fierce debate. There was already blood on the carpet of many scientific institutions, and more preciously held theories were to be sacrificed. Science does not change its world view without pain, and pain there was for some of the great minds of the nineteenth century. Learned and religious men who had been bastions of received wisdom for decades found themselves defending the basic principles they held most dear against young academics who had time and hard evidence on their side. This was a momentous era in science and John walked innocently into a maelstrom, which he would enthusiastically embrace, and to which he would contribute, not however without being bruised and battered in the storm.

In the mid-nineteenth century, geology and biology were still part of Natural Theology: in other words, scientific interpretation was commonly used to support a biblical interpretation of God. Hence many esteemed academics were also theologians or ordained ministers and it was completely acceptable to talk about the creator in scientific papers, as indeed did Charles Darwin. Increasingly, however, fresh ways of explaining the physical forms and diversity of life were moving the agenda towards a secular scientific community that excluded Christianity from guiding their work.

John found himself studying red-hot subjects as the academic see-saw rocked. Slowly but surely the evidence was amassing, tipping opinion away from a world where a narrow interpretation of the Bible had to be supported. It is hard to overestimate how groundbreaking this period was. At the beginning of John's time at the university Darwin's ideas on the evolution of species were just sinking in, profoundly challenging the way biologists looked at the world outside their university windows. The diversity of life, from the birds in the trees to the oxen in the fields, even to human beings themselves, was now believed to have come into being through one long process of selection of traits, and nothing was immutable. No longer could it be possible that life had appeared in six days, fully formed, just a few thousand years ago. Evolution required time in abundance and life was shaped by forces beyond our control. Humanity became a very small part of a vast process that stretched back through time and onwards into an unknown future. We came out of past life forms and were still subject to change. Almost overnight the human family appeared small and vulnerable in a dynamic and changing world. John's farm-world view, handed on by his Creationist father and preached from the pulpit, must have been shaken to its foundations.

Geology too was challenging the idea that great deluges, such as Noah's flood, created the landforms of the present age. Not so, said the new generation of glaciologists; slow-acting ice sheets, grinding away for millennia, were the only explanation. It was unbiblical and shocking, yet evidence was amassing daily. These ideas, combined with advances in astronomy, stretched time away from humanity in all directions, dizzying, disconcerting, and challenging to the core.

The only science teacher at Wisconsin was Professor Ezra Carr, who held the Chair of Natural Sciences. He was a young, ambitious, and controversial thinker, not afraid to take on the establishment. He was certainly religious himself, yet he embraced these emerging ideas and fed them to his receptive students, including John. He was a popular teacher but courted criticism from the University for his progressive notions about what education was actually for. Carr believed passionately that learning should be useful and prepare students for a life of contributing to the practical activities that were making America great, such as forestry, agriculture, and mechanics. He sincerely acknowledged that studying the sciences was a good way to discern the mind of God, but held that the old ways of thinking were strangling the future, not contributing to it. In his inaugural lecture he proclaimed:

> Somewhere along the electric chain, which binds the different classes of community together, the laborer at his plough, to the thinker in his quiet study, there are rusted links... Let our educational system be

constructed in accordance with our national ideas, let their utility and economic value be fully illustrated, and our institutions will speedily become intellectual hearts, whose systole and diastole would alike vitalize and invigorate the whole body politic.[11]

The University didn't agree. Within the walls of the great bastions of higher education, it was believed that pure knowledge was gained for its own sake and must remain unsullied by the needs of industry. Carr started off on the wrong foot and stayed there. The fact that he refused to go to daily worship didn't help his cause.

As science was less compartmentalized than today, Carr's classes covered a range of subjects from anatomy to atomic theory to microscopy. John absorbed them all and was intrigued by the astonishing complexity of the world. The earth began to look like one of his inventions, many intricate parts fitting together to produce a harmonious whole, but envisioned by the mind of God, not a mere mortal.

Just as importantly, however, Ezra Carr was the husband of Jeanne, the mother of one of the boys he had jettisoned out of his bed at the Madison Fair. Ezra mentioned John to her as an unusual young man who had appeared in his classes and who showed promise in science. One day John went to visit the Carrs' house, taking with him a violin, a collection of old Scottish ballads to sing, scriptural quotations, and his joyous personality. A whole morning was spent in front of the fire drinking coffee and discovering just how much they had in common. It was his first, fruitful morning with Jeanne Carr. She was thirty-six, a mother of four boys, small in stature, softly spoken, highly intelligent and well educated. She loved plants, and like John she saw the beauty in nature and in people. She was impressed by his kind, sparkling personality and obvious intelligence. From then on the Carrs welcomed this rustic young genius into their home and their lives.

To Jeanne Carr, John was as extraordinary, and as rare, as a beautiful orchid. Like the collection of plants in her conservatory, she took time to nurture and love him into fruitfulness. In him she found a mixture of scientific understanding, technological creativity, wit, religious depth, insatiable curiosity, and a true love of nature. These were ingredients that could, given the right introductions and the right reading material, amount to a recipe for greatness. Like John, Jeanne was a Christian who saw God in all things. This great divine force was a powerful presence that infused the world with meaning. The earth and all that was found on it was like a book that pointed the way to greater truths. This "feminine" view of the world was truly appealing to John, and he and Jeanne were soulmates, intellectually mated yet physically separate. Jeanne believed that very few people are called to dedicate their lives to "the pure and deep communion of the beautiful, all-loving Nature",[12] and so any that showed promise had to be encouraged. The letters they exchanged span their forty-year friendship and are intimate and warm. John called her his Earth Mother; she was his mentor, friend, teacher, and confidante.

Written throughout John's pilgrimages to wild places, the letters speak of an intensity that few find in their lives. It would be tempting to think that the intimacy of their exchanges belied a deeper relationship, but his letters to her were freely shared with her husband and friends, and some were published. In this example John was in the Yosemite Valley in the Sierra Nevada in 1871 and wrote, "O Mrs Carr, that you could be here to mingle in this night moon glory!... In the afternoon I came up the mountain here with a blanket and a piece of bread to spend the night in prayer among the spouts of the fall. But now what can I say more than wish again that you might expose your soul to the rays of this heaven?"[13] Jeanne Carr replied, "Your moonlit letter was a beam from the upper sky – I take it out into the cool dewy moonlights – where the large oaks are looking their beautifullest and sitting down upon a root think it over!"[14] They were lovers, but of nature rather than each other.

Whenever she could in the following decades Jeanne Carr introduced John to many acclaimed intellectuals and socially influential people of the time. The Carrs allowed him the use of their library and he described their home as being "filled with books, peace, kindliness and patience".[15] She gave him tutorials on the plants in her private collection and encouraged him to keep notes and records of his own thoughts and findings. She also introduced him to the writings of the Transcendentalists such as Ralph Waldo Emerson and Henry David Thoreau. There is no understanding John Muir without recognizing the influence of Jeanne Carr.

Through the writings of Emerson et al., John began to hear a different message from the one that had long been drummed into him by his father. He also heard echoes of the literature he had secretly read on the farm. His fundamentalist upbringing had taught that he should always bow to the authority of the teachings of the Bible and the church elders. Now he read that an individual's heart is good and true. That a reliance on personal experience and judgment is the only basis for greatness. That, despite toil and disappointment, great succour can be found in the vastness of creation which lifts the spirit from the daily physical realm to a much higher plane of spiritual understanding. Emerson's words were transforming the hearts of many Americans:

> So shall we come to look at the world with new eyes. It shall answer the endless inquiry of the intellect, — What is truth? and of the affections, — What is good?... Build, therefore, your own world. As fast as you conform your life to the pure idea in your mind, that will unfold its great proportions. A correspondent revolution in things will attend the influx of the spirit.[16]

This is what Jeanne Carr had in mind for John Muir, and from the earliest opportunity she was there to help in whatever way she could.

Although Transcendentalism was a broad term encompassing a range of ideas, all its great thinkers taught self-reliance and a personal experience of nature as pure ways to God. Their words were already driving green and lush chasms through the bare, capitalist wastelands that were eroding the beauty of North

America. They were subversive and challenging and represented the burgeoning of a type of American literature that was unique. It was a view of nature formed in a land not yet completely subdued and could still hold out a vision of wild, divine beauty untarnished by humanity. Here was a different relationship with the natural world that was based not on exploitation, extraction, slaughter, and money, but on a transporting experience of creation. Through their words John could hear faint reverberations of a book of the Bible with which he was familiar, Job: "But ask the animals and they will teach you, or the birds of the air and they will tell you; or speak to the earth and it will teach you, or let the fish of the sea inform you" (NIV). But these were not men who wanted obedience to an established authority; rather, they stressed a personal journey of discovery through contact with raw nature.

John's university experience was mind-blowing. New ideas in science combined with beautiful, challenging literature began to weaken his ties to his fundamentalist faith. No wonder Daniel was worried about his son's moral well-being inside the walls of a university when there was no one from the Disciples of Christ to protect him from so many beguiling influences.

If Jeanne Carr encouraged John's innate lyricism, then an earnest young man, renowned for his annoying habit of always trying to teach people, set John's sails for a course of study he would follow for the rest of his life, field botany. Early in his university life a student with the wonderful name of Milton Griswold saw John sitting on some steps beneath a locust tree. Here was a soul who seemed to have time on his hands, and Griswold's urge to instruct was overwhelming. He questioned John on his knowledge of the form of the tree next to him. Was it similar to anything else? Yes, said John, it appeared similar to a weedy pea bush, but couldn't possibly be related, as what he could see in front of him was thick, sturdy and tree-like, while the other was straggly and puny.

No matter, assured Griswold, it is the characteristics that bind, not superficial outward appearances. A locust tree may not appear to be like a sprawling, clinging pea plant, but if one looks carefully it is possible to discern the identical characteristics in the flowers, even down to the taste of their leaves. God, not man, has seen to it that life is ordered. "Man has nothing to do with their classification," exhorted Griswold. "Nature has attended to all that, giving essential unity with boundless variety, so that the botanist has only to examine plants to learn the harmony of their relations."

John was hooked and was sent "flying to the woods and meadows in wild enthusiasm... Now my eyes were opened to their inner beauty, all alike revealing glorious traces of the thoughts of God, and leading on and on into the infinite cosmos... My eyes never closed to the plant glory I had seen."[17] To some, Griswold may have been a pedantic show-off, but to John he was another messenger from God. From then on he botanized as often as he could and his room filled up with jars of specimens.

It was the sciences that fired John, not the "grave-tangled Greek and Latin" that he was also studying, though he was impressed with the teacher. James Davie Butler, the first Professor of Greek and Latin at Wisconsin, was an eccentric scholar of the old school who disliked the modern trend of separating subjects, preferring to see knowledge as a whole with everything informing everything else. He was a prolific writer and, although not a particularly acclaimed academic, he contributed original and well-sourced ideas on many aspects of life. His family, like the Carrs, recognized the brilliance in John Muir and they became much-loved friends who would remain in contact with him for many years.

Academia was enriching and revealing but it was not enough. John yearned to know his future path; was it to be medicine or inventing? Perhaps a career in science, but how would that work? Where should he live? His eclectic meandering around subjects he liked rather than studying a set course didn't help make the decision any easier. Throughout 1862-3 he went on excursions to collect plants and then, with the encouragement of Ezra Carr, enrolled as a medical student at the University of Michigan, where he intended to start studying in the autumn.

To the outside world that seemed like a good plan, but inside he was in turmoil. Everywhere the peace of nature was thrown into sharp contrast by the snarling, savage beast of war that was snapping perilously close to his ankles. The American Civil War was now in full flow and the University of Wisconsin became embroiled in fighting talk. The area where the Fair had been held became a training ground for new recruits. Here hot-blooded young men revelled in the glory and friends went off to slaughter their fellow men, as John saw it. He was a pacifist and was deeply distressed by the pomp and ardour that so often cover the gruesome reality of blood and grief. He was no supporter of slavery, and yearned for national harmony, but could not see how killing could help promote peace.

Partly to clear his mind and partly to avoid being drafted, he went on a long excursion with friends in the summer of 1863. They began by travelling through south-western Wisconsin and then crossed into Iowa. Here among the picturesque gorges and strata packed with fossilized shellfish he began to find balance. He saw nature at peace with itself and bathed in glorious summer sunlight. With his newly found scientific knowledge he saw not only beauty but also truth revealed through form and structure. He glimpsed back through time to an ancient era when the land was covered by ocean and filled with strange creatures. He mused about that primordial sea and wondered at the storms that might have raged above his head and the strange creatures that would have swum by. He then marvelled at the steep ravines and how they had been formed by water. Geology became a living subject and presented itself as an exciting book, full of mystery and revelation. John left anxiousness behind and felt free and full of curiosity.

The trip was shorter than the group had hoped, but it was enough to energize him again. It did not, however, send him back to complete a degree at the University of Wisconsin. For reasons never explained, neither did he take up his place at Michigan to study to be a doctor. On his return he packed his bags and left Madison. In an emotionally charged paragraph that concludes his book on his early years he acknowledged how much his time at the University had given him, but realized it was time to move on.

> From the top of a hill on the north side of Lake Mendota I gained a last, wistful, lingering view of the beautiful University grounds and buildings where I had spent so many hungry and happy and hopeful days. There with streaming eyes, I bade my blessed Alma Mater farewell. But I was only leaving one University for another, the Wisconsin University for the University of the Wilderness.[18]

In the autumn of 1863 John left behind his nurturing friends with their walls lined with books and once again headed alone into the unknown, as he had three years earlier as an innocent young inventor sitting on the cowcatcher of a train leaving Pardeeville. His head held more information, his heart more desires, but he still had no formal plan. Wisconsin had served him well by providing so much varied education, but at this moment he felt more like a cork bobbing on an ocean than a man with a mission to fulfil.

In 1875 Professor Butler wrote an article commending public libraries and the great service they provided for the good of all. He could well have been describing what the University of Wisconsin at Madison did for John in the five terms he spent there. "All truths being inter-dependent, every road will lead to the end of the world, and so while studying one subject a man becomes interested in others, and his range of inquiry expands. When he kindles one dry stick, many green ones will catch, and his brightest blazes are lit up by unexpected sparks."[19]

Connections had been made at Wisconsin and sparks flew off from poetry to science to ancient languages. They all contributed to John's eclectic mind and prepared him for a life interpreting nature. His eloquence with words and encouragement from Jeanne meant he wrote down what he found in beautiful, inspiring prose. Without the catholic education he had received at the hands of the likes of the Carrs and Butler John would have struggled to find the words to become the great unifying voice for the protection of the natural world. And so he bade Madison farewell and stepped into the future. He wrote to Emily Pelton, "Goodbye – I feel lonely again."[20]

Chapter 6

A Long Way from Home

"Joy is to fun what deep sea is to a puddle. It's a feeling inside that can hardly be contained."

Terry Pratchett, *A Hat Full of Sky*

Over 22,000 years before John Muir existed, a huge sheet of ice over one mile thick lay across Canada and most of North America. It scoured the land, gouging out great valleys in the mountains and deep depressions in the bedrock. Later these would fill with meltwater to form the Great Lakes. The legacy of the ice was a denuded landscape, scraped and scratched, glistening with many thousands of pools, piles of gravel, bog land, and boulders. Slowly scrub, mosses, and ferns established themselves to form a vast tract of impenetrable bushy swamp over large areas of southern Canada. It was into this inhospitable environment that John Muir ventured in the spring of 1864. In the flat lands north of Lake Ontario he faced his fears in a watery wilderness.

Botanizing around the shores of the lakes was mostly enjoyable, but there were times of extreme loneliness and homesickness. This was nothing like the softness of Wisconsin and the endless bog offered no home comforts. John trudged wearily through an area called Holland Marsh, forty miles north of Toronto. Today it is drained and forms rich arable farmland, but then it was a wet, thick, dense scrub.

Late one afternoon he felt demoralized, wet, tired, and hungry. He could find nowhere to stay. His food had run out and he was faint with exhaustion. He began to plan a long, damp night lying in a makeshift bed in a fork of the branches of a tree, as the ground was too sodden to lie on. As the sun began to set, however, he was visited by an overwhelming sense of joy – what C. S. Lewis would later phrase as being "surprised by joy".[1]

Nearby, as though gently whispering to him to visit them, a patch of tiny white and purple flowers, nestled in a bed of moss, nodded gently in the evening breeze. They were Calypso borealis, orchids of cold and wet places: delicate jewels embedded in bog. He described them as the most spiritual of all the "flower people" he had ever seen, and they evoked great yearnings for something indescribable and remote, a feeling of joy almost akin to pain in its intensity. It was a profound moment and he was moved to tears as he gazed at these transcendent beings until it was almost dark. How could such fragility move creatures as large and clumsy as a human? The following year John put his feelings on paper to Jeanne Carr, describing the moment when these tiny floral fireworks lit up the moor and dissipated loneliness and hunger. His passion flows out through his words:

> I did find Calypso — but only once, far in the depths of the very wildest of Canadian dark woods, near those high, cold, moss-covered swamps... I never before saw a plant so full of life; so perfectly spiritual, it seemed pure enough for the throne of its Creator. I felt as if I were in the presence of superior beings who loved me and beckoned me to come. I sat down beside them and wept for joy.[2]

John carried on wandering in this land of glacial majesty, his spirit refreshed by Calypso, but his emotions swayed like the pines in the wind. When he came across bands of men clearing the forests to establish farms, as his own family had done in Wisconsin, he lamented the loss of so many trees. He knew, however, that there was no other way to make a living. The eternal tension between people and nature is at its most raw when pure survival is at stake. In a letter to Jeanne Carr in 1865 he wrote ruefully:

What you say respecting the littleness of the number who are called to "the pure and deep communion of the beautiful, all-loving Nature," is particularly true of the hard-working, hard-drinking, stolid Canadians. In vain is the glorious chart of God in Nature spread out for them. So many acres chopped is their motto, so they grub away amid the smoke of magnificent forest trees, black as demons and material as the soil they move upon.[3]

These woodsmen were tough survivors but they were also generous, and he often found a warm welcome at the tables of these steely frontier families. What they lacked in their sensitivity to nature they made up for with giving hearts; something he recognized in his own farming community back home. People, he decided, were at once a curse upon nature and a source of goodness that flowed from God, and John was again faced with contradictory feelings that were hard to reconcile.

By the beginning of the winter of 1864 he had settled with a family called Trout, also devout Disciples of Christ, in Meaford, Ontario. They ran a family business manufacturing farm tools out of wood, a trade John knew a lot about. This hard-working, sociable family employed both John and his brother Dan, who was independently exploring Canada. Dan moved on fairly quickly but John stayed for another year to help expand the business and invent new, more efficient equipment. Machines drew him away from wilderness, and his mind became consumed with devising and building ever better ways to make hay rakes and broom handles. He still gazed at the thick forest that surrounded the factory on his walks to church on Sunday, wondering where his heart really lay.

The correspondence with Jeanne Carr began in September 1865 with her suggestion that they have "an exchange of thoughts". This first letter is lost but his reply admits to loneliness and laments the short span of human life, far too short to accomplish all the things that pulled at his heart. It shows a torn, uncertain soul. He could find no place to put down roots in the flatlands of Canada and had no clearer sense of purpose. Should he revisit the idea of studying medicine? Was inventing the way forward, or perhaps going back to university to study science more thoroughly?

Little had been resolved since he had left Madison, and despite all the joy of collecting plants and seeing God in an orchid he had not yet found peace. Jeanne Carr offered him memories of comfort and a feminine softness amid the harshness of Canadian life. "Oh Mrs Carr, when lonely and wearied, have I wished that like some hungry worm I could creep into that delightful kernel of your house, your library... and verdure of your little kingdom of plants, luxuriant and happy as though holding their leaves to the open sky of the most flower-loving zone in the world!"[4]

It is through his letters to Jeanne that we see John Muir beginning a transformation. Like the chrysalises that Jeanne kept in her conservatory so that, come the winter, beautiful butterflies would flutter "like winged blossoms" about her plants, so John was slowly metamorphosing in his cocoon in Canada. He was changing from a hard-line Presbyterian into a more diffuse spiritual being who could "take more intense delight from reading the power and the goodness of God from 'the things which are made' than from the Bible".[5] It was not a rapid process, though, and it would take another couple of years before John could flit among the flowers of nature rather than the industry of man. In the meantime he still had machinery in his blood and was constantly drawn back to technology.

In a letter to John in September 1865, Jeanne encouraged him by admiring his talents for invention: "A great mechanical genius is a wonderful gift, something one should hold in trust, a kind of seal and private mark which God has placed upon souls especially his own." She believed he was contributing to the greater good of humanity, not just in the here and now, but for future generations. These blessed children of the future could be relieved of the burden of work and take more time to rest in nature because of people like John. He was heartened and accepted he could create useful things, and his employment with the Trouts continued.

In March 1866, however, disaster struck. A fire broke out in the factory and raged through the workshop. The machines and the 30,000 broomhandles he had helped make went up in flames. Despite desperate attempts to save their livelihood, the Trouts lost everything. John saw it as a sign to change, but to what? What he was sure of was that his time in Canada had come to an end. The increasing division between his developing religious beliefs and those of the devout Trouts had put a strain on their relationship, and he felt confined. He bade them farewell, leaving them some money to help begin their lives again, turned south, and headed towards Indianapolis.

This rapidly expanding centre of industry housed well over a million residents. Smoke bellowed from chimneys and sawmills filled the air with screeching and grinding. Here was a chance to make his mark with wood, steel, and smoke, and hopefully reap a fortune in the process.

By now, mid-1866, the Civil War was over; Abraham Lincoln had been killed by an assassin's bullet, and Andrew Johnson was in office. The victorious North showed promising prospects as it expanded its industrial prowess. Indianapolis was a culture shock after the wilds of sparsely populated Canada, but it was a canny choice, for as soon as he arrived John found a job. Turning wood into planks for housing, fence posts, pit props, and all the other uses required by the burgeoning industries of America was the bedrock of Indianapolis's success. As steam power replaced water, around the time John arrived, mills were no longer confined to rivers but spread out into the heart of woodland. The depletion of the forest cover was dramatic. Concern for the disappearance of forests had arisen as early as 1799, when legislation was passed that imposed a fine "for felling or boring any walnut, oak, whitewood, poplar, cherry, ash, chestnut, coffee or sugar tree on another person's land without permission".[6] But laws were not enough to save the magnificent hardwood forests. In 1800, 19.5 million acres of Indiana was forested. By 1900, that had been reduced to 1.5 million.[7]

Ironically, Osgood and Smiths, like the Trouts' factory, also made agricultural tools from the vast forests that John so loved. Like the spirals of DNA, wilderness and machinery were entwined in his nature, but they never sat harmoniously. Hardwood came in to one end of the factory; tools came out of the other. On Sundays John went for solitary walks into forests to refresh his spirit and draw plants in his notebook, but he always went back to work on Monday. This classic cognitive dissonance produced stress and it tore at his soul.

Believing, however, that inventing was his only means of making money, as well as his Christian duty, he suppressed his desire to explore the wilds and continued to be a fine employee. He wrote to his brother Dan declaring that it was impossible to escape machines and so he was resigned to focusing his talents on technology. He made money fast. As soon as it entered his pocket his commitment to Christian charity meant that he gave most of it away to the needy in the city and to his family. Even so, his frugal lifestyle meant he was building up savings.

Relentless, noisy, and dirty, factory work slowly began to crowd out other thoughts and tighten its grip. Jeanne was worried by this turn of mind and her letter in October 1866 asked, "Did you not feel more at home there (in Canada) than here in the human element surrounding you?"[8] She pleaded with him to leave the city and come and stay with them in Madison, where she would introduce him to her new-found passion, fungi: "Their perishable nature adds to their interest for me – it allies them to the clouds and the morning and evening light."[9] But John stayed in Indianapolis and slogged away in the grime. Until, that is, events took a dramatic turn.

When Aristotle proclaimed, "The ideal man bears the accidents of life with dignity and grace, making the best of circumstances," he couldn't have had a character like John in mind. When an industrial accident turned John's world black, he was inconsolable. In March 1867 he was mending a piece of machinery when a file flew out of his hand and pierced his right eye. He immediately went back to his room in fear and anguish. Fluid flowed out of his damaged eye and his left eye went dark "in sympathy". John was blind. He was distraught and unable to accept comfort, even from Jeanne.

> What can I do now, while you are so far from us but whisper some of those sweet promises which fasten the soul to the source of light and life?... So I do not know how to be useful to you in this extremity – except just to speak the words of hope and faith and courage of which my heart is full... Let us believe that nothing is without meaning and purpose which comes from the Father's hand.[10]

Friends immediately rallied round and doctors advised him to lie in a darkened room. In a dictated reply to Jeanne he wrote, "The sunshine and the winds are working in all the gardens of God, but I – I am lost. I am shut in darkness. My hard, toil-tempered muscles have disappeared, and I am feeble and tremulous as an ever-sick woman."[11] He could see no hope. No matter that Jeanne told him he had an extraordinary God-given gift that enabled him to see without physical vision. He had, she declared, an "eye within the eye, to see in all natural objects the realized ideas of His mind".[12] But John could not be comforted. Without being able to gaze upon the beauty of the earth, all was for nought. Despair overtook him and God was a distant memory. He was far from stoic.

For weeks he was confined to a dark room, supported by friends who cared for him with tenderness. Slowly but surely his sight did return in both eyes, but it had been a terrible experience. He replied to Jeanne, "During those dark weeks I could not feel this (that there was a purpose behind it all), and, as for courage and fortitude, scarce the shadows of these virtues were left me. The shock upon my nervous system made me weak in mind as a child."[13]

Perhaps Jeanne was right about divine providence. It was because of the accident that the metamorphosis that had begun in Canada now entered its next phase: John Muir the engineer emerged out of the darkness as John Muir the man of nature. The time alone with himself in grief and pain had expunged any desire to stay among the works of man. Now he desired only to spend the rest of his life wandering in God's garden and to decipher the mind of the great inventor of the earth. No more cogs, belts, oil, and steam; only nature, pure and simple. In his memoirs he would later recall this time as a profound change in direction: "I bade adieu to mechanical inventions, determined to devote the rest of my life to the study of the inventions of God".[14]

Remembering the wondrous travels of the naturalist and explorer Alexander von Humboldt, John planned a thousand-mile walk from Madison to Florida. He knew this was not without risks – after all, the southern states were only just surfacing from a bloody war – but he was restless and driven. He wrote to Jeanne, "I wish I could be more moderate in my desires but I cannot and so there is no rest."[15] He gathered his belongings and went back to Fountain Lake Farm to, once again, say his goodbyes.

If John was expecting tearful farewells with hugs and blessings, he was sorely disappointed. His parents lectured him on the folly of wandering about in the wilderness instead of doing useful work, and Daniel admonished him constantly for his sinfulness in studying something as deeply evil as geology. He offered no financial support whatsoever and even ordered John to pay for his board and lodging during his stay. A young friend who accompanied John to the farm pulled no punches in describing Daniel as a bigoted fundamentalist who hated Catholics and any science that challenged Creationism. It was not a happy reunion and John left, assuring Daniel it would be a long time before they would see each other again. It would be eighteen years.

John also called in to Madison to say goodbye to the Carrs, the Butlers, and his other university friends. Here he did find encouragement to follow his soul and reach into the heart of nature.

John's plan for the thousand-mile walk from Indianapolis to the Gulf of Mexico in September 1867 was simple: "push on in a general southward direction by the wildest, leafiest and least trodden way I could find".[16] The route would take him through Kentucky, Tennessee, Georgia, and Florida. He set off carrying little but a change in underwear, a few of his favourite books such as Burns' poetry, the New Testament, a book on botany, and a plant press. His mood was joyous and he felt free from all that had harnessed him to civilization. The factories, church duties, wage packets, and the expectations of society were the "golden or silver fetters" of Henry David Thoreau, and he wanted to break free. He had no desire to be one of those men that "live lives of quiet desperation", whom Thoreau so pitied.[17] John took the hermit of the pond's advice wholeheartedly: "A man is rich in proportion to the number of things he can afford to let alone."[18]

This trip was to serve three functions: it was a journey to shed the constraints of civilization, a scientific expedition to study botany, and a pilgrimage that would allow his spirit to be enriched by immersion in wilderness. All three were equally important. His attempts to conform to society had so far led to disappointment and frustration. He found he could not commit himself to inventing because it required him to sell his soul to the city. He had no personal relationship to tie him to anyone's needs than his own.

Any thoughts of returning to the farm were dispelled by his poor relationship with Daniel. Academia was not gritty enough for a young man who thrived on physical exertion and working with his hands. Machines intrigued him but did not nurture his spirit. Everything he had tried so far seemed to lead to a dead end and a deadened soul. This walk, then, was a period of renewal, a time to let go of clocks and courses and simply to wander in a world that spoke of God. "No portion of the world is so barren as not to yield a rich and precious harvest of divine truth."[19]

John was well equipped to gather in that harvest. He was now twenty-nine years old and had amassed enough valuable experience to take on this type of challenge. He possessed the same passion for plants that the famous John James Audubon had for birds. "I never for a day gave up listening to the songs of our birds, or watching their peculiar habits, or delineating them in the best way I could,"[20] wrote Audubon, who had also wandered in the forests of the south. But, in order to study birds, Audubon had to shoot them. "I wish I had eight pairs of hands, and another body to shoot the specimens."[21] John would not have found this palatable. Luckily plants don't fly away, however, and there was no need to carry a gun. The bloodiness of the Civil War, with its 600,000 casualties, had intensified his pacifism and John found any destruction of life, other than for pure necessity, increasingly difficult to stomach. The gentleness of botany was well suited to a peace-loving soul.

All of the skills he had so far amassed in his diverse life would now be useful. To help scientific recording he carried Alphonso Wood's *A Class Book on Botany*, which he had used at university; it was a book he would keep close by for most of his life. He would also have to employ his naturalist skills to detect the different smells, tastes, and shapes of plants, and to find the more elusive ones he would need to search with sharp eyes that were tuned to minute detail. These were skills he had honed around the meadows of the farm or on the high moorland of Canada.

John the inventor was called to the fore too. As Milton Griswold back in Madison had demonstrated, plants of very different physical forms could well be related at a fundamental level. Size was no indication of status; a small cog is as important as a large one if the engine of life is to function harmoniously. John was about to examine a machine of vast complexity and he wanted to work out how it fitted together. To discover wild connections he would have to employ the same instincts that enabled him to create clever machines.

Botany was also deeply appealing because of the theological lessons to be learned from contemplating the life of plants: "God never made an ugly landscape. All that the sun shines upon is beautiful, so long as it is wild," he would write later.[22] Plants, as part of that landscape, were incapable of being anything other than a display of beauty on a grand and a small scale. Even those with thorns and poisons were treasured in God's eyes.

Great truths could also be gleaned from simple facts. The largest of trees arise from a tiny seed buried in the ground, removed from light and fresh air, yet giants emerge towards the sun and grow to magnificence. As though urged on by a divine force they completely change form, producing leaves, stems, trunks, and branches that stretch over the earth. All they have to complete this miraculous transformation is what the sun and the soil provide at no cost: the gifts of a benevolent creator. Individual plants live and die in accordance with a rhythm not set by humanity. The great mysteries of life and death blend harmoniously in the world of plants. Once a perfect specimen has graced the earth with its presence and has fulfilled its purpose it disappears, giving back to the soil the nutrients it has taken out without the morbid fuss or grief so common among people. All of this provided rich, spiritual food for thought.

This journey was therefore a complex intermingling of all that constituted John Muir. It was not purely a spiritual contemplation amid mountains and daffodils, as Wordsworth had done in the Lake District, nor was it the botanical equivalent of Wilson's or Audubon's great works on birds. This trip demanded physical endurance and scientific knowledge, which John would use to season the poetry and the theology he so loved to read.

In many ways it was a mental pilgrimage too. As he physically journeyed south he would also delve into regions of his psyche not yet explored. Starting with the familiar he would venture deeper into unknown landscapes that would be strange and threatening. Physical demands would test his resolve and stamina to their limits. He would face near-starvation and disease and have to hold his nerve. Through hardship and danger he would be asked to honestly define his idea of a benevolent God and reassess his place in the natural order. This was much more of an odyssey than a trip down south.

His first few days were spent walking through the groves of ancient Kentucky oaks and his cares fell away like the leaves of autumn. He was buoyed by the magnificence of the forests that "spread their arms in welcome". Despite a few passing shadows of loneliness, John had no doubts this was what he was meant to do. God's "plant people" would be his constant companions from now on and plant people, unlike the human version, demanded nothing of the fellow traveller other than to be left to live and die in peace. "Kentucky," he wrote, "is the greenest, leafiest State I have yet seen. The sea of soft temperate plant green is deepest here."[23] The very first night of his journey he spent sleeping in bushes amid "magnificent flowing hill scenery", and when he awoke strange birds and plants seemed to look him straight in the face to delight his opening eyes. He had awoken in heaven and spent his first few hours lingering among the "trees, and soft lights and music". These early days drew out the scientist and the seeker of religious truths but they also sparked his quirky humour and his keen eye for character. He recorded not only the plants but also the curious people and conversations he had along the way.

The famous Kentucky caves form an immense underground labyrinth in the limestone-rich hills that dominate most of the northern part of the state. John marvelled at the cold-loving mosses and ferns that grew around the mouths of caves, enabled by the cool air that flowed from underground. In an otherwise hot state these cave entrances were miniature northern environments supported by air from the underworld. Mammoth Cave is the most famous and John was keen to find it, so asked a local the way. The man told him it wasn't worth the ten-mile journey, as it was nothing but a hole in the ground. Rather scathingly John wrote, "He was one of the useful, practical men – too wise to waste precious time with weeds, caves, fossils or anything else he couldn't eat."[24]

The hotel at Mammoth Cave provided an early lesson in the inability of mankind to compete with nature in creating beauty; a theme John would return to many times. The fine lawns and tended gardens of the hotel were adorned with plants, "cultivated to deformity, and arranged in strict geometric beds, the whole pretty affair a laborious failure side by side with Divine beauty".[25] In John's eyes humanity's attempts to design miniature natural worlds only proved what poor and conceited co-creators we are. He was already forgetting how much he had admired the tended lawns and gardens of the University.

In many places en route he saw woodsmen hard at work removing the ancient oaks, along with the abundance of life that depended on them. Large trees, homes to whole ecosystems of their own, were regarded as nothing more than lumber to be turned into dollars. It was a constant reminder that the growth of America depended purely on its natural heritage and required an unsentimental, some would say brutal, approach to other life. Whether an America filled with John Muirs could ever be a successful and productive industrial giant is not a question he asked himself directly at the time, but very soon he would have to face it. A battle was breaking out throughout America as the incipient conservation movement went head to head with industrial development, and trees were on the front line. As John absorbed the beauty of the forested landscapes of Kentucky he stored up a passion that he would later release as he pitched himself with full force into the fray.

Spurred on by Henry David Thoreau's seminal 1854 book *Walden: or, Life in the Woods*, the more educated Americans were beginning to support a conservation mentality. This was one man's eloquent plea to forge a new, spiritual, relationship with the natural world. "I would that our farmers when they cut down a forest felt some of that awe which the old Romans did when they came to thin, or let in the light to, a consecrated grove," Thoreau wrote.[26] Along with Emerson (Thoreau's hero and close friend) and the other Transcendentalists, he spearheaded the new American consciousness, leading many to nurture their feelings rather than their bank balances and to experience primordial joy. And John took it all to heart.

> The woods are made for the wise and strong. In their very essence
> they are the counterparts of man. Their beauty – all their forms
> and voices and scents – seem, as they really are, reminiscences of
> something already experienced.[27]

This was not the way of the foresters of the south, though. While
intellectuals at Harvard believed that "[m]ost of the luxuries, and
many of the so-called comforts of life, are not only indispensable,
but positive hindrances to the elevation of mankind",[28] the loggers
of the southern states preferred to raise themselves from poverty. It
was a battle destined to rage on, and in the twenty-first century it still
shows no sign of finding a solution. John, however, walked his leafy
way towards the coast, too consumed with plant life to engage in
this titanic struggle for nature conservation just yet. He was certainly
aware that it was happening, but for now he turned away from the
sound of axes and found the least disturbed route he could.

The tree choppers themselves, as John had found before, were
mostly friendly and generous and he relied on their hospitality, as
well as on that offered by the well-to-do and the freed slaves. If
no one would take him in for the night he slept in the woods and
fell asleep "muttering praises to the happy abounding beauty of
Kentucky". In this first week he felt the turmoil of the previous
years slowly fall away. On his last day in the state he sat on a hill and
looked out over streams, canyons, and deep woods. "The soft light
of morning falls upon ripening forests of oak and elm, walnut and
hickory, and all Nature is thoughtful and calm." A sense of ease was
beginning to seep into his soul.

> I [often] had to sleep out without blankets, and also without supper
> or breakfast. But usually I had no great difficulty in finding a loaf of
> bread in the widely scattered clearings of the farmers. With one of
> these big backwoods loaves I was able to wander many a long, wild
> mile, free as the winds in the glorious forests and bogs, gathering
> plants and feeding on God's abounding, inexhaustible spiritual beauty
> bread.[29]

Tennessee offered the Cumberland Mountains, the first hills of any substance John had climbed. He was somewhat disconcerted that it took him six or seven hours to reach to the top. It was worth it, though, because hard work brought great delight in the form of creeks and waterfalls: "There is nothing more eloquent in Nature than a mountain stream… Every tree, every flower, every ripple and eddy of this lovely stream seemed solemnly to feel the presence of the great Creator."[30] These were the first inklings of the God-loving mountaineer to come. Overpowering beauties lay ahead in California, but this gentle mountain habitat was a perfect introduction.

As he pressed on further south, the ravages of war became more apparent, both in the fields and in the people, who distrusted strangers from the north. Here John's ability to be a "contumacious quibbler," the trait that had so irritated his father, proved to be useful. Always good for a chat, John could often natter his way into people's trust. His in-depth knowledge of the Bible also helped in this deeply Christian state. One evening, he called at a house to ask if they could put him up. The burly blacksmith householder challenged him as to why he was not working in these hard times. Surely he had something more useful to do than wander about looking at flowers? "Picking up blossoms doesn't seem to be a man's work at all," he remonstrated.[31] John held his eye and earnestly explained that Solomon wrote a book about plants and that Christ himself had told his disciples to "consider the lilies". Who, then, enquired John, should he listen to, a blacksmith or the Bible? For a God-fearing, hard-working man these were convincing arguments, and John got a meal and a bed.

In the morning the blacksmith warned him not to carry on but to turn back to Wisconsin. Since the war nothing was stable, he warned. Bands of guerrillas hid in the mountains and would rob or even kill for very little money. John carried on regardless.

The blacksmith was right, though. Very soon a band of threatening men on horseback blocked his way and stared aggressively, but his eccentric dress and poor appearance convinced them he was nothing more than a wandering medicine man, and they let him pass. On a few occasions on the journey he had lucky escapes from people, both black and white, intent on robbery. These were desperate times as old securities were dismantled and a shaky new social order was assembled. Poverty and bitterness were rife among blacks, plantation owners, and Native Indians. With memories so fresh it was only the foolhardy and the brave who ventured into the wilds.

Alongside violence, however, often comes kindness and generosity, which John records with a great sense of humour. A desperately poor Negro family welcomed him into their home for a meal of string beans, buttermilk, and cornbread, but unfortunately the only chair they offered had no seat. As weariness overtook him from a long day's walk, he sank further and further into the hole and his knees were pressed ever closer against his chest. Eventually his chin was level with his plate, his bottom almost on the floor and his knees by his ears. Ever the optimist, he wrote, "But wild hunger cares for none of these things and my curious compressed position prevented the too free indulgence of a boisterous appetite."[32]

As he walked through the village of Philadelphia (which he thought was filthy) and Madisonville ("brisk"), he saw more mountain scenery that took his breath away. Further on, he gazed with wonder at "an ocean of wooded, waving, swelling mountain beauty and grandeur... What perfection, what divinity in their architecture! What simplicity and mysterious complexity in their detail!"[33] It would not be exaggerating to say that John was as near to heaven as he had ever been. Even the fearsome, man-catching briars that tore his clothes and his skin couldn't dampen his joy.

On his last day in Tennessee he describes walking along an undulating road and coming across "a shackly wagon that seemed to be held together by spiritualism, and kept in agitation by one very large and one very small mule". Riding inside were an old woman, a man, and a young woman. The wagon was so loosely attached to the mules that as the road (which had many ups and downs) followed the contours the travellers were unceremoniously thrown backwards and forwards. They were constantly rolling around, and crashing into the boards at either end of the wagon. As they landed, they formed tangled and undignified heaps. All the while they carried on chatting about everyday events and the old lady held on to a small bunch of marigolds.

As John left Tennessee for Georgia, he entered another world, which became increasingly unfamiliar and disconcerting. His notes record many rattlesnakes, Negroes picking cotton, and tangles of vines heavy with sweet grapes as well as the "stately banana". He feasted on a strange fruit, "a many chambered box full of translucent purple candies", the peculiar-looking, yet delicious, pomegranate.

Deep fears were beginning to surface, however, made more intense by the landscape: "Strange plants are crowding about me now. Scarce a familiar face appears among all the flowers of the day's walk."[34] There was still much to amaze him and many beauties to record, but there is a discernable change of tone in his writing. On 30 September no one would take him in and he had to walk on to the town of Augusta, "more than forty miles without dinner or supper". He was so hungry that his stomach was sore and he was beginning to weaken. The next day he remarked on the wondrous Spanish moss draped like a beard over many of the branches of the trees, something he had never seen before. And then he entered the cypress woods. These dense forests have a flat top, "as if each tree had grown up against a ceiling". Very little light penetrated to the path. He couldn't recognize any of the birdcalls and the plant people seemed like aliens from another world. Homesickness and hunger were beginning to take their toll: "The winds are full of strange sounds, making one feel far from the people and plants and fruitful fields of home. Night is coming on and I am filled with indescribable loneliness."[35]

John had delved deeper into his fears. The comfort of the familiar lay many miles to the north; what lay ahead he could only guess, but he had crossed the Rubicon and there was no route back.

Chapter 7

The Best Laid Plans

"All human plans are subject to ruthless revision by Nature, or Fate,
or whatever one preferred to call the powers behind the universe."

Arthur C. Clarke, *2010: Odyssey Two*

The journey so far had mostly been a nurturing meander through welcoming forests and inspiring accessible mountains. Apart from some uncomfortable nights on school benches or out of doors, and a few missed meals, it had been more of a botanical holiday than a testing expedition. Three weeks into the trip, however, John was getting tired and the increasingly strange alien scenery jarred his nerves. Physical exertion combined with his lack of interest in food meant he was increasingly malnourished. Money too was running low and his wallet was almost empty.

When he reached the town of Savannah on the coast of Georgia he was down to a couple of dollars and desperately needed funds to arrive from his brother. When nothing was in the post office all he could do was wait. To pass the time he set off down "a smooth, white shelled road" towards Bonaventure Cemetery, about four miles outside the town. He passed dreary fields and broken huts: "These little fenced fields look as if they were intended to be for plants what cages are for birds."[1]

Eventually, just beyond the last houses, he found an abandoned old mansion house surrounded by white marble gravestones: Bonaventure Cemetery. Here was the most exquisite mingling of natural and man-made nature he had ever seen. Magnificent planted avenues of evergreen oaks were swathed with ten-foot-long drapes of Spanish moss that waved in the wind like funeral shrouds. The ornate graves dedicated to the great and good of Savannah were surrounded by thousands of shrubs and bushes that thronged with butterflies and buzzing insects of all kinds. The land sloped down to the river and its marshy reeds full of birds gave the whole graveyard a fringe of singing, waving fronds. Bald eagles roosted noisily in the waterside trees. "Bonaventure to me is one of the most impressive assemblages of animal and plant creatures I ever met."[2]

The first night John slept with his head on the mound of a grave, his slumber disturbed only by the bites of mosquitoes and prickly-footed beetles running over his hands and face. When he awoke he began to absorb his surroundings. The wild beauty of the cemetery was intertwined with a deliberate attempt to lay out a fine resting place for the dead. Throughout the nineteenth century graveyards were increasingly seen as places to contemplate life and death in picturesque surroundings. Inspired by the English Romantic movement, cemetery designers wanted to elicit what Wordsworth described as "the spontaneous overflow of powerful feelings".[3] Increasingly, technology and money were seen as erasing the finer attributes of mankind, and so these lovely places of death were a deliberate reaction to the increasingly overcrowded and industrialized towns and cities.

As old church graveyards filled up, the dead were remembered in carefully designed wild parks that were often used by families for Sunday walks and picnics. By 1867 Bonaventure had fallen into disrepair. "Even those spots which are disordered by art, Nature is ever at work to reclaim and to make them look as if the foot of man had never known them". Wild nature was now slowly conquering the attempts at human grandeur, which was fading fast.

How assiduously Nature seeks to remedy these laboured art blunders. She corrodes the iron and marble, and gradually levels the hill which is always heaped up, as if sufficiently heavy quantities of clods could not be laid upon the dead. Arching grasses come one by one; seeds come flying on downy wings, silent as fate, to give life's dearest beauty for the ashes of art; and strong evergreen arms laden with ferns and tillandsia drapery are spread over all – Life at work everywhere, obliterating all memory of the confusion of man.[4]

There was no way of knowing how long it would take for the money to arrive from David, so John had no choice but to stay put. With the cash in his pocket dwindling, he realized he could well face starvation among the long-dead dignitaries of Savannah. With time on his hands and the possibility of an eternity to face, John contemplated the meaning of life and death in his rambunctious graveyard.

After building a tiny shelter, well concealed from prying and possibly malicious eyes, he gazed at the plethora of butterflies adding colour to the rusting iron railings and slabs of stone. He listened to the melodious songs of warblers and the harsher screams of the bald eagles. It was a fitting place to ponder on the teachings on death that he had heard in church and to compare them with the reality of what he saw. His conclusion was uplifting and his writings on Bonaventure provide us with a beautiful example of John Muir at his best: "Bonaventure is called a graveyard, a town of the dead, but the few graves are powerless in such a depth of life." Bonaventure, said John, "is one of the Lord's most favoured abodes of life and light." He concluded that only those who ignore the lessons of nature regard death as something to fight against. The Victorian religious doctrines he had been taught railed against what is most natural. They urged people to see death as a punishment for sin and instilled fear and dread when the bell tolled. Strange, then, thought John, that nature doesn't see it that way. He wrote, "On no subject are our ideas more warped and pitiable than on death."

In a powerful and often-quoted passage he contrasts nature with the religious orthodoxy of the time and challenges the reader to assess for themselves the reality of death and the confusion that surrounds it. How come we can glory over the slaughter of thousands in a war, yet wail over a relative who has died a peaceful and timely death? To what end do we insist on a black dress code and sing the words of mournful hymns? What are the "imaginary glooms and ghosts of every degree" that cause us to quake and go pale at the thought of our last breath? What is the meaning behind the deathbed utterance "I fear not to die"? If we could only turn our eyes to see how nature deals with the end of life, we would see no reason to fear.

"Come," writes John and see "the beautiful blendings and communions of death and life, their joyous inseparable unity, as taught in woods and meadows, plains and mountains and streams of our blessed star… death is stingless indeed and as beautiful as life, and that the grave has no victory, for it never fights. All is divine harmony."[5]

All this eloquence may have contained an element of John comforting himself, as the possibility of dying unseen among the graves was getting closer with every penniless day. He was reduced to nibbling on dry crackers at breakfast, and then nothing more. With time on his hands, deep in thought, and surrounded by Bonaventure's stately line of trees standing tall amid a tumbling mass of beauty, he settled down to send his musings to Jeanne Carr:

> I gazed at this peerless avenue as one newly arrived from another planet, without a past or future, alive only to the presence of the most adorned and living of the tree companies I have ever beheld. Bonaventure is called a graveyard, but its accidental graves are powerless to influence the imagination in such depths of life.[6]

His own body was feeling far from lively, however. He was becoming dangerously hungry and delirious. He staggered as he walked and the streams seemed to flow uphill. Eventually, after five days, the money did arrive, but he couldn't get it without one last effort. His famous contumacious quibbling was called for again to convince the post office that he was indeed the intended recipient. The clerk was worried that the letter John showed him from his brother, stating that money was on its way, had been stolen, and wanted more identification. John resorted to arguing that the letter described him as a botanist, and he challenged the clerk to test him on anything to do with plants. Surely that would prove he was the right person. Perhaps it was his wan face and dishevelled look that brought out feelings of pity, as the money was duly released and John feasted on gingerbread from a passing Negro lady. He then headed straight for a boat to Florida, stopping first at a restaurant to buy a very large meal.

The steamship took John to Fernandina in Florida, just over the state line. This was the state he most wanted to visit. Long-held dreams were now becoming reality as the ship "paddled like a duck" as it negotiated the islands close to the shore. In his mind he would spend the next few days walking into a three-dimensional version of a William Morris print, "a close forest of trees, every one in flower, and bent down and entangled to network by luxuriant, bright blooming vines, and all over a flood of bright sunlight".[7] When he stepped onto the rickety pier, however, he was faced with a low-lying, dark confusion of impenetrable vegetation: not at all what he had imagined.

Needing a place to sit for breakfast, he eventually found a small dry patch and ate some bread. The Bonaventure fast had seriously weakened his mind and body and his mood was sombre and uncharacteristically nervous: "Everything in earth and sky had an impression of strangeness; not a mark of friendly recognition, not a breath, not a spirit whisper of sympathy came from anything about me and of course I was lonely. I lay on my elbow eating my bread, gazing, and listening to the profound strangeness."

John knew he was not in the best state of health and needed rest to build himself up again, so when the bushes behind him rustled his mind imagined all kinds of horrors and he panicked – "In this half-starved, unfriended condition I could have no friendly thought" – and was convinced that at any moment the jaws of an alligator would clasp him and drag him to watery depths. In fact, out of the darkness stepped a beautiful white crane, "handsome as a minister from spirit land".[8] This unusual jumpiness worried John: anxiety and hunger had really taken their toll.

He spent the first day gathering what specimens he could by wading chest-deep in the water, trying not to be intimidated by the thought of snapping alligators. As this thousand-mile journey took him physically further away from familiarity, so it also took him spiritually away from the religious orthodoxy of his youth. The process that had begun in Canada, where he dared to write that nature was teaching him as much about God as the sermons from the pulpit, continued and deepened in this far south swamp. It was not that he was leaving God behind, far from it: ecstatic homilies seemed to be preached from the beak of every bird and every blowing tree sang praises. More than ever before God was manifest in the very stuff of creation but the divine was starker and more challenging. The biting, stinging, stinking swamps were not a gentle bosom. Instead of resting at ease under an oak he was forced to strive for comfort and had to search for a nurturing hand to guide him.

Florida may not have been what he had hoped, but it matured his understanding of God. When he came across the palm palmetto he experienced another moment of divine joy, akin to his Calypso experience. It stood alone, twenty-five feet tall, on a patch of grass. Its long fronds were gently ruffled by the wind as they draped down from the crown. Its rounded, broom-handle like trunk was grey and straight giving it the impression of calm certainty. Although not as beautiful as a Wisconsin oak, its presence was beyond its physical form. "This palm was indescribably impressive and told me grander things than I ever got from a priest… it has a power of expression not excelled by any plant high or low I have met in my whole walk so far."[9] The details of the grand things it told him he doesn't record, but his spiritual feelings for the wealth of nature he saw poured out of the page. "Though lonely tonight amidst this multitude of strangers, strange plants, strange winds blowing gently, whispering, cooing, in a language I never learned… yet I thank the Lord with all my heart for his goodness in granting me admission to this magnificent realm."[10]

Spiritual food he had in abundance, but bread was more difficult to come by. In the 1860s, Florida was scarcely populated, and only 140,000 people lived in the state's 64,000 square miles.[11] Eighty per cent of those were concentrated around the northern boundary where sugar and cotton plantations were plentiful. Time and again, John was forced back to roads and villages to replenish his stocks. "A serious matter is this bread which perishes, and, could it be dispensed with, I doubt if civilisation would ever see me again."[12]

How true this statement is is far from certain. He may have wanted it to be so, but the reality was he yearned for company. Loneliness was an increasing problem and he writes as keenly about the people he met as he does about many of the places he visited. John was intrigued by the diverse, quirky, mass of humanity that populated his trail. Their lives were so different to his own he took in every detail. Vivid encounters with Florida locals are dotted through his notes.

These included loggers, who were "the wildest of all the white savages I met... for downright barbarism these Florida loggers excel".[13] They nonetheless shared their meal with him. White alligator hunters bragged of their conquests. Negros, too poor even to have a hut, gave him water from a gourd. Their young child lay directly on the mud, awaking from sleep to eat a meagre meal of hominy, "rising from the earth naked as to the earth he came. Had he emerged from the black muck of the marsh, we might easily have believed that the Lord had manufactured him like Adam, straight from the earth."[14]

A white couple in a pretty cottage gave him food, even though they were both suffering from malaria. Dirt impregnated their skin and clothes in such a cloying way he was appalled. "The most diseased and incurable dirt that I ever saw... Dirt and disease are dreadful enough when separate, but combined are inconceivably horrible."[15] Both the poor and the rich extended hands of friendship to John, a few desperadoes tried to rob him, all were as much a part of this journey as the plants. To say he would rather have removed himself from all human contact seems to be more an outburst of frustration than genuine misanthropy.

Through these encounters, he discovered the broken, weary world of post-Civil War southern America and the goodness that was almost always close to the cracked surface. He compared people in the south to a forest that had been destroyed. The damaged trees were like the older people who had experienced the worst humanity can inflict on each other. The younger generation, like young saplings, grew up around them and carried none of this burden. On their strong limbs and fresh minds they carried the hope for the future.

Constantly warned of the dangers of wandering vagabonds with ill intent he dared not light a fire in the evenings, despite often being cold and wet. Hungry, night prowling alligators were also a concern, so much so that when he became desperately thirsty after a long day's walk he only dared drink from, "slimy pools groped for in the grass", rather than wade out into cleaner water. A Florida swamp was no place for a vulnerable, soft-bodied, warm-blooded creature at night.

John's fear of alligators was fuelled by the legion of stories he was told by white "gator" hunters who confidently stated that an alligator's favourite meal were dogs and Negroes. There was no way to prove that but John was far from convinced they were innately evil creations of the devil and thus deserved to die. He saw them as fellow beings with a right to inhabit their watery kingdom without being persecuted.

> How narrow we selfish, conceited creatures are in our sympathies! How blind to the rights of all the rest of creation! With what dismal irreverence we speak of our fellow mortals! Though alligators, snakes, etc., naturally repel us, they are not mysterious evils. They dwell happily in these flowery wilds, are part of God's family, unfallen, undepraved and cared for with the same species of tenderness and love as is bestowed on angels in heaven or saints on earth.[16]

Such heresy wasn't confined to alligators. Sport hunting too, that great foundation stone of frontier America, made little sense. He was put up for a few nights by Captain Simmons, an ex-Confederate army captain, who had little sympathy for the North, but who was nonetheless kind and hospitable. With a local judge he took John hunting for deer in the local woods. Perhaps, he suggested, they could even have a shot at bear and wolf if they found them?

Despite being grateful for a bed and food for a few days, his disgust at their glorying in killing was unrestrained. "God's cattle", as he called deer, were not put on earth to provide sport. Certainly it was fitting for Native Indians to hunt, as they had always done, and for ordinary families to put a well-earned meal on the table, but for pure aristocratic pleasure, absolutely not. He deplored the fact that "these self approving preachers", killed wildlife at will because it pleased them, but let a beast, "kill the most worthless person of the godlike killers", then revenge must be exacted.

Perhaps John was also thinking back to his farm days and the purging of the wildlife in the woods around Fountain Lake Farm by bands of boys, the slaughter of the passenger pigeons and the execution of poor Watch for eating chickens. Perhaps too he was remembering his visit earlier in the journey to a place where Cherokee Indians had been rounded up and sent off on their Trail of Tears, many of them to face death through starvation and hypothermia. The arrogance and hypocrisy of some sectors of humanity, who he termed "Lord Man", towards other fellow humans and wildlife seemed as prevalent as ever. "I have precious little sympathy for the propriety of civilized man, and if a war of races should occur between the wild beasts and Lord Man, I would be tempted to sympathize with the bears."[17]

John had entered Florida on 15 October 1867 and had spent eight days walking from the east coast to the west, to the port of Cedar Key, where he hoped to get a passage to Cuba and then on to South America. The Sunshine State had provided much food for thought on the relationship between people and nature and had brought a growing uneasiness with the belief that humanity had a God-given authority over all of creation. His conviction that man was failing to respect his "fellow mortals" (a phrase he borrowed from Robert Burns) was growing by the day. In his opinion, the earth was for sharing and God's love was poured down on all.

This led to the problematic conclusion that planet earth was not necessarily a comfortable place to live on, and not everything on it was for the benefit of humanity. Both people and wildlife had a right to have a home and find food, even if that meant that sometimes humans lost out. His alligator ponderings led him to believe that, even if they took an occasional human, then so be it: we were venturing into their realm. Getting rid of alligators, bears, wolves, or anything else that posed a danger was simply a dereliction of our moral duty to live humbly and with respect for a diverse, living, breathing natural world.

It would be easy to level the criticism that these were the observations of a young, fit man who had no family to care for, enough money to get by, and a secure home to return to should times get difficult. Those who were living cheek by jowl with dangerous creatures, or were trying to forge a living out of inhospitable land, could be forgiven for holding a less idealized, more practical view. Had the Scottish writer and political reformer Samuel Smiles, a contemporary of John, been walking alongside him at this point, he would perhaps have made use of one of his most famous quotes: "The very greatest things – great thoughts, discoveries, inventions – have usually been nurtured in hardship, often pondered over in sorrow, and at length established with difficulty."[18] In other words, a true test of these loving but high-minded beliefs would be adversity, to see just how robust they really were. And that test was about to be met.

As the road led away from the deep swamps and towards the sea, the air was filled with the long lost aroma of salty air. Immediately he was lifted out of the steamy atmosphere of Florida and transported back a quarter of a century to the bracing shoreline of Dunbar in Scotland. He could hear the cry of the gulls and see them soaring on stiff wings over the rough, cold sea. He was splashing through the rock pools finding strange mini beasts and scaling the walls of the old black castle. He could visualize the churches, his grandfather's butcher's shop, his school, and Bass Rock in the Firth of Forth. The magnolias, vines, palms, and anything humid had disappeared. "I do not wonder," he wrote, "that the weary camels coming from the scorching deserts should be able to smell the Nile."[19] He was filled with a yearning for the coolness of Scotland.

When he arrived at the harbour it was empty of ships, so he found work at a small sawmill, owned by a Mr Hodgson, with the aim of getting a place on a steamer due to arrive in two weeks to take lumber to Texas. From there he would somehow reach the West Indies and then, maybe, he would finally get to South America and reach the place he most longed to see, the Amazon rainforest. Robert Burns, however, was already whispering in his ear, "The best laid schemes o' mice an' men, gang aft a-gley" (the best laid plans of mice and men often go astray).[20]

The next day, 24 October 1867, John had a headache and his senses were dulled. He had an overwhelming desire for something sour and bought lemons. The day after, a leadenness came over his limbs and he found it difficult to walk. He carried on at the factory and tried to shake off the feelings by bathing in the sea, refusing to believe he was ill. For twenty-nine years he had relied on his strong body. He had proved he could endure physical hardship and scarce food. He had even survived pneumonia. On his third day in Cedar Key he couldn't eat but was desperate for lemons. On his way back from town, "the fever broke on me like a storm, and before I had staggered halfway to the mill I fell down unconscious on the narrow trail among the palmettos".[21] John had malaria.

This devastating disease is caused by a parasite which is injected into the bloodstream of the victim via the bite of a particular species of mosquito, the Anopheles mosquito. This insect was already present in America before Europeans arrived, but the parasite probably wasn't native. It seems likely that Europeans brought it over from southern England, France, Spain, Portugal, and Italy, where it was common.

It was slow to get a foothold at first, but when slaves arrived from the west coast of Africa, where the parasite was also present, it became firmly established and spread rapidly. As Europeans cut down forests, dug canals, cleared savannahs, and cultivated large areas for rice and sugar cane, the standing water the mosquitoes needed to breed appeared over much of the country. By 1850 malaria was established throughout vast areas of North America and for the next fifty years it was a major killer. Ten thousand Union troops died of it during the Civil War, a conflict that exacerbated the spread of malaria from the South to the North. The freeing of slaves, along with the general disruption, caused many fields and plantations to be abandoned, providing further ideal breeding pools for the mosquitoes. There were two types of malaria that John could have caught, Plasmodium vivax and Plasmodium falciparum, as both were present in the southern states. P. vivax is the less serious type and rarely fatal, although certainly incapacitating. Fortunately, he probably suffered from this type.

Working backwards, it was most likely in the glorious setting of Bonaventure Cemetery that a mosquito injected its debilitating parasite into John's bloodstream. The actual cause of malaria would not be discovered until 1880, and even then diagnosis and treatment were not common until the 1920s. At the time John was being bitten as he lay in his flowery bower it was thought that bad air emanating from swamps, literally "mal air", caused the severe bouts of fever, sickness, headaches, and exhaustion. He certainly knew about the dangers of exposing himself to swampy air when deciding on the graveyard for his waiting room: "If I am to be exposed to unhealthy vapours, I shall have capital compensation in seeing those grand oaks in the moonlight,"[22] he wrote, but little did he know at the time just how ill it would make him.

The natural world is lovely indeed but even the most beautiful face can mask utter indifference to human suffering and disease. If God smiles down on all his creatures, great and small, that beneficence must include the ugly, irritating insects that can cause so much pain and death. John had written eloquently about humanity being a part of the great cosmic creation but not until now had he faced the reality of what that meant.

For three months the kindly Hodgson family took on the role of hospital and nurse. They took him into their own home and poured quinine down him in vast quantities. He was desperately ill. He had no doubt he owed his life to these angels of the south. By January he was well enough to walk down to the woods and would lie for hours under a tree, just staring at the birds and listening to the wind:

It is delightful to observe the assembling of these feathered people from the woods and reedy isles; herons white as wave-tops, or blue as the sky, winnowing the warm air on wide quiet wing; pelicans coming with baskets to fill, and the multitude of smaller sailors of the air, swift as swallows, gracefully taking their places at Nature's family table for their daily bread. Happy birds![23]

He even managed a short trip in a boat to the myriad islands that dotted the bay. He noted down that the main trees were evergreen oaks, juniper, and long-leafed pine, and many were knee-deep in flowering magnolias. Soberly dressed mocking birds sang in their branches alongside robins and many other unidentified musicians. Bluebirds scudded past like patches of blue sky. Nature was a balm during his recovery, as well as the curse that caused his illness in the first place.

His rising spirits were further lifted by the throngs of waders that swarmed around the mudflats like living clouds. They twisted and turned in unison in mind-defying synchrony. His sense of humour returned too as he watched herons standing alone on the shore:

A few lonely old herons of solemn look and wing retire to favorite oaks. It was my delight to watch those old white sages of immaculate feather as they stood erect drowsing away the dull hours between tides, curtained by long skeins of tillandsia. White-bearded hermits gazing dreamily from dark caves could not appear more solemn or more becomingly shrouded from the rest of their fellow beings.[24]

Jeanne Carr sat in Madison and worried about him. She had heard from him in November when he sent a feeble note telling her of his illness and slow road to recovery: "I am just creeping about getting plants and strength after my fever... Will you please write me a long letter?... I have written little, but you will excuse me. I am wearied."[25] She replied, "I also feel very keenly the loss of you in my life. I am not a little heavy hearted about you, what have the tropic weeks done to our dear pilgrim youth?"[26] He longed more than ever for her wise counsel and motherly attention.

These days of torpor were not wasted, though. They provided long hours of reflection on what he had experienced and allowed him the time to gather his thoughts. He had travelled 1,000 miles to meet as many plant people as he could, and many were as wonderful, if not more so, than those he knew as friends at home. But he had learned that not all of nature is as sweet as the meadow flowers that had brightened his farming days. Down south some plants possessed aggressive characteristics. The ones he had feared most on his journey so far were the catbriars. Their claws could undress you in minutes and rip the flesh off your bones, as he had found when trying to wade out to a grove of palmettos in Georgia. In Florida these catty plants were accompanied in their seeming spitefulness towards humans by the terrifying Spanish bayonet. Even the steeliest explorer could be undressed and filleted in the blink of an eye by these butchers working in unison. They were as effective at defrocking and dismembering a human body as any alligator. The Spanish bayonet is a type of yucca and the edges of its thick, rigid leaves are serrated and can easily tear the toughest clothing and slice into flesh. In addition, each leaf ends in a stiff, dagger-like point. Any unwary traveller who tries to wander through a patch of Spanish bayonets will soon find that these garrisons of plant soldiers "will saw his bones, and the bayonets will glide to his joints and marrow without the smallest consideration of Lord Man".[27]

John was left with the inescapable conclusion that God's idea of a diverse world is not one that humanity would have designed for itself. The natural world had caused a disease that almost extinguished an otherwise healthy young man. No matter if it was caused by gas from a swamp or the bite of an insect, it was still the result of being surrounded by nature in the raw. Who was this God who distributed life and death irrespective of species? If nature really was created purely for people, as his Christian teachers believed, then how come such dangers lurked unseen in the midst of beauty? Could they be simply viewed as the result of our sin and a fallen world? These southern climes held many attractions as well as perils, and his musings on alligators, spiky plants, and malaria led to some of his most famous writings:

> Nature we are told, was made especially for man – a presumption not supported by all the facts. A numerous class of men are painfully astonished whenever they find anything, living or dead, in all God's universe, which they cannot eat or render in some way what they call useful to themselves.[28]

With this perverted idea of our own importance and place on earth, wrote John, it is no wonder that the traditional image of God is so distorted. In a passage that at once dismisses the religious teachings of his youth and the oppression of the English over the Scots, and much of the rest of the world, he wrote that the conventional God

> is regarded as a civilised, law-abiding gentleman in favour of either a republican form of government or of a limited monarchy; believes in the literature and language of England, is a warm supporter of the English constitution and Sunday schools and missionary societies; and is as purely a manufactured article as any puppet of a halfpenny theatre… Now, it never seems to occur to these far-seeing teachers that Nature's object in making animals and plants might possibly be first of all the happiness of each one of them, not the creation of all for the happiness of one. Why should man value himself as more than a small part of the one great unit of creation? And

what creature of all that the Lord has taken the pains to make is not essential to the completeness of that unit – the cosmos? The universe would be incomplete without man; but it would also be incomplete without the smallest transmicroscopic creature that dwells beyond our conceitful eyes and knowledge.[29]

From the viewpoint of a society with a more advanced scientific understanding, these sentiments may now seem naïve. The eradication of a "transmicroscopic creature", for example the smallpox virus in 1979, brought to an end a great deal of suffering. It would be hard to argue that the world is worse off for its disappearance. For his time, however, these sentiments were revolutionary and would have won him no friends in the orthodox religious circles still so prominent in civil society.

John's interest in geology also added to his ideas on where we stood in the grand scheme of the life of planet earth. He now saw the era of the dominance of humans as no different from that of the age of the dinosaurs or the time when trilobites were one of the commonest creatures on earth. "This star, our own good earth, made many a successful journey around the heavens ere man was made, and whole kingdoms of creatures enjoyed existence and returned to dust ere man appeared to claim them."[30] Humanity too will one day be no more than a layer of fossils in a cliff face. We will have played our part and the universe will move on without us. Heresy indeed. Daniel would have been apoplectic if he had known how far his son had wandered from the path of righteousness.

One day John felt strong enough to climb to the top of the house and sit on the roof to take in the magnificent view of the forests and blue sea. On the horizon he spotted a white schooner, bouncing on the waves, as though beckoning to him. It was the *Island Belle* and it was on its way to Cuba with a load of lumber, docking in Cedar Keys for a very short time to replenish water supplies. John scrambled down and immediately secured a passage for twenty-five dollars. He was still far from well, but knew he had to shake himself free from the clamminess of the Florida coast.

His hasty and sorrowful goodbyes to the generous Hodgsons were laced with heartfelt thanks for all the care he had been given, and they would remain friends for many years. As the ship left harbour, he gloried in the bracing air and revelled in the sway as it made the open ocean. The boat rode the swell "like an exulting war horse to battle". After a while a storm blew up and tossed the ship hither and thither. Most would have retreated inside but John held on to a rope and listened to the wind's "mysterious voice… gathered from a stormy expanse of crested waves and briny tangles".[31] No doubt the captain and crew were glad when the gale died down, but for John it was all too short; he was desperate for coolness and vigour after so many weeks of sticky, humid torpor.

It was a Sunday afternoon in January 1868 when John stepped ashore in bustling, Catholic Havana, and it was the busiest day of the week. "Cathedral bells and prayers in the forenoon, theatres and bull-fight bells and bellowing in the afternoon! Lowly whispered prayers to the saints and the Virgin, followed by shouts of praise or reproach to bulls and matadors!"[32] Cuba was a confusion of piety and ribaldry, and as far from his sober Protestant roots as it was possible to get. He had found another tropical paradise of flowers, shells, white beaches, and sumptuous fruits, but he also saw cruelty on a scale so far unseen. He was sickened to his stomach by the way the Cubans treated animals:

I saw more downright brutal cruelty to mules and horses during
the few weeks I stayed there than in my whole life elsewhere. Live
chickens and hogs are tied in bunches by the legs and carried to
market thus, slung on a mule. In their general treatment of all sorts
of animals they seem to have no thought for them beyond cold-
blooded, selfish interest.[33]

He spent a month sleeping on the boat but his days were spent walking the beautiful gardens and white beaches close to the city. As in Florida, the exuberance of tropical plants astonished him; they put Lord Man in his place and refused to bow down to the will of farmers. "In tropical regions it is easy to build towns, but it is difficult to subdue their armed and united plant inhabitants." In Wisconsin he had seen how the plough and the hoof had destroyed the fragile wildflower meadows he loved to play in. Acres of colourful tapestry were turned to monoculture within one season. Here it was different.

> The plant people of temperate regions, feeble, unarmed, unallied, disappear under the trampling feet of flocks, herds and man, leaving their homes to enslavable plants which follow the will of man and furnish him with food. But the armed and united plants of the tropics hold their rightful kingdom plantfully, nor, since the first appearance of Lord Man, have they ever suffered defeat.[34]

This image of a strong floral army defiantly holding out against the spread of humanity pleased him, but he still needed bread. Thank goodness some plants were "enslavable" and edible. The battle of Nature versus Man was a dichotomy he faced every day of his wanderings in the wilds.

Enchanted by the gorgeous exuberance of wild Cuba, he longed to explore further afield, but his health was far from good. Fevers kept returning and he was too weak to venture inland. After a month of Cuban vivacity, even the tenacious John Muir admitted defeat. The humidity was draining him and he found it impossible to build up strength. He yearned to rest in a cool climate. Attempting to head for South America began to appear more foolish by the day, and anyway no boat appeared in the harbour to take him. While scouring the newspapers, however, he did find a cheap deal to California via New York. It meant sailing far to the north to go back south again, but the ocean had proved to be invigorating and he had fine sea legs. He promised himself that once he had recovered he would resume his odyssey to the Amazon rainforest, but for now he needed freshness and recuperation.

Luck was on his side and a small oak schooner waited impatiently in the harbour, her cargo of oranges packed ready for delivery to

New York. The captain was willing to take an extra passenger, despite there being no time to obtain the official papers for travel. John Muir was about to exchange the crowded world of tropical plants for high mountains and open meadows, and in doing so make history. The transformation from farm boy to explorer had been long, slow, and at times painful, but the time had almost arrived for him to break out of his cocoon and fly.

Chapter 8

Coming Home

"People from a planet without flowers would think we must be mad with joy the whole time to have such things around us."

Iris Murdoch, *A Fairly Honourable Defeat*

A stiff northerly wind carried the small schooner, loaded with its cargo of oranges and an ailing naturalist, out of Havana harbour on a bright, mid-February day. Its compass was set towards the now wintry metropolis of New York. John hid below decks to avoid being seen by the port officials. Luck was on their side and the schooner was waved through without inspection. When he felt the heaving of the waves he emerged to see the shoreline retreating and the vast untrammelled ocean stretched ahead: "The Castle towers, the hills, the palms, and the wave-white strand, all faded in the distance and our mimic seabird was at home in the open stormy gulf, curtseying to every wave and facing bravely to the wind."[1] This was the new start he needed. The wind and the waves were an energizing beginning to an adventure that would last for the rest of his life. The deadening heat of the tropics was literally blown away and out to sea.

He had revelled in stormy seas on his previous voyages but this time the ocean added a dazzling aerial display. Flying fish shot into the air, their bodies glistening in the sunshine, pursued by living torpedoes: dolphins. "These fish-swallows rose in pretty good order, skimmed swiftly ahead for fifty or a hundred yards in a low arc, then dipped below the surface. Dripping and sparkling, they rose again in a few seconds and glanced back into the lucid brine with wonderful speed, and without apparent terror." Once the dolphins had gained on the fish, however, panic broke out and "all order was at an end".[2] The dolphins were an embodiment of powerful elegance and showed "their splendid colours" as they launched into the air. Some of the panicked fish attempted to soar right over the deck but fell short, landing among the oranges, and were devoured by the ship's dog before any of the sailors could reach them.

Such energy and freedom were exactly what John needed. All around him new life sparkled in the sea or glided on the wind, and it told of a mysterious world removed from human influence. He wondered at the vastness of the ocean and its untameable depths and its secrets yet to be uncovered. He marvelled at the physical strength of the wind that came and went at will, evading control and understanding: "I like to cling to a small chip of a ship like ours when the sea is rough, and long, comet tailed streamers are blowing from the curled top of every wave."[3]

As the boat rose and fell with the waves he felt as though he were climbing and descending mountains. He drank in the "unsullied country of ever changing water", and had to keep reminding himself that this land was not meant for humans: "I almost forgot at times that the glassy, treeless country was forbidden to walkers." Yet he longed to explore it as he had the woodlands and wetlands on his thousand-mile walk, to take specimens of the plants of the sea and study the soaring birds:

To sleep in wild weather in a bed of phosphorescent wave-foam, or briny scented seaweeds; to see the fishes by night in pathways of phosphorescent light; to walk the glassy plain in calm, with birds and flocks of glittering flying fishes here and there, or by night with every star pictured in its bosom![4]

The winds sang and moaned as they whipped the water and tugged at the rigging. What was their message? Was it meant for his ears?

"The substance of the wind is too thin for human eyes, their written language too difficult for human minds, and their spoken language mostly too faint for human ears."[5] John longed to be able to interpret the sounds of the sea and felt both insignificant and privileged to be allowed a glimpse of this mystery.

These ocean wind-songs did not leave him lonely and isolated as they had when unbidden gusts stirred the leaves of the palms in Florida; rather, they served to reawaken his spirit and suggest new questions about the cosmos and humanity's place in it. He was even more sure of his conclusion that man was a part of nature, albeit a blessed part, but was not the purpose of its existence. How can we be the focus of the entire universe when so much is hidden from our senses? Even on our own planet we know so little about the landscapes beneath the sea, he mused, so how can it be for us?

His experiences on his journey so far, of sickness, danger, and joy, had left him certain that people are a vulnerable part of a vast universe, whose ultimate purpose is for God's understanding alone. There was still much to discover about the nature of our "blessed star" and the role of man as it whirled through space and time.

Concern was never too far away, though, and he worried that some day even this ocean terrain would fall prey to the insatiable desire of Lord Man: "In view of the rapid advancement of our time, no one can tell how far our star may finally be subdued to man's will."[6] The command to conquer and subdue could yet extend beyond the already degraded shorelines and estuaries, many of which had been built on and drained. The fish of the sea had made many rich over the past hundred years in America from harvesting unprecedented amounts of (mainly) cod, despite growing concern for diminishing stocks. In just two years' time, Congress would write "… the most valuable food fishes of the coast and the lakes of the U.S. are rapidly diminishing in number, to the public injury, and so as materially to affect the interests of trade and commerce…"[7] Yet still the fleets left the ports with no sign of restraint. The leviathans of the oceans, the whales, were daily being hunted in unsustainable numbers and American lamps were still largely lit by whale oil. It would take a few more decades before coal and oil would give these giant mammals some respite.

How long would it take for less-accessible resources to be discovered, John wondered? How many years before the buried treasures of the seas would be opened up for business? "We are apt to look out on the great ocean and regard it as but a half-blank part of the globe – a sort of desert, 'waste of water.' But land animals though we be, land is about unknown to us as the sea, for the turbid glances we gain of the ocean in general through commercial eyes are comparatively worthless." But this was the age of science and industrial growth. John had seen how machines, science, and muscle power were transforming the land everywhere from the prairies to the coast and new discoveries of wealth-making resources were being made all the time. He had no doubt that opportunistic eyes would turn their gaze to the sea if it were shown to hold the potential for making money: "We may at length discover that the sea is as full of life as the land. None can tell how far man's knowledge may yet reach."[8]

It took twelve days to reach New York. Every day took them further into cold air, and when they finally approached New York the snow painting the leafless trees was an alien yet welcome sight. The sailors pulled on woollens but John stood and faced the icy air blasting off the land: "For myself, long burdened with fever, the frosty wind, as it sifted through my loosened bones, was more delicious and grateful than ever was a spring scented breeze."[9]

For ten days John waited at the quay for his ship to set sail for Aspinwall-Colón in Panama. From there he would cross the Isthmus by train and then board another steamer to California. He was little prepared, though, for the noise and bustle of this great city. Illness and isolation from mainstream society had left his confidence at a low ebb and he dared not leave the harbour in case he got lost and missed his departure. He had lived with plant people for many months, but this mass of two-legged humanity was too much: "I felt completely lost in the vast throngs of people, the noise of the streets, and the immense size of the buildings. Often I thought I would like to explore the city if, like a lot of wild hills and valleys, it was clear of inhabitants."[10]

Just up the road the newly built Central Park, with its 4 million trees and plants, lakes, and rocky bluffs, might well have soothed his jangled nerves, but he was too timid to venture out of sight of the water. Forty dollars bought him a steerage-class ticket and at last, with a sigh of relief, he set sail south again in the ship *Nebraska*. This time his travelling companions were "a barbarous mob" who disgusted him with their table manners and rowdy behaviour.

John records little of this return voyage to Panama other than a few jotted notes in which he revisited his ideas of stepping out of the boat and wandering through the sea as one would through a beautiful landscape. If, he mused, he could walk on the sea floor, the foamy wave-tops would be like the clouds, the fish would be as brilliant as the birds, and their flights through the water would be "lighted and marked with stars".

He contrasted the cleanliness of nature with the dirtiness of the humans around him. Only animals are clean, he decided. Filth is a result of civilization, and the more a society develops, the more complex the type of filth it can produce, layering through time to give an archaeological record of dirt. It seems he was not enjoying his human companions very much at all and was glad to take his leave of them when *Nebraska* docked at Aspinwall-Colón.

As his train crossed the Isthmus of Panama, John stared out of the window at a profusion of plant life, which was even more exuberant than he had found in Florida or Cuba. Colourful flowering trees beckoned, surrounded by a lush tangle of vegetation, but he could not stop and follow their call: "I fairly cried for joy and hoped that sometimes I should be able to return and enjoy and study this most glorious of forests to my heart's content."[11] Their mysterious beauty did not seem to be for human eyes to behold, he decided, so unknowable were the forests he could only glimpse.

The train took him to Plaza Cinco Mayo and from there he found another wharf with a steamer bound for San Francisco. On 1 April 1868 he sailed into the Sunshine State along with an amiable English companion he had met on board, Joseph Chilwell (who called John "Scottie"). Together they set out to explore the land that John thought would be his convalescent base for a year. In fact it was to be his home for the rest of his life. Once settled, he would write to Jeanne, "Fate and flowers have carried me to California, and I have revelled and luxuriated amid its plants and mountains for nearly four months."[12] That four months would turn into more than forty years.

California is more of an island than a state. It is biologically the richest part of America, containing one-quarter of the biodiversity of the whole continent. Guarded by mountains, rivers, and the ocean, it has more endemic flora and fauna than anywhere else. Giant redwoods and giant sequoia trees, the largest organisms on earth, join carpets of flowers, rushes, and mosses to produce a land of plant extremes. The largest bird, the Californian condor, soars over the mountains and the smallest, the calliope hummingbird, flits between blossoms. The original Native Indian cultures were just as varied. Fully 100 different languages were spoken by maybe 500 different tribes before they were devastated by the diseases and guns of European invaders.

The tribes split the state between them, occupying different niches provided by the mountains, plains, and coastline. To provide what they needed they worked the land by a variety of methods, including burning, planting, irrigating, and hunting. Burning kept the meadows and savannahs open, creating the right conditions for the growth of nutritious herbs and acorn-laden oaks. After the fires had passed through the tribespeople collected a bonanza of roasted grasshoppers and insect larvae, which they viewed as a delicacy. Fruits, nuts, seeds, game, and fish provided a rich table. The Native Indians were an active, creative part of the Californian landscape, not just passive occupiers. Before the Spanish arrived in the sixteenth century it is thought 300,000 Native Indians lived there. The diseases brought in by the settlers wiped out half of that population, but in 1845 there were still around 150,000.[13] Like the rest of North America the Wild West was indeed wild, but it was not an untouched wilderness.

When John and Joseph stepped off the boat in the early spring of 1868, California was going through an upheaval of immense proportions. The "barbaric mob" that had accompanied John on the steamer from New York on a cheap passage west gave a hint of who was increasingly settling there. In 1848 the population of San Francisco numbered around a thousand permanent residents, and California was a quiet backwater. Just four years later, in 1852, the city had grown to 25,000 residents and in total around 300,000 people made their way to the state between 1849 and 1854. By the end of the century the population of California would increase by 3 million.[14] What followed this influx was a lawless frenzy brought on by the prospect of gold.

In 1848 gold nuggets were found in the foothills of the Sierra Nevada Mountains at Coloma. News spread astonishingly fast, considering there was little transport and no telecommunications. Nothing got in the way of those who could smell the tantalizing aroma of dollars. The gold rush made a few very rich, broke the hearts of many more, and produced, according to naturalist and film-maker Steve Nicholls, in his 2009 book *Paradise Found, Nature in America at the Time of Discovery*, "one of the worst episodes of environmental vandalism in American history". It also caused the near annihilation of the Native Indians. In 1857, only eight years after the gold rush had begun, J. Ross Browne, the government's Investigator of Indian Affairs, produced a report on the fate of the beleaguered tribes in the region. His findings make shocking reading.

> The wild Indians inhabiting the Coast Range, the valleys of the Sacramento and San Joaquin and the western slopes of the Sierra Nevada, became troublesome at a very early period after the discovery of gold mines. It was found convenient to take possession of their country without recompense, rob them of their wives and children, kill them in every cowardly and barbarous manner that could be devised, and when that was impractical drive them as far as possible out of the way.[15]

The statue of John Muir as a boy on Dunbar High Street. It was designed by the Ukrainian artist Valentin Znoba and presented to the town in 1997 (© Mary Colwell).

The coastal town of Dunbar and the rocky foreshore where John Muir played as a child (© Mary Colwell).

Dunbar harbour with the castle wall in the background where John Muir learned to climb as a boy (© Mary Colwell).

Above: Mount Shasta, a 14,179 feet volcano situated at the southern end of the Cascade Range in California. John Muir almost died here, trapped on the summit for 17 hours by a snowstorm that made, "the fire of life smoulder and burn low" (© Dr. Marli Miller/Visuals Unlimited/Corbis).

Right: Calypso borealis, a member of the orchid family found in undisturbed northern and montane forests. John Muir described them as "the most spiritual of all the flower people I had ever met" (© skibreck/ iStockphoto)

Above: The Yosemite Valley in the Sierra Nevada, forever associated with John Muir (© Thomas Vergunst).

Right: Map of the San Joaquin Valley bordered on the west by the Coastal Range on the east by the Sierra Nevada (© United States Environmental Protection Agency).

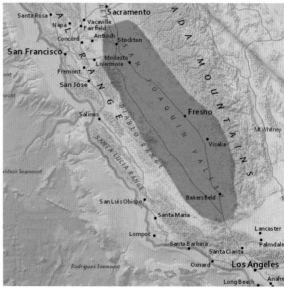

Left: The highest waterfall (2,400 feet) in the United States, the Yosemite Falls. John Muir shuffled along a narrow ledge on his heels, his back to the rock, to stand next to the falling water at the top of the cliff (© ejs9/iStockphoto).

Below: Mount Ritter (13,149 feet) in the Sierra Nevada. John Muir made the first recorded ascent, solo, in October 1872 (© Mel Stoutsenberger/Flickr).

Left: John Muir, *c.* 1875, aged 37 by Carleton Watkins (© Fotosearch/Getty).

Below: John Muir with John Burroughs on a glacier in Alaska in 1899 (© Corbis).

A portrait of John Muir, *c.* 1910 (© Bettmann/Corbis).

It is estimated that in the twenty years from the start of the rush 100,000 Californian Indians died, 4,500 of whom were murdered.[16] Many succumbed to starvation as the mining processes destroyed the natural resources they relied on. Rivers where gold was found were blocked by mud and silt from blasting. Chemicals such as mercury poisoned life for miles around. Dams and river diversions changed the landscape and dried up once biologically rich areas. Water-blasting eroded rock faces, leaving debris and devastation. In *The Sacramento Bee* in 1998, historian Chris Bowman wrote of the period, "But more than anything, it was the 32-year period of intense hydraulic mining that changed the face of the landscape. At the peak of hydraulic mining in the late 1870s, single nozzles up to 9 inches in diameter were discharging up to 25 million gallons of water in 24 hours, the equivalent of filling 1,250 backyard swimming pools."

Forests were clear-felled to provide pit props, buildings, and fuel. Riverbanks were trampled by settlement and panning and by dam-bursting to carry the logs downstream. It was an unprecedented onslaught. It didn't end there; all these miners needed food, and the marshes and savannah areas were fast coming under cultivation. Wildlife was killed and eaten. The coastal cliffs and outlying islands where seabirds nested provided eggs by the million. As the cultivation of crops and introduction of livestock increased, any "pests" were quickly eliminated.

When John started his exploration of southern California the gold rush was still in full flow. How much he knew about the murder and destruction is hard to discern, but he was certainly aware to some degree. Perhaps this helped guide his choice of route away from San Francisco. With no time constraints and no one to meet at any particular place, he could sojourn anywhere. John and Joseph Chilwell chose a route that took them away from the concentration of mines, which were mainly in the northern and central regions, and headed in a southerly direction.

Perhaps also the words of Jeanne Carr were whispering in his ear. In a letter written in 1867, when he lay blinded in bed in

Indianapolis, she had told him about a sublime valley of sun-kissed domes and waterfalls she had read about in a magazine article: "Oh this home of our Father! I would like to know all its mansions – and often to meet and compare notes with you, who love it with the same fervent love."[17] She was talking about the Yosemite Valley deep in the Sierra Nevada Mountains. In his reply he said, "You know my tastes better than anyone else." Now he was, relatively speaking, just a stone's throw away, and had his chance to do as Jeanne wished.

Southern California can be thought of as a high-sided oval basin, with ranges of mountains either side of the central San Joaquin Valley. The Coast Range forms the western rim and is lower, less than 6,560 feet, and is forested by conifers and ferns. The Sierra Nevada forms the eastern rim and towers to over 13,120 feet and is capped by snow. Although only 400 miles long and at most 80 miles wide, the Sierras punch above their weight as regards spectacle. They contain the highest peak in the contiguous United States, Mount Whitney, the granite-domed Yosemite Valley, spectacular glacial lakes such as Mono and Tahoe, giant sequoia groves, and sublime high meadows brimming with flowers.

The most popular way of reaching the Yosemite at that time was by heading directly east out of San Francisco to Stockton, and then on to the Yosemite by stagecoach and horseback. John and Joseph's indirect, flowery route went immediately south, following the foothills of the southern coastal range to Gilroy and into the San Joaquin Valley via the Pacheco Pass. They then followed the Merced River into the mountains. John thought the Coast Range impressive enough:

They were robed with the greenest grass and richest light I ever beheld, and were coloured and shaded with myriads of flowers of every hue, chiefly purple and golden yellow. Hundreds of crystal rills joined songs with the larks, filling the valley with music like a sea, making it Eden from end to end... And hills rise over hills and mountains over mountains, heaving, waving, swelling, in most glorious, overpowering, unreadable majesty.[18]

He felt like "a crushed insect" in the face of such beauty. And just when he thought his senses could take no more he entered the San Joaquin Valley, a vast plain that stretched out before him, watered by sparkling rivers and in the distance the tantalizing snowy peaks of the Sierra Nevada. Here was the Garden of Eden he had been searching for. He had hoped Florida would be the land of flowers but its treasures were often hidden in strange, dark swamps and guarded by inaccessible, sometimes hostile, tangles of vines. In Cuba the flowers he sought were piled together in a jumbled heap of glowing confusion. Here, however, bright blooms were laid out like jewels on a velvet blanket. All he had to do was wander at will and each footstep brought more gems:

> ...side by side, flower to flower, petal to petal, touching but not entwined, branches weaving past and past each other, yet free and separate – one smooth garment, mosses next the ground, grasses above, petaled flowers between.[19]

John had found heaven on earth. He wrote to Jeanne in July 1868 in fulsome Muir prose, exulting in the range of flowers he had found in just one square yard of the valley floor. Compsitea, the daisy family, formed the greater part of the display, as its clusters of bright yellow flowers carpeted the valley floor. He knelt down and counted the flower heads in that one square yard and recorded thousands of heads of daisies and sunflowers, members of the pea family, umbellifera, and herbs of many types as well as grasses and mosses. He likened them to a mass gathering, as though many flower tribes had gathered together for worship:

> The valley of the San Joaquin is the floweriest piece of world I ever walked, one vast, level, even flower-bed, a sheet of flowers, a smooth sea, ruffled a little in the middle by the tree fringing of the river and of smaller cross streams here and there, from the mountains.[20]

At last he did tear himself away from the flowers and they carried on with their planned journey to the Yosemite Valley, but it seems to be the flowers that entranced John in the beginning rather than the splendour of the rocky fortress deep in the Sierras. He mentions to Jeanne that he went to the Yosemite, acknowledging its splendour: "It is by far the grandest of all the special temples of Nature I was ever permitted to enter."[21] But he does not fall into an almost ecstatic state when describing it. He forgot to say a bear scared him, and he failed to mention that when the pair decided to buy a gun for protection he accidentally shot Joseph Chilwell in the shoulder during target practice! There is no hint that the high mountains pulled at his soul in the way the flowery plains had done. In the biography *A Passion for Nature: The Life of John Muir* (2008), the environmental historian Professor Donald Worster wrote of John's first trip into the Yosemite: "He came, he trembled at the sight of a bear, and he left again, writing little about any of it."

When he returned to San Joaquin from this first trip into the mountains, reality hit. Again he was faced with the fact that a passion for flowers was not enough to keep body and soul together. Pesky bread and a roof over his head were necessities and John knew he had to find work. Joseph Chilwell left California and John turned to what he knew well, and became a farm labourer. Eventually he branched out from odd-jobbing and took on a new role, shepherding.

A sheep farmer called John Connel, known as "Smoky Jack", needed someone to care for his flock over the winter in a truly delightful spot called Twenty Hill Hollow in the flowery valley. This sunken area of the valley floor, surrounded by grassy knolls, formed "a charming fairy land of hills". Streams meandered between the grassy domes and then united to form a larger stream, Hollow Creek. Less than a mile in length, it provided a compact, undulating landscape, "seen only by hunters and shepherds, sunk in the wide bosom of the plain, like undiscovered gold". Here John moved into a leaky shepherd's hut, ate beans, flapjacks, and homemade sourdough bread, and began to absorb the rhythm of the lowland wildlife that buzzed and pottered about the flowers.

At this stage he preferred to be in Twenty Hill Hollow rather than the overpowering Yosemite. "Here are no Washington Columns, no angular El Capitans."[22] Still suffering from occasional bouts of fever, and no doubt quite weak, he needed the balm of a green hollow rather than an adventure in mountains.

This fairy dell was soothing to the eye and could be absorbed with simple joy rather than demanding awe and wonder. The dimensions were restful and he could imagine the watery forces that had carved the rounded hills, rather than have his powers of imagination challenged by the immense upheavals required to fashion the granite domes and deep-set valleys of the Sierra. Yellow and purple flowers carpeted the ground; ferns and mosses provided a darker hue in the shadier nooks. There was only one bush that formed such a striking feature in an otherwise smooth landscape that John's sheepdog thought it was a bear and constantly barked at it. For the first time in months John stopped moving, settled down with a cool wind in his hair and warm sun on his face, and just gazed. He also thought about Jeanne Carr.

In a letter written to Jeanne in February 1869 he confessed to missing her presence amid such beauty: "I have thought of you hundreds of times in my seasons of deepest joy, amid the flower purple and gold of the plains, the fern fields in the gorge and canyon, the sacred waters, tree columns, and the eternal sublimities of the mountains." He sent her a pressed flower. In return she wrote to him at Easter, "My thoughts are unto you ward, dear shepherd, and there is no other soul with whom I would prefer to keep this spotless day sacred to the holiest memories and hope." She told him she was planning a visit to him, now that her family had left Madison and moved to California, where Ezra Carr was to work at the newly founded university. They must arrange to meet and see the Yosemite Valley together. "You and I are of those who must leave the spiritual laws to bring us together as they surely will... I hear your voice in the undertones of life." She was worried, however, that his solitude was too much: "But you must be social. John, you must make friends among the materialists, lest your highest pleasures taken selfishly become impure."[23] Ever the friend, mentor, and spiritual advisor, Jeanne touched John in ways no one else ever did. The news that the Carrs now resided in the same state was a joy; his life was coming together once again. She alone would understand what he was thinking and feeling about this wondrous Californian Eden.

The lovely Hollow views were accompanied by the music of streams and larks: "An inspiration this song of the blessed lark, and universally absorbable by human souls. It seems to be the only birdsong of these hills that has been created with any direct reference to us." He pondered on all the melodies that were not audible: the wind creating tunes around sand grains, or gently buffeting the stamens of flowers and ruffling the feathers on birds. The Hollow was filled with music that human senses were not sophisticated enough to detect: "Fancy the waving, pulsing melody of the vast flower congregation of the Hollow flowing from myriad voices of tuned petal and pistil, and heaps of sculptured pollen. Scarce one note is for us; nevertheless, God be thanked for this blessed instrument hid beneath the feathers of a lark."[24]

Jackrabbits were hunted by visiting eagles. Ducks alighted on pools and herons stalked the creeks. Occasionally he noted a coyote or a Californian wolf, "but they are not numerous, vast numbers having been slain by the traps and poisons of the sheep-raisers". The ground squirrel that chatted and busied about the grass was persecuted too because of its love of grain: "What a pity that Nature should have made so many small mouths palated like our own!"[25] And what a pity that the sheep he tended ate his beloved flowers and trampled the ground.

Again, the dichotomy of the practical versus the ideal struck deep. People needed employment to provide housing and food, and for John it was sheep that allowed him to live in this delightful garden, free from civilization and all its confining expectations. But sheep also destroyed what he so loved. He felt ensnared by sheep, yet indebted to them. He despised them, calling them, "hooved locusts", and considered them half-manufactured, half-alive constructs of Lord Man. In a letter to Jeanne Carr he described them as his "mutton family".[27] He had no alternative, though, but to depend on them.

Despite his troubled relationship with sheep, we get a measure of his improving health at the end of his writings on Twenty Hill Hollow. One senses a rebuilding of his old powers after so long travelling and languishing in an exhausted, feverish state. He at last feels full strength returning. "I am well again, I came to life amidst the cool winds and crystal waters of the mountains," he wrote to Jeanne.

John was living the American version of the pastoral idyll of Wordsworth. These luxuriant days would appear years later in an article, "The Bee Pastures of California". They were also important in inspiring his first outreach to readers. In *A Thousand-Mile Walk to the Gulf*, a travelogue of his trip, rather than simply describing nature he begins to urge anyone coming to the area to take a detour away from the well-trodden path to Yosemite Valley and seek out this haven: "If you wish to see how much of light, life and joy can be got into a January, go to this blessed Hollow. If you wish to see a plant resurrection – myriads of bright flowers crowding from the ground like souls to a judgement – go to Twenty Hills in February." April, however, was a time for unsurpassed flower glory:

Few have any conception of its amazing richness... you will find that there are from one to ten thousand upon every square yard, counting the heads of Compositae as single flowers. Yellow Compositae form by far the greater proportion of this goldy-way. May well the sun feed them with his richest light, for these shining sunlets are his very children – ray of his ray, beam of his beam! One would fancy that these California days receive more gold from the ground than they give to it. The earth has indeed become sky; and the two cloudless skies, raying towards each other flower-beams and sunbeams, are fused and congolded into one glowing heaven.[28]

This passage is quintessential John Muir: made-up words infused with religious imagery and overflowing with a love of nature that welled up from within. He had no desire to keep his findings to himself; he was an evangelist who urged others to find their healing in nature, whether they were sick in body or in spirit. For those who are ill he advises staying away from doctors and hiding in the hills: "lave in its waters, tan in its golds, bask in its flower-shine and your baptism will make you a new creature indeed. Or, chocked in the sediments of society, so tired of the world, here will your hard doubts disappear, your carnal encrustations melt off, and your soul breathe deep and free in God's shoreless atmosphere of beauty and love."

It is in this small temple of green and gold that he experienced what can only be interpreted as a moment of religious ecstasy. He describes the almost painful beauty of the star-spangled rivers fringed with glowing flowers: "The Hollow overflowed with light… The ground steamed with fragrance. Light of unspeakable richness, was brooding the flowers." Behind him stood the towering majesty of the Sierras, bands of hills rising in shades of purple and blue to the highest snowy peaks that pointed to heaven. Staring at them, he didn't sense them as distant rocky crags, separated by miles from his sunken kingdom, but as part of him: "To the lover of the wild, these mountains are not a hundred miles away. Their spiritual power and goodness of the sky make them near, as a circle of friends." The Hollow had done the trick. His gaze turned to the Sierras and he was lost in love and prayer. In a meditative state he wrote, "You bathe in these spirit beams, turning round and round, as if warming at a camp fire. Presently you lose consciousness of your own separate existence: you blend with the landscape, and become part and parcel of nature."[29]

John's understanding of his relationship with nature deepened during this time as a solitary shepherd in the Central Valley. No longer was nature "out there", but indistinguishable from his own flesh and blood. His body had become transparent, a glass receptacle that was filled with the wonder of the world surrounding him. John Muir and nature were one.

His thousand-mile odyssey came to an end in California, and he found his home in the light and colour of the West. The twentieth-century essayist and cartoonist James Thurber created a little ditty that captures this point in his life:

All men should strive
To learn before they die
What they are running from, and to, and why.[30]

He had certainly been running long and hard away from the many constraints of his home and religion. Their stranglehold loosened as he walked south to Florida and was eventually released through feverish nights and languid days of weakness and self-analysis. He was running to a place of freedom from expectations and authority, to places where he could be alone with his ideas, his own image of God, and his beloved plants, his "fellow mortals".

And why was he running? The contradictions he had experienced so far – the conflict between machines and nature, the God of authority and the God of the woodlands, the beauty of nature and the dangers of disease and death from that same wilderness – tore him apart. He needed time to think and above all to understand man's relationship with all things non-human. He thought he would find everything he needed entangled in vines or in the waving fronds of palms in the tropics; he had no idea he would find it in the floweriest land of all, California. The Hollow had reinvigorated him. He was now ready for the next phase of his physical and spiritual journey. The Sierra Nevada, the Range of Light beckoned.

Chapter 9

John of the Mountains

"One touch of nature makes the whole world kin"

William Shakespeare, *Troilus and Cressida*

John Muir is often called "John of the Mountains". His name is synonymous with the Sierra Nevada, the "Range of Light"[1] as he called them, the towering, snowy-peaked, sunlit mountain range that filled his peripheral vision in Twenty Hill Hollow and whose call to him to visit grew stronger day by day. He is especially associated with the Yosemite Valley, a hall of grandeur nestled in the heart of the mountains 4,000 feet above sea level, guarded by granite buttresses. "I am hopelessly and forever a mountaineer,"[2] he wrote to Jeanne as he emerged from his shepherd cocoon and stretched his wings among the mountains and high meadows.

His next five years would be spent almost entirely in the Range of Light, communing with the spirit of the rocks and pines, lost in contemplation and wonder. He was filled with a love that flowed out through every word he scribbled in his notebooks and letters, and his most inspired writings came out of this immersion. But to say that it was some kind of divine impulse that drove him to the high mountain passes in the early summer of 1869 would be misleading. It wasn't a heavenly call; it was sheep. As much as he continuted to hate them, it was a fuzzy, bumbling flock of flower-munchers that led the way to his destiny.

After his contract with Smoky Jack in Twenty Hill Hollow had finished, another sheep farmer, John Delaney, offered him a job that seemed to be a solution to the eternal problem of finding food in the wilderness. "The bread problem" was still a major block to freedom and John had been toying with ideas on how to "live like the wild animals, gleaning nourishment here and there from seeds and berries".[3]

Delaney then stepped into the picture. This affable Irish, ex-Catholic seminarian turned out to be a surprising ally. He needed someone reliable to accompany his lazy and dull shepherd, Billy, plus 2,050 sheep, into the high Sierra pastures. They were to trek to a height of 9,000 feet above sea level, to the headwaters of the Merced and Tuolumne rivers, and feed the flock on an area of pasture north of the Yosemite. John would not be required to do much shepherding, just to keep Billy on track. A hunter asked if he would take his dog, a St Bernard called Carlo, to relieve the poor animal of a summer of intense heat on the plains, and he gladly agreed.

Delaney seemed to instinctively understand John and admired his writing. He assured him there would be plenty of time to explore the mountains and study flowers. On 3 June 1869 the band of sheepherders left the Delaney ranch. It comprised Delaney, John Muir with Carlo, Billy, and two extra hands, a Chinese and a Native Indian, employed to help them for the first few weeks. John and Billy were to stay on and were not due to return until September. John took a notebook and pencils and little else. Gone were the flower press and the Bible, as well as his books on Milton and Burns; he travelled light and opened himself to the experience. Delaney accompanied them as far as Pilot Peak Ridge, a few days into the journey, and then turned back, promising fresh supplies in midsummer.

When the going was good they made progress of about a mile a day, but the intense heat and the slow sheep made anything more ambitious impossible. In the lowlands they passed over brushy hills dotted with ceanothus, Adenostoma fasciculatum (greasewood) and azaleas. Occasional blue oaks gave welcome shade to the panting, overheated sheep. Gone now was the golden carpet of spring flowers. The intense heat transformed the moisture of life to bare, cracked earth. "The poor dust-chocked flock" became increasingly distressed.

In the evening, John and his companions made a campfire and ate and smoked, "and under the influence of fullness and tobacco the calm that settled on their faces seemed almost divine, something like the mellow meditative glow portrayed on the countenances of saints".[4] Only one of the group stayed apart: "The Indian kept in the background, never saying a word."

At dawn the group breakfasted on coffee, bacon, and beans. Stands of the Sabine pine began to appear among the blue oaks, reminding John more of a palm than a pine. Its long, straight trunk is undivided for fifteen or twenty feet and then branches outwards, but its straggly form gives little shade. The cones, however, are huge, six or seven inches long and five wide, and the wood provides richly scented fires. The nuts, the size of hazelnuts, were nutritious and eaten by the local Native Indians: "food and fire fit for the gods from the same fruit".

By 6 June they had reached a higher plateau where the trees began to change to yellow and sugar pine. With the increasing altitude the heat was less intense and views began to open out, giving tantalizing vistas of waves of mountains stretching as far as the eye could see, "a glorious wilderness that seemed to be calling with a thousand songful voices". The vegetation changed with height. It became more densely packed, giving the rocks a rich, plush coat of green: "How wonderful the power of its beauty! Gazing awestricken, I might have left everything for it… Beauty beyond thought everywhere, beneath, above, made and being made forever."

As John lay under the stars at night the presence of the high peaks was powerful: "The night wind is telling of the wonders of the upper mountains, their snow fountains, and gardens, forests and groves." He felt altitude in his bones and his spirit began to fly. Now they had reached the edge of the great coniferous forest, the gateway to the higher reaches. Here he wrote one of his most beautiful passages, echoing the transcendent experience in the Hollow:

We are now in the mountains and they are in us, kindling enthusiasm, making every nerve quiver, filling every pore and cell of us. Our flesh and bone tabernacle seems transparent as glass to the beauty about us, as if truly an inseparable part of it, thrilling with the air and the trees, streams and rocks, in the waves of the sun – a part of all nature, neither old nor young, sick nor well, but immortal.[5]

Although John hadn't been to church since leaving for his thousand-mile walk, he was not lacking in theological lessons. The plant people expounded eternal truths from their rocky pulpits along the mountain trails and the trees waved their branches like worshippers. The divine was everywhere he looked, resonating with the words of a contemporary poet, Mary Dow Brine, who walked the country lanes of New York State:

And the flowers preached their sermon
By the wayside – sweet and fair,
Breathing out their subtle fragrance
On the Sabbath morning air.[6]

These divine contemplations were, however, constantly interrupted by the sound of baaing. The rambling mass of wool reminded him of a grey cloud slowly ascending the mountain. He grabbed time here and there to sketch and make notes, but was forever pulled onwards. He longed to sit at the feet of a globe lily (or fairy lantern), a "plant saint" as he called it, that blessed all those who passed by and made them pure: "It is not easy to keep up with the camp cloud while such plant people are standing preaching by the wayside."[7] But he had a job to do and he had to move on. His sense of interaction with nature deepened. He was no longer an outside observer but felt part of something immense and mysterious: "The whole wilderness seems to be alive and talkative, sympathetic, brotherly. No wonder when we consider that all have the same Father and Mother."[8]

He felt the connection with all of life, from stones to trees, from squirrels to bears. Here were his kith and kin. In a letter to a friend he wrote:

> Rocks and waters, etc., are words of God and so are men. We all flow from one fountain Soul. All are expressions of one Love. God does not appear, and flow out, only from narrow chinks and round bored wells here and there in favoured races and places, but He flows in grand undivided currents, shoreless and boundless over creeds and forms and all kinds of civilizations and peoples and beasts, saturating all and fountainizing all.[9]

This first summer in the Sierra Nevada marked the end of the transformation that had begun in Canada. He was a different man from the one who had set out in 1864 to botanize around the shores of the Great Lakes. Now completely healthy, he found he could spend every day revelling in new and inspiring landscapes. The higher the group climbed, the more intense those feelings became. The snowy peaks were the frost icing on an unimaginably rich Sierra cake made of gorges, waterfalls, meadows, and wildlife. Sunny days, cool breezes, and starlit nights are the stuff of poets, and the notes he kept became some of his best-known writings:

> Another glorious Sierra day in which one seems to be dissolved and absorbed and sent pulsing onward we know not where. Life seems neither long nor short, and we take no more heed to save time or make haste than do the trees and stars. This is true freedom, a good practical sort of immortality.[10]

Again and again he used religious terminology to express the wonders that now touched his soul daily. He wrote like a preacher but his congregation was as yet undefined and his words restricted to letters and his notebook. As if seeing everything with new eyes, delight was everywhere he looked – apart, that is, from when his gaze fell upon Billy and the sheep.

John's dislike of sheep grew as they trampled and munched the vegetation: "Sheep, like people, are ungovernable when hungry… almost every leaf that these hooved locusts can reach within a radius of a mile or two from camp has been devoured."[11] At night, penned in a corral, he said they looked like a grey blanket; in the day they were a "crawling sheep cloud". They were "silly" as well as destructive: "Sheep brain must surely be poor stuff… A sheep can hardly be called an animal; an entire flock is required to make one foolish individual."[12]

He feared that, as increasing amounts of money could be made from them as the human population of California grew, the numbers of sheep coming into the mountains would escalate, exposing ever more of this Eden to their "blighting touch". Although they couldn't eat the trees they could easily damage tender seedlings and munch through beautiful lilies and other wild flowers:

> Only the sky will then be safe, though hid from view by dust and
> smoke, incense of a bad sacrifice. Poor, helpless, hungry sheep,
> in great part misbegotten, without good right time to be, semi-
> manufactured, made less by God than man, born out of time and
> place, yet their voices are strangely human and call out one's pity.[13]

He despaired as the sheep trampled blindly through a particularly beautiful meadow where larkspur and columbine fringed a swathe of waist-high lupins: "And so the beauty of lilies falls on angels and men, bears and squirrels, wolves and sheep, birds and bees, but as far as I have seen, man alone, and the animals he tames, destroy these gardens."[14] The sheep had a lot to answer for.

But then Billy showed little more understanding of where he was than did his charges. He seemed totally incapable of appreciating beauty and showed no interest at all in his surroundings. In the daytime he never stopped to look at the scenery and he was scathing about tourists who paid good money to travel to the Yosemite. At night, rather than make a bed out of sweet-scented boughs and lie in the fresh air, he chose to sleep in a hollow in the soil next to the sheep pen, where he breathed in dust scented with urea. His trousers were never washed and were stiff with the congealed fat that dripped off the mutton he tied to his belt for lunch. Layering grease upon dirt for year upon year, they trapped insects, wool, mud, and food scraps. The layers were so thick that John fancied his trousers might have geological significance.

Billy's clothes mirrored his mind: inflexible, lacking colour, and full of the mundane detritus of grubby living. He could see no wonder in the tumbling waterfalls or towering snowy peaks. When John tried to persuade him to view the Yosemite waterfall plunging 3,000 feet over a rocky ledge to the valley below, Billy refused, saying it was just a hole full of rocks and most likely very dangerous. Far from being a place of sublime beauty, it was to be kept well away from. And anyway there were plenty of rocks to look at where he sat and chewed his mutton. "Such souls, I suppose, are asleep, or smothered and befogged beneath mean pleasures and cares," opined John.

John blamed the lifestyle of Californian shepherds in particular for this dullness of mind and he distanced them from the noble profession he had seen back in Scotland or read about in the Bible or Wordsworth's poetry. The honourable and tragic shepherd Michael in Wordsworth's *A Pastoral Poem,* the hillside seer who lived in and through the landscape, could not have been more different to Billy.

> An old man, stout of heart, and strong of limb.
> His bodily frame had been from youth to age
> Of an unusual strength: his mind was keen,
> Intense, and frugal, apt for all affairs,
> And in his shepherd's calling he was prompt
> And watchful more than ordinary men.
> Hence had he learned the meaning of all winds,
> Of blasts of every tone; and, oftentimes,
> When others heeded not, he heard the South.[15]

John mused on this dignified man of the hills and then looked upon Billy: "If ancient shepherds were so intelligent and lute-voiced, why are modern ones in the Lord's grandest gardens usually so muddy and degraded?"[16] John saw British shepherds as seamless characters in a tranquil landscape, their lives honed through centuries of tradition and steeped in an understanding of nature passed down through the generations. Their flocks were manageably small, nothing like the throngs of the hooved locust that traipsed where they liked with little appreciation on the part of their guardians of where they were or what damage they might be inflicting. British shepherds, thought John, read books lying on a green hillside, "and conversed with kings".

American sheep drovers, on the other hand, had no time for self-improvement, such were the distances they had to travel to find pastures and the dangers they had to guard against in the form of wolves, coyotes, and bears. They spent too long alone in squalid cabins with poor food and no entertainment, dreaming only of making money. Eventually all senses were extinguished except those they needed for sheep-tending. They went insane as their minds were smothered with woollen blankets that insulated them from the rest of society. They went blind to the surrounding beauty as thick wool slipped over their eyes. They became deaf to the music of the mountains as the incessant baaing of sheep blocked all other sounds. Thus the Californian shepherd was a dullard, the British shepherd a romantic sprite of the countryside.

It was a harsh judgment and an idealized view of shepherding in Britain. Indeed, John Clare and Robert Burns were farm labourers, but they were exceptions and Clare lamented his loneliness and isolation from others who found his interest in poetry unfathomable. As regards the landscape, Britain had been through the destructive phase inflicted by grazing sheep and had settled into a new order that accommodated their impact. Wolves and bears had been exterminated in Britain long ago to protect livestock. For John, however, it was undeniably painful to watch nations of his beloved plant people being chewed and digested in great swathes along a mountain track while their guardian failed to notice even one lovely thing.

If Billy was no romantic figure of old, he also stood in stark contrast to the brooding figure of the Indian helper, a "Digger Indian", so-called because they dug up roots for food. This silent man is given no name or age and is portrayed as sullen and unfriendly. He spurned all unnecessary contact with the group, ate his meals at a distance, and rarely spoke. One cold night they offered him blankets but he refused, instead lying apart on bare ground in clothes that were damp with sweat from the day's work. He rebuffed any attempt at friendship and John was at once full of bemusement and admiration at his ruggedness: "A fine thing to be independent of clothing where it is so hard to carry. When food is scarce, he can live on whatever comes his way – a few berries, roots, birds' eggs, grasshoppers, black ants, fat wasp or bumblebee larvae, without feeling that he is doing anything worth mention, so I have been told."[17]

John makes no reference to the treatment of the Native Indians at the hands of the Forty-Niners, which was easily within living memory and in many places ongoing. Who knows what horrors this man had seen and what resentments he held?

On one level the Indians were impressive in their ability to live off the land with ease, as this man could. He also envied the way they moved lightly through the landscape. One morning an old Indian man appeared in the camp at daybreak and stood silently, staring at John while he was sketching. John was shocked to see him when he looked up, as he had made no sound, even getting past the camp dogs undetected. He was

> grim and silent within a few steps of me, as motionless and weather-stained as an old tree stump that had stood there for centuries. All Indians seem to have learned this wonderful way of walking unseen… Indians walk softly and hurt the landscape hardly more than birds or squirrels.

He compared the ways of Indians with those of the Forty-Niners who were shattering the landscape some miles to the north:

> How different are most of those of the white man... roads blasted
> in solid rock, wild streams dammed and tamed and turned out of
> their channels and led along sides of canyons and valleys to work in
> mines like slaves... Long will it be ere these marks are effaced, though
> Nature is doing what she can... patiently trying to heal every scar.[18]

On the other hand, when an old woman played the same trick, appearing silently near John as he sat by a river, she disgusted him. She had been looking at him for who knows how long before he noticed her. She was dirty and the dress she wore was made of the rags of white men's clothes. "But from no point of view that I have found are such debased fellow beings a whit more natural than the glaring tailored tourists we saw that frightened the birds and squirrels."[19] Or indeed the ragged band of sheep and shepherds of which John was a part.

Indians, therefore, were a contradiction; they seemed to occupy two worlds. One was in nature, in tune with their surroundings and beating to the same rhythms and seasons as wildlife. Yet on the other hand they appeared dirty and shambling, often begging for tobacco and alcohol, and as unsightly and as much out of place as Billy.

The way of life of the native peoples was so removed from the experience of the incomers that many of their actions were misinterpreted. Most Californians mistook eating grubs and insects for savagery and did not see it as a wise use of protein that was easily available. Many saw their apparently relaxed approach to life as laziness rather than as a sign of a fulfilment that was free from the tyranny of making money. Most of all, the majority missed their invaluable contribution to the landscape. The Sierra Indians undoubtedly influenced the vegetation and wildlife through their management but most incomers failed to fully recognize it, John included.

It is no wonder, though, that John envied the Indian his ability to live off the land, as bread, as ever, was a problem. For weeks the group were forced to eat just mutton and tea as they waited for Delaney to return with supplies of flour. He was surprised by how much it affected him, even dreaming about bread at night: "Man seems to have more difficulty in obtaining food than any other of the Lord's creatures," he lamented.[20]

As he stood on the shores of the magnificent Lake Tenaya, he longed to be like the cheery and hardy bushes: "I wish I could live like these junipers on sunshine and snow, and stand beside them on the shore of Lake Tenaya for a thousand years!"[21] If he were a tree, he fancied, he could carry all the food and drink he needed in the bark around his body and be freed from even carrying a bag. As a mighty pine he could hold his head high enough to view the wonders of the mountains, and with his feet dipped into cool lakes or rocky soil he could get all essential sustenance from above and below. He fancied he would be forever happy and never lonely. His outstretched arms would welcome birds, his canopy would offer shelter to lumbering bears and elegant deer, his trunk would be a home for myriad insects, and the cheeky, "condensed nugget of fresh mountain air", the squirrels, would scamper busily about his body. He would never be alone and even his human friends would appear close by as the mountains gathered all to themselves, making miles irrelevant. "One would be at endless Godful play," he wrote wistfully.

As John and the band slowly herded the sheep ever higher, Jeanne Carr had arrived in the Yosemite Valley below to search for him. Her family were now settled in Oakland, just across the water from San Francisco, and Ezra Carr had taken up a professorship at the University of California. This was her first chance to reconnect with her protégé. Unfortunately her letters telling of her arrival had failed to reach him, and so John was miles away as she swooned at the vistas and the magnificence around her. She left notes in various places in the hope they would find each other but it was not to be:

> Not less than eight letters and notes are travelling around in search of you and having up to this moment followed your directions as nearly as I could, I can only simply acquiesce in the inevitable and

go away without seeing you until in God's own time and way we are once more permitted to enjoy face to face communion.[22]

John may have missed the one person he wanted to share his joy with, but he did catch up with Professor Butler, a reunion that was not planned at all. As John sat high above the Yosemite, a strange and powerful feeling – which he could only describe as a premonition – made him race down the mountain to meet him. Although he had had no idea Butler would be there, he became convinced he was not far away. He found him by a river, to everyone's astonishment, but it was a scratchy, unsatisfying reunion as Butler was constantly harried by his travelling companion to move on. John pleaded with him to stay so that he could show him some of the delights very few visitors even knew about, but he left quickly, seeing almost nothing. He was a little put out that Butler didn't think him worth more time. To Jeanne he wrote, "I am glad the world does not miss me and all of my days with the Lord and his works are uncounted and unmeasured."[23] Jeanne was furious: "It makes me so mad that he should have found you! Mad at both of you."[24]

Failing to meet Jeanne was a severe blow: "I need not tell you how sorely I am pained by this bitter disappointment... Thus far all of my deepest, purest enjoyments have been taken in solitude, and the fate seems hard that has hindered me from sharing Yosemite with you."[25] She alone would have understood what he was experiencing in this temple of endless bliss. In a future letter he would confide that she was never far from his mind: "In all my wanderings through Nature's beauty, whether it be among the ferns at my cabin door or in the high meadows and peaks or amid the spray and music of the waterfalls, you are the first to meet me and I often speak to you as verily in the flesh."[26]

John's combination of robust health and the sense of immortality gained from his transcendental experiences were, however, often a dangerous combination. On 15 July he explored the area above the Yosemite Valley. The view was beyond description, with its sublime domes and canyons, dark sweeping forests, and glorious array of white peaks deep in the sky, every feature glowing, radiating beauty that pours into our flesh and bones like heat rays from a fire. Sunshine all over; no breath of wind to stir the brooding calm. Never before had I seen so glorious a landscape, so boundless an affluence of sublime mountain beauty.[27]

He followed the Yosemite Creek, which flows along a narrow channel before plunging over the edge of a terrifying precipice to a pool 1,500 feet below, and then onwards a further 700 feet to the bottom of the valley. In all, the river falls half a mile, producing the much-photographed and acclaimed Yosemite Falls, the highest waterfall in North America. John was overcome with a desire to see just how closely he could tether his spirit to the wild. Not content with marvelling from a distance, he wanted to stand next to the falling water, to see "the forms and behaviour of the falls all the way down to the bottom". To do this he had to get very close to the watery column as it leapt out from the cliff into thin air.

After studying any likely looking rock faces he realized the only way was to shuffle on his heels with his back to the rock along a wet ledge only three inches wide, which led to the side of the falling water. Everything in him screamed stop, "[b]ut in the face of Yosemite scenery cautious remonstrance is vain; under its spell one's body seems to go where it likes with a will over which we seem to have scarce any control". He made his way to the ledge and, planting his heels as firmly as possible, he inched across the sheer rock face. After thirty feet or so he arrived at the edge of the waterfall, balancing precariously. "Here I obtained a perfectly free view down into the heart of the snowy, chanting throng of comet-like streamers into which the body of the fall soon separates."[28] He chewed on sour leaves in a hope they would stem his dizziness.

He must have made a heart-stopping sight, if there had been anyone there to see him other than Carlo the sheepdog, who looked on in great alarm. John was not aware of being scared as the roaring of the water smothered his senses. He couldn't tell how long he stood there, a tiny dot perched on a thin slippery ledge, inches from a cascade of water, thousands of feet above a rocky valley. Eventually he shuffled back again and made his way back to camp. Only later did his body revolt against the extreme danger, keeping him awake with nightmares of falling. His nerves were badly shaken, but, far from deciding that that was enough, it was just the start of many more mountain escapades that narrowly avoided death. This wild spirituality was no longer a passive contemplation of flowers; it demanded a full submission to the physicality of the mountains. To engage fully, though, he had to free himself from sheep.

When the group finally arrived back in the lowlands before the first winter snows, John gave up any plans for leaving to carry on with his original journey to South America. He wanted to see the valley in the hush of winter when all the tourists and sheep had gone and the place was becalmed under a blanket of snow. The Amazon could wait. There was work to be done here, important work. To earn money he took employment with James Hutchings, who ran the first hotel in the Yosemite Valley.

The Yosemite Valley lies 150 miles due east of San Francisco and hangs high in the mountains. It is a mile wide and seven and a half miles long, giving it an enclosed yet airy feel. Many streams tumble over the high walls, some of which tower 4,000 feet above the valley floor. These streams combine to form the Merced River, which flows out of the valley in the west, winding its way through lush meadows. The valley was to be a stunning base camp for the following years of mountain immersion.

After abandoning machines for so long, the old skills resurfaced and he made use of the fast flowing water to make a small, water-powered sawmill to cut planks out of trees that had been blown down in storms. These were used to repair and extend the hotel, and he also made himself an eccentric cabin that stretched over the stream. Here he could rest to the sound of running water and tread softly on the ferns that grew on the floor. In December he wrote to Jeanne,

I am feasting in the Lord's mountain house, and what pen may write my blessings? I am going to dwell here all winter magnificently "Snowbound". Just think of the grandeur of a mountain winter in Yosemite! Would that you could enjoy it also!... I am dead and gone to heaven.[29]

From now on, over the next few years, whenever he could, he left the valley bottom and headed to higher, hidden places, often spending weeks alone. He needed nothing but bread and time. "Every day opens and closes like a flower, noiseless, effortless. Divine peace glows on all the majestic landscape, like a silent enthusiastic joy that sometimes transfigures a noble human face."[30]

Cold, wet, exhausted, and hungry, he defied his own comfort and put himself into the very heart of the mountains whatever the mood of the weather. He was young, now fully fit, and full of zeal. With the foolhardiness of a young adventurer he took a host of risks, which make nerve-tingling reading.

Mount Ritter is an isolated, 13,000-foot mountain of dark rock, lying to the east of the Yosemite Valley. The San Joaquin and Owen Rivers spring from its glaciers and its summit can be reached only by precipitous climbing. With no ropes and no companion, sustained only by tea and a slice of bread, John made the first ascent in the autumn of 1872.

At length, I found myself at the foot of a sheer drop in the bed of the avalanche channel, which seemed to bar all further progress. The tried dangers beneath seemed even greater than that of the cliff in front; therefore, after scanning its face again and again, I commenced to scale it, picking my holds with intense caution. After gaining a point about halfway to the top, I was brought to a dead stop, with arms outspread, clinging close to the face of the rock, unable to move hand or foot either up or down. My doom appeared fixed. I must fall.

There would be a moment of bewilderment, and then a lifeless tumble down the one general precipice to the glacier below. When this final danger flashed in upon me, I became nerve-shaken for the first time since setting foot on the mountain, and my mind seemed to fill with a stifling smoke. But the terrible eclipse lasted only a moment, when life burst forth again with preternatural clearness. I seemed suddenly to become possessed of a new sense. The other self – the ghost of by-gone experiences, instinct, or Guardian Angel – call it what you will – came forward and assumed control.[31]

On a few occasions he stood face to face with bears, having disturbed them as he rambled through meadows and forests. Once he found a grizzly, feared everywhere for their attacks on people. "He came on within a dozen yards of me and I had a good, quiet look onto his eyes." Luckily the bear decided John was of no interest. In a later article he described the meeting: "In my first interview with a Sierra bear we were frightened and embarrassed both of us, but the bear's behaviour was better than mine."[32]

Intrigued by avalanches, he often went out after heavy snow to watch and listen as the snow tumbled down the mountains:

Most delightful it is to stand in the middle of Yosemite on still, clear mornings after snow-storms and watch the throngs of avalanches as they come down, rejoicing, to their places, whispering, thrilling like birds, or roaring and booming like thunder.

Most people find watching an avalanche at a distance exciting enough; not many choose to throw themselves into one. After one particularly heavy snowfall, John had laboured to the top of a canyon in waist-deep snow, when suddenly the whole mass of snow and ice gave way.

When the avalanche started I threw myself on my back and spread my arms to try to keep from sinking… On no part of the rush was I buried, I was only moderately imbedded on the surface, or at times a little below it… This flight in what might be called a milky way of snow-stars was the most spiritual and exhilarating of all the modes of motion I have ever experienced. Elijah's flight in a chariot of fire could hardly have been more gloriously exciting.[33]

Throughout all this time he was writing and making notes. After long days mountaineering he would return to his cabin and write into the night, his emotions pouring onto the page. Some scribblings he sent to Jeanne and, with his permission, they began to appear in magazines from 1871. One of his most popular stories told of an event in December 1874, in the middle of a violent storm. It was a bright day after much rain. The wind howled and the different trees bowed and swayed in varying degrees of submission. "The force of the gale was such that the most steadfast monarch of them all (a silver pine two hundred feet high) rocked down to its roots with a motion plainly perceptible when one leaned against it." To savour the storm fully he climbed to the top of a Douglas fir 100 feet tall, tied himself on, and swayed in the wind while trees uprooted themselves and crashed around him: "The slender tops fairly flapped and swished in the passionate torrent, bending and swirling backward and forward, round and round, tracing indescribable combinations of vertical and horizontal curves, while I clung with muscles firmly braced, like a bobolink on a reed."[34]

Some escapades were entered into with full awareness; others were the result of misjudgment or simply being lost in a reverie. He had already explored the top of the Yosemite Falls, getting too close for comfort to the falling water. Now he wanted to pray next to it, lower down where the force of the water was intense, and meditate by the light of the moon.

One night in the spring of 1872 he went to see the soft light through falling water. Overcome by intense feelings, he crept onto a narrow ledge behind the waterfall to view the full moon filtered through thousands of gallons of streaming water and spray. It was a beautiful sight as long as the wind sucked the water away from his perch, less so and extremely dangerous when it shifted direction, pushing the whole column of water on top of him and pummelling him with hard, watery rods. Humbled, sore, and chilled to the bone, he eventually escaped in a temporary respite, "better, not worse, for my hard midnight bath".[35]

Adherents to John Muir's "natural piety", as Wordsworth would phrase it, needed a strong constitution and a death-defying spirit. This was how John lived his faith, far from pews and the quiet sobriety of churches. It was only by experiencing the range of moods of nature that one could know God, the audacious creator of a stunning planet that administered fear and wonder in equal measure.

It was also the only way to get to the places where the mountains could reveal the secrets of their formation. As well as being filled with wonder, he was also burning with a desire to understand. To Jeanne he wrote,

> No scientific book in the whole world can tell me how this Yosemite granite is put together or how it has been taken down. Patient observation and constant brooding above the rocks, lying upon them for years as the ice did, is the way to arrive at the truths which are graven so lavishly upon them.[36]

He was convinced that the grand forms of the Yosemite were the result of glacial action and not due to dramatic earth movements, as many established geologists believed. Time and again as he wandered the Sierra he found smooth, ice-polished rocks and deep scratches caused by the movement of ice, and strewn everywhere he saw erratic boulders. These rock orphans, ripped from their homeland and transported for miles by ice, littered the meadows and plains; "strangers in a strange land," John called them. From the Three Brothers, a rock formation in the heart of the valley, he wrote, "Glacial action even on this lofty summit is plainly displayed. Not only has all the lovely valley now smiling in sunshine been filled to the brim with ice, but it has been deeply overflowed." He knew his theory was unpopular and he was determined to gather proper evidence to show the world how the Yosemite was formed.

Understanding the valley now became an obsession that filled his thoughts and kept him awake at night. Science and the religion of nature possessed him and he was determined to be a faithful servant to both. He expressed his overpowering feelings to Jeanne in a letter in 1871:

> The grandeur of these forces and their glorious results overpower me, and inhabit my whole being. Waking or sleeping I have no rest. In dreams I read blurred sheets of glacial writing or follow lines of cleavage or struggle with the difficulties of some extraordinary rock form. Now it is clear that woe is me if I do not drown this tendency toward nervous prostration by constant labour in working up the details of this whole question.

Pages of detailed notes and drawings show a fine mind, missing nothing, trying to grasp the essence of ice on rock. For months he wandered, free and unencumbered, "like a butterfly or bee", avoiding the people in the Valley below. The higher he climbed, the more he discovered, and one autumn day in 1872 he made a phenomenal discovery, which he described to Jeanne in a letter:

> One of the yellow days of last October, when I was among the mountains of the Merced group, following the footprints of the ancient glaciers that once flowed grandly from their ample fountains, reading what I could of their history as written in moraines and canyons and lakes and carved rocks, I came across a small stream that was carrying mud and observed that it was entirely mineral in composition and fine as flour, like the mud from a fine-grit grindstone. Before I had time to reason I said, "Glacier mud, mountain meal." Following it higher I found a snow bank and moraine. I shouted "A living glacier."

Now he had a real glacier to work with, not just the remains of those long dead. From then on he studied it intensely, marking its progress with stakes and recording every detail. Here was creation in action – further proof, alongside Darwin's revolutionary work on species, that the earth is in constant formation and not a done deal. Everything changes constantly, responding to forces acting all around, whether on lifeless rocks or on breathing creatures. It was an exciting step forward and his philosophy and spurred on his literary ambition to share his insights with the world. "Now, in the deep, brooding silence all seems motionless, as if the work of creation were done. But in the midst of this outer steadfastness we know there is incessant motion."[37]

Any visits he made to the deadened, befogged, choking city were short and he felt the need to cleanse himself in the purity of mountain air on his return. The trips were useful, though, as a prerequisite to get some of his articles into print, with the invaluable help of Jeanne. People marvelled at this eloquent yet wild mountain man. Science and adventure mingled effortlessly in his lyrical prose and many wished to meet him. Some of the greatest minds of the late nineteenth century trekked to the Yosemite to see if the truth really did match the words, and none went away disappointed. They met him at his cabin, or walking in the hills, or in hotels. Ralph Waldo Emerson arrived in 1871, at the suggestion of Jeanne Carr. The Sage of Concord, as he was known, had been an inspiration for John ever since Jeanne had introduced him to his Transcendental poetry and philosophy back in Madison days. Emerson wrote:

> Nature is a language and every new fact one learns is a new word; but it is not a language taken to pieces and dead in the dictionary, but the language put together into a most significant and universal sense. I wish to learn this language, not that I may know a new grammar, but that I may read the great book that is written in that tongue.[38]

These were words that could have been written by John Muir himself as he sketched and pondered the glacial rocks.

Overcome at the thought of meeting such a famous and influential man as Emerson, John stayed in his cabin, sending a short note of invitation. When Emerson arrived in the ferny, stream-filled cabin the two men immediately formed a strong bond.

Emerson was the most serene, majestic, sequoia-like soul I ever met. His smile was as sweet and calm as morning light on mountains. There was a wonderful charm in his presence; his smile, serene eye, his voice, his manner, were all sensed at once by everybody. I felt here was a man I had been seeking. The Sierra, I was sure, wanted to see him, and he must not go before gathering them an interview! A tremendous sincerity was his. He was as sincere as the trees, his eye sincere as the sun.[39]

For his part, Emerson thought John more authentic than the famous wild man, Henry David Thoreau, and put his name on a list of "my men". But bitter disappointment followed when Emerson's companions refused to allow the ageing (sixty-eight) and failing sage to sleep out of doors amongst the sequoia. All John could do was accompany them out of the valley after such a short visit and his last image of Emerson was of him lingering at the back of the train of horses. When the others had gone ahead, Emerson stopped and turned round. He removed his hat and waved to the solitary John Muir standing on the edge of a forest of giant trees. "I felt lonely, so sure had I been that Emerson of all men would be quickest to see the mountains and sing to them."[40] After he left John spent the night in "the wrinkle of the bark of a Sequoia".[41]

Joseph LeConte, a professor of geology at Berkeley University, also made his way to the valley in 1870. He had heard about the wild mountain man via Jeanne Carr. The two men spent ten days in the Yosemite and John pointed out the glacial features he had discovered. LeConte remembered him as

a most passionate lover of nature. Plants and flowers and forests, and sky and mountains seem actually to haunt his imagination. He seems to revel in the freedom of this life... a man of strong earnest nature and thoughtful, closely observing and original mind.[42]

They became lifelong friends, despite LeConte incorporating John's ideas and observations in papers he presented at scientific meetings, without giving him credit. Jeanne was angry; John was hurt but magnanimous: "I have not heard anything concerning LeConte's glacier lecture… I cannot think he will claim discovery, etc. If he does, I will not be made poorer."[43]

LeConte was not the only plagarist. In his 1872 book *The Wonders of the Yosemite Valley, and of California*, Professor Samuel Kneeland of the Boston Society of Natural History, who had also been given a personal tour, drew directly from what he had been shown. John noted dryly that he "gave me credit for all of the smaller sayings and doings, and stole the broadest truth to himself".[44] Taking academics into his confidence was obviously a risky business, but he continued to share openly and generously.

Asa Gray, the first professor of botany at Harvard, travelled to the Yosemite, as did the artist William Keith. The great and the good, the ordinary and the lowly arrived in the years John lived and worked in his hermitage, many through Jeanne's introduction. There is no doubt he had a profound influence on any that spent time with him, and he corresponded with the greatest minds of his time. Ordinary tourists hired him as a guide on nature walks; others listened to his tales told in a broad Scottish brogue. Still others carefully considered his scientific theories and pondered their verdict on the nature of the earth. Jeanne sat in her parlour in San Francisco and glowed with pride in her wild, eccentric friend and did whatever she could to enhance his reputation as the nature prophet of California. If anyone she admired could not make it to the valley, she lauded John and showed his work, as she did to the eminent glaciologist Louis Agassiz.

John was an unusual mountain hermit. He treasured his time alone but often signed off his letters with a remark about being lonely. He was a sociable solitary and missed his good friends and intelligent, jovial chatter. But he also wanted others to share his joy. Far from wanting to keep the mountains to himself, he urged all to come and be filled with life and light. By far the best way to entice them was to write, and to do that he needed a more practical base with lighting and a desk. Slowly the power of the mountains to keep him fastened in his cabin was loosening: "Heaven knows that John the Baptist was not more eager to get all his fellow sinners into the Jordan than I to baptize all of mine in the beauty of God's mountains."[45]

And, as John the Baptist left the desert to proclaim his message, so John left the Yosemite for the worldliness of the city.

Chapter 10

Out of the Wilderness

"If you would not be forgotten as soon as you are dead, either write something worth reading or do something worth writing."

Benjamin Franklin

Kairos, a moment in time of great significance, occurred for John Muir in 1873. He turned 35 and ideas that had been swirling through his consciousness began to coalesce into something more solid and definable. Inspired by his enthusiasm and uplifting spiritual message, many friends and acquaintances urged him to spend more time writing. Rather than being restricted to thoughts expressed in private letters and barely readable jottings in a notebook many believed more formally written lyricism could help turn the nature-blind American public back to the wild. He was also amassing fascinating and invaluable evidence for glaciation in the Yosemite, which his scientific supporters wanted to see validated and given due credit. In 1872 he had written to Jeanne, "I am approaching a kind of fruiting-time in this mountain work and I want very much to see you. All say write, but I don't know how or what." He longed for her support and advice.

As he scribbled away at articles to send to Jeanne, cogitating on a career as a writer, he carried on exploring more of the region's exquisite places, including further afield to the south of the Sierra range in Kings Canyon, the Inyo Mountains, and the headwaters of the Kings River. In the Kings Canyon, another magnificent valley, John saw more evidence of glaciation with the same features he had seen in the Yosemite. He was also overawed by the giant sequoia groves that forested the slopes. He made his first ascent of Mount Whitney, the Sierra's highest peak, in October. All of this added to his growing pile of notes and he knew he had to fashion them into something suitable for print. But this year also saw a change in his relationship with Jeanne Carr.

James and Elvira Hutchings ran the hotel and sawmill where John had worked and lodged for a while at the beginning of his stay in the Yosemite. Elvira was twenty years younger than her irascible husband and felt increasingly lonely and restless in their marriage. Living in such an isolated spot meant that John, who was ten years older, was the only sympathetic ear. Just how sympathetic and to what extent he reciprocated her feelings is unknown, but she seems to have fallen in love with him. She accompanied him on many walks, painted the flowers of the valley, and poured out her heart. Elvira was also a friend of Jeanne Carr and during her visits to Oakland, and in letters, she revealed their special friendship. The details were obscure, hidden behind flowery language and mysterious phrasing, leaving it wide open to speculation. Jeanne profoundly disapproved that her protégé-on-a-pedestal could be involved with a married woman and mother, if indeed that is what had happened. She wrote to John that he had disappointed her expectations of him and that she could no longer guarantee to help him with his work or indeed visit him in the summer as planned.

It is unlikely that John and Elvira's relationship was physical, given his religious beliefs, but Jeanne assumed whatever it was went beyond what was considered proper. It also added more bitterness to John's relationship with James Hutchings, which had soured two years earlier when John found him to be a difficult employer. Elvira did leave James and they were divorced in 1874, but how much John contributed to the split remains unknown. Relations between John and Jeanne were eventually restored and the planned mountain trip did go ahead in June 1873, and was a great success. In 1909 John expurgated the crucial letter from Jeanne, which may have revealed all. Suffice to say the whole episode was damaging.

It was as well that their relationship was healed. On 23 October 1873 the Carrs' son, Ezra Smith Carr, was crushed between two railroad trucks and killed at a station in Alameda, California, where he worked as a brakeman. John wrote to them both, "I received the news of your terrible bereavement a few moments ago, and can only say that you have my heartfelt sympathy and prayer that our Father may sustain and soothe you."[1] As he knew the family well he grieved with them, and this perhaps helped his decision to leave the Yosemite in the autumn of 1873 and head to Oakland, planning to return in the summer.

It is not easy to define the impetus that led John Muir to walk away from the purity of his mountain monastic cell and head for the chaos of a burgeoning railway town. Probably many factors came together. Jeanne and Ezra were dear friends and he must have wanted to be near them at such a difficult time. There is no doubt that Sierra winters were tough and confining. Deep snow kept him from many of the places he wanted to study. He was also beginning to experience a measure of success with his writing and needed a better workspace to lay out his notes and books. Jeanne had delivered some of his work to Benjamin P. Avery of the magazine *Overland Monthly* and articles on Hetch Hetchy Valley and the Tuolumne Canyon appeared that year. The editor and public were hungry for more, and by the end of 1873 he was considered to be a major contributor. Perhaps the city gave him the amount of emotional and physical support he needed to put his thoughts on paper.

Hetch Hetchy, which appeared in an article in March 1873, was a magnificent and remote valley north of the Yosemite, which he had explored in 1871. It too had been carved out by glaciers, leaving towering walls and tumbling waterfalls, but was more inaccessible to the ordinary visitor. John reckoned that only 7,000 people had ever seen it, although how he worked that out is unknown. Very few people took the time to leave the beaten trail to make the forty-mile journey along a single track, and it remained a quiet treasure used only seasonally by the occasional sheepherder and the Native

Indians. The ferocious mosquitoes that swarmed its meadows in the summer and the difficult access kept it low on the European agenda.

John's eloquence and enthusiasm for the place struck a chord. His writing was so personal and intimate that it allowed the reader to relive his experiences. They could be there with him as he studied fresh bear prints in the mud, praise with him as he marvelled at the beauty of the rock walls and flowery meadows, and then, when the snow began to fall, crouch with him under a rock as though sheltering in a small house. From here, with a few branches as protection from the wind, John and the reader could peer out between the twigs at the surrounding forest as the snow swirled around the trees:

> Scores of firs in my front yard were over 200 feet in height. How nobly and unreservedly they gave themselves to the storm. Heart and voice, soul and body, sang to the flowering sky, each frond tip seemed to bestow a separate welcome to every ward of the wind, and to every snowflake as they arrived. How perfectly would the pure soul of Thoreau have mingled with those glorious trees, and he would have been content with my log house.

For those starved of elemental excitement and the purity of the wilderness this was tantalizing stuff, and he made it seem so accessible.

> Tourists who can afford the time ought to visit Hetch Hetchy on their way to or from Yosemite… and it certainly is worth while riding a few miles out of a direct course to assure one's self that the world is so rich as to possess at least two Yosemites instead of one.[2]

If Hetch Hetchy provided grandeur, his words about the Tuolumne Canyon, which led into the northern part of Hetch Hetchy, touched the spiritual desires of the reader, urging them to go beyond the physicality of the granite and tree bark and find a manifestation of the smile of God, who was still joyously at work fashioning the earth. It was pure transcendentalism lifted out of Harvard University and into the homes of ordinary Americans:

> I used to envy the father of our race, dwelling as he did in contact with the new-made fields and plants of Eden; but I do so no more, because I have discovered that I also live in "creation's dawn". The morning stars still sing together, and the world, not yet half made, becomes more beautiful every day.[3]

In all, *Overland Monthly* published eighteen articles, helping its readers to see with different eyes that mountains were suppliers not just of gold but also of pure joy. John wanted others to share his vision and in increasing numbers they did, though perhaps not up to his grand expectations.

Throughout his time living in the Yosemite he had watched with concern the rising number of tourists as they explored the valley and its surroundings. Over a thousand had made the trek in 1870 and that number would double in ten years. In his opinion the vast majority were there to tick a box, "to do the valley" rather than to spend any time being at one with the experience. His comments were sometimes far from kind. In a letter to Jeanne he wrote an unflattering description:

> All sorts of human stuff is being poured into the Valley this year, and the blank, fleshly apathy with which most of it comes in contact with the rock and water spirits of the place is most amazing...
> They climb sprawlingly to their saddles like overgrown frogs pulling themselves up a stream bank.[4]

Jeanne had expressed dismay that such people were now desecrating a holy place, and told him that if they were ever rude about it in her hearing she would be tempted to throw them off a cliff. John assured her they did not disturb him, "for the tide of visitors will float slowly about the bottom of the valley as a harmless scum, collecting in hotel and saloon eddies". This was not only an exclusive attitude to nature but also disingenuous, as John had met many fine minds and influential people in those same hotels and had valued the company and stimulation they gave him. They may not have been as spiritually sensitive as he was, but at least they had made the effort to make the arduous journey. The way most of North American society was heading, this collection of overgrown frogs represented the converted.

The industrialization of America had certainly brought wealth to a few, but it meant a life of drudgery for many. It had taken people away from nature in droves. Increasingly it was the city streets and saloons that soaked up the continent's 38.6 million people.[5] In Chicago, for example, the nation's fastest-growing city and the centre of its railway network, the population grew from 100,000 in 1860 to 1 million in 1890. Likewise the population of San Francisco had reached nigh on 250,000 people by the 1870s.[6] Mud coated the streets and lawlessness was rife. It was a time of unprecedented technological advances but the majority of Americans were working-class and 40 per cent of them lived below the poverty line.[7] Most people's eyes and hearts were focused on money, not beauty, with worrying consequences for America's natural resources.

A number of signs showed that all was not well: forests disappeared, rivers silted up, soil became less productive, and wildlife thinned out across the continent. Concern for wilderness grew and was expressed in different forms. The Transcendental writings of Thoreau and Emerson, the art of painters such as Thomas Cole, George Catlin, and William Keith, and books on conservation such as *Man and Nature; or, Physical Geography as Modified by Human Action* (1864) by George Perkins Marsh all infiltrated society and a gradual sea change was under way, particularly among the more educated.

It was into this degraded yet increasingly concerned society that John launched his writing career, but he didn't find it easy. Even though he had so much to say, every word was an effort. He expressed his despondency in a letter to his sister in 1876:

My life these days is like the life of a glacier, one eternal grind, and the top of my head suffers a weariness at times that you know nothing about. I'm glad to see by the hills across the bay, all yellow and purple with buttercups and gilias, that spring is blending fast into summer, and soon I'll throw down my pen, and take up my heels to go mountaineering once more.[8]

He also hated the mucky, wet streets and the lack of beauty in the city. He longed for the summer months so that he could escape and explore, but there was much to write about, keeping him at his desk. *Overland Monthly* went into bankruptcy in 1875 and he began to contribute to the newspaper *Evening Bulletin*. In one of his first articles in 1874 he described a visit to a hatchery that raised salmon from fertilized eggs from migrating fish that travelled along the McCloud River, which flowed down from Mount Shasta in the Cascade Range in the north of California. The young salmon were then transported across the continent, and even abroad, to restock the increasing numbers of exhausted rivers. It was a profitable business. Wintu Indians, the traditional people of the river, who believed that once the salmon stopped swimming humanity would die, helped to catch and strip the fish of their milt and roe.

Salmon were struggling to survive not only because of overfishing but also because the clean, gravelly rivers they depended on to breed were becoming increasingly choked with silt and pollution. In the case of the rivers flowing out of the Sierras it was the debris from hydraulic mining that destroyed their breeding grounds. It was a salutary reminder that America's resources were not inexhaustible and that seemingly robust and extensive nature was easily damaged.

The forests were suffering badly too. Clear felling of woods was not controlled and magnificent trees, some thousands of years old, were destroyed for a few dollars each. Both types of giant redwood were harvested. Giant sequoia (Sequoiadendron giganteum) grew in groves along the western slopes of the Sierra Nevada, between three and eight thousand feet, and craggy old stalwarts can grow to be the largest organism on earth by volume. At a lower altitude and along the slopes of the Coast Range the coast or California redwoods (Sequoia sempervirens) formed silent cathedrals of trees that are the tallest on the planet. Both of these unique Californian giants often shattered as they hit the forest floor, rendering most of the tree unusable. It was a terrible waste. Ever since John had set eyes on the coastal and mountain redwoods he had viewed them with wonder.

In 1870, he wrote to Jeanne about the days he spent in a giant sequoia grove around the Yosemite. Only to her could he write in such effusive, religious terms:

> Do behold the King in his glory, King Sequoia! Behold! Behold! Seems all I can say. Some time ago I left all for the sequoia and have been and am at his feet, fasting and praying for light, for is he not the greatest light in the woods, in the world? ... But I am in the woods, woods, woods and they are in me-ee-ee. The King and I have sworn eternal love – sworn it without swearing, and I've taken the sacrament with Douglas squirrel, drunk Sequoia wine, Sequoia blood, and with its rosy purple drops I am writing this woody gospel.

Later, when he explored what was to become the Sequoia National Park in 1873, he wrote:

> A magnificent growth of giants… one naturally walked softly and awe stricken among them. I wandered on, meeting nobler trees where all are noble… this part of the Sequoia belt seemed to me the finest, and I then named it "the Giant Forest".[9]

Yet his "Kings" and "Giants" were being sacrificed in unsustainable numbers on the altar of rampant commercialism, and it broke his heart. In an article entitled "God's First Temples" in the *Sacramento Daily Union* in February 1876, he describes witnessing at least five mills located near the town of Fresno alone and one of those had processed 2 million feet of sequoia wood in one season. No forest, no matter how extensive, could withstand this attack. It wasn't just the lumbermen who destroyed forests; the sheepherders spread fire to clear pathways and encourage pasture for their flocks that killed young seedlings. John's article was a measured, level-headed plea to save California's woodland treasures. For millennia the trees had stood firm, now in just a few decades they were disappearing.

> A few minutes ago every tree was excited, bowing to the roaring storm, waving, swirling, tossing their branches in glorious enthusiasm like worship. But though to the outer ear these trees are now silent, their songs never cease. Every hidden cell is throbbing with music and life, every fibre thrilling like harp strings, while incense is ever flowing from the balsam bells and leaves. No wonder the hills and groves were God's first temples. And the more they are cut down and hewn into cathedrals and churches, the farther off and dimmer the Lord himself.[10]

Photographs, paintings, and engravings of the felled trees appeared from the mid-nineteenth century and helped people realize what was happening in the wilderness beyond the city streets. The cutting down by gold prospectors in 1853 of Mammoth Tree, a jaw-dropping 302 feet high and 96 feet in circumference, created outrage when people saw the images of triumphant loggers standing on the trunk. In a final act of disrespect the level stump was made into a dance floor that held forty people. Samuel Manning, an English minister and travel writer, drew it for his book *American Pictures*,[11] and James Hutchins actually witnessed the act of destruction and described it as "a botanical tragedy" and "an act of desecration". He reported that it took five men a full twenty-two days to fell it. "In our estimation it was a sacrilegious act," he wrote.[12]

It didn't stop there. Another magnificent giant sequoia, standing even taller than Mammoth Tree at 321 feet and affectionately named The Mother of the Forest, was stripped of its bark, which was then sent to England to be displayed as a curiosity in the Crystal Palace, where it was eventually destroyed by fire. The tree was later proved to be 2,500 years old. For many people, enough was enough.

Calls for the protection of America's astonishing natural treasures increased in tempo.

In a widely read and influential magazine, *Gleason's Pictorial Drawing-Room Companion*, the Boston-based editor, Maturin M. Ballou, wrote on 1 October 1853, in grand Muir style:

> To our mind it seems a cruel idea, a perfect desecration, to cut down such a splendid tree… In Europe, such a natural production would have been cherished and protected, if necessary, by law; but in this money-making, go-ahead community, thirty or forty thousand dollars are paid for it, and the purchaser chops it down, and ships it off for a shilling show! We hope that no one will conceive the idea of purchasing the Niagara Falls with the same purpose!… But, seriously, what in the world could have possessed any mortal to embark in such speculation with this mountain of wood? In its natural condition, rearing its majestic head towards heaven, and waving in all its native vigour, strength and verdure, it was a sight worth a pilgrimage to see; but now, alas, It is only a monument of the cupidity of those who have destroyed all there was of interest connected with it.

John's was not a lone voice in raising awareness of what was happening to American nature, but it was an influential one. Blind short-termism ruled and the government seemed unable and unwilling to take action. This was a battle John continued to fight all his life and with every fibre of his being.

He was increasingly convinced that acts of vandalism such as the felling of giant trees could be stopped only if people learned to love and respect the land they inhabited. Laws would only go so far; much more effective would be a sense of wonder and excitement about the wilderness. Stepping onto soft pine needles, breathing scented air, resting by rivers, and laughing at squirrels would do more for conservation than worthy lectures and penalties.

Despite his earlier comments about frogs and scum he was heartened by the rise in tourism, which helped spread the word about America's beauty. In 1876, the nation's hundredth birthday, he proposed the freeing of the "urban slaves" whose lives were dulled by endless work, allowing them time to explore. When it came to children, he wrote, "compulsory education may be good; compulsory recreation better". Everybody should feel the benefit of wilderness, no matter what age, colour, creed or state of wealth.

> Go now and then for fresh life… Go whether or not you have faith… Go up and away for life; be fleet! I know some will heed the warning. Most will not, so full of pagan slavery is the boasted freedom of the town, and those who need rest and clean snow and sky the most will be the last to move.[13]

He urged people not to travel quickly but to take time, to sit by a tree all day perhaps, and simply observe the life around them:

> I would advise sitting from morning till night under some willow bush on the river bank where there is a wide view. This will be "doing the valley" far more effectively than riding along trails in constant motion from point to point. The entire valley is made up of "points of interest".[14]

Leave the guidebook at home, suggested John; all that is needed is a calm heart, and delights will reveal themselves everywhere. His articles spoke to the overworked public, who found comfort and excitement in his words.

The work of John Muir was becoming a tour de force for the wilderness. He had the ability to reach through the page, take the reader by the hand, and guide them to singing streams, towering trees, intimate conversations with wildlife, and ranges of mountains so beautiful they made him fall on his knees in prayer. He was the voice of the wild and the tip of his quill glowed with divine love. Wilderness, however, is not just about soaring spirits that bathe in nature's loveliness; he also showed that nature can be as ruthless as it is nurturing.

In a letter in February 1873, Jeanne responded to the news of an accident John had suffered. He had slipped and fallen, knocking himself out and nearly tumbling over a steep cliff. Suppose he had died, "and a great sob from the Valley pines had reached me and a call had come from the soft-voiced one to find you, missing and always to be missed." Then, said Jeanne, she would have covered him in rocks and moss and left him to Nature's kindliness. But if he had been found, "bruised, broken limbed, unable to defend yourself from creatures that had tortured you", then nature would wear a darker robe and speak of untold angst and pain. No longer would mountains be fountains of light but urns of darkness.

Her words were touching and almost prophetic, because in 1874 he very nearly did succumb to the darker face of the mountain. Mountaineering as a sport was taking off in Europe and increasingly in America. Magisterial beauty could be found in the Sierras that was no less inspiring than that of the Alps. John had been climbing solo for years by now and in the autumn of 1873 and spring of 1874 he climbed the rugged and inaccessible volcano Mount Shasta three times to collect data for the Coast and Geodetic Survey. In the April ascent he had one of his most gripping adventures. He and a fellow climber, Jerome Fay, became trapped by a snowstorm on the summit. John, as usual, was only in shirtsleeves, as he found coats cumbersome. His companion, fortunately, had a warm top coat. The account of what happened in the article "Snow Storm on Mount Shasta", published in 1877, makes terrifying reading. The day began in sunshine, but with no warning they were enveloped by a storm:

A few minutes after 3 P.M. we began to force our way down the eastern ridge, past the group of hissing fumaroles. The storm at once became inconceivably violent, with scarce a preliminary scowl. The thermometer fell twenty-two degrees, and soon sank below zero. Hail gave place to snow, and darkness came on like night. The wind, rising to the highest pitch of violence, boomed and surged like breakers on a rocky coast. The lightning flashed amid the desolate crags in terrible accord, their tremendous muffled detonations unrelieved by a single echo, and seeming to come thudding passionately forth from out the very heart of the storm.[15]

The two men survived by lying next to hot acidic pools. Their backs and hips were scalded by the steam; the fronts of their bodies were frostbitten. It was a miracle they didn't die. They were rescued on their way down the next day – weak, lame, and barely alive. John wrote to Jeanne in May: "The intense cold and the want of food and sleep made the fire of life smoulder and burn low." His experiences on Mount Shasta became deeply embedded and he referred to them many times in his writing:

Mountains. When we dwell with mountains, see them face to face, every day, they seem as creatures with a sort of life – friends subject to moods, now talking, now taciturn, with whom we converse as man to man. They wear many spiritual robes, at times an aureole, something like the glory of the old painters put around the heads of saints. Especially is this seen on lone mountains, like Shasta, or on great domes standing single and apart.[16]

The snowstorm adventure saw Mount Shasta in a particularly bad mood. It highlighted a less loving side of the Sierra, brooding and menacing. Human life was naught to a mountain: "Man's life's as cheap as beasts", as Shakespeare put it in *King Lear*. Mountains, however, represented the pinnacle of art, poetry, physicality, and spirituality to many in the late nineteenth century.

These wild adventures stirred the hearts of John's readers. Not only did this land of business opportunity give dollar-producing resources, it also took people to the edge of existence in savage terrain. Beauty was there, but death-defying exploits could be had for those who were courageous enough to leave the parlour fireside. The wilderness became an adventure playground as well as a spiritual temple.

In this decade of intense article writing, he extended his outreach by publishing in magazines such as *Scribner* and *Harper's Magazine*.

He was paid to wander the country and report on topics as diverse as the Mormons in Utah and the bees in California. Natural history and humanity's effect on the landscape were entering stylish American homes, enlightening the lives of those who loved his personal and expressive style.

For his part, John's experiences in the wilderness were so real and intense that they kept his spirit fire burning, and his pen scribbling, through the desolate winter days of writing in the city, when he often came down with coughs and colds: "Civilization and fever and all the morbidness that has been hooted at me has not dimmed my glacial eyes, and I care only to entice people to look at Nature's loveliness."[17]

He also tried to write up his notes on glaciation. He was determined to impress the scientific community and change their minds about the importance of ice. His first published article, "Yosemite Glaciers", which appeared as early as 1871 in *The New York Tribune*, had sparked controversy. In it, he celebrated his theories on the role of glaciers in forming the valley:

> The great valley itself, together with all its domes and walls, was brought forth and fashioned by a grand combination of glaciers, acting in certain directions against granite of peculiar physical structure. All of the rocks and mountains and lakes and meadows of the whole upper Merced basin received their specific forms and carvings almost entirely from this same agency of ice.

John's glacial ideas were based on painstaking evidence he had collected over years. He had noted down the scratches, boulders, piles of debris, and the angles of the valley sides in an impressive set of field notes. All these features are typical of glacial scenery. To him it was self-evident that glaciers had shaped the Yosemite as they spread out, carving the granite and scouring out depressions to form the many lakes. His recordings were highly accurate but his method of collecting data was less conventional. In an article in 1873 for *Overland Monthly* he described a day collecting his evidence:

I drifted about from rock to rock, from stream to stream, from grove to grove. Where night found me there I camped. When I discovered a new plant, I sat down beside it for a minute or a day, to make its acquaintance and try to hear what it had to say. When I came to moraines, or ice scratches upon the rocks, I traced them, learning what I could of the glacier that made them. I asked the boulders I met whence they came and whither they were going.

This eccentric method of scientific recording produced wonderfully detailed maps of the Yosemite and the surrounding area. Yet far from being grateful for such accurate work, produced for nothing, the chief of the California Geological Survey, Josiah Whitney, was furious. Whitney's theory was that the Yosemite was the result of a cataclysmic earth movement wherein the bottom of the valley had literally fallen away, collapsing into a "void" underground, leaving the dramatic features seen today. Ice could not account for the towers and domes, only earthquakes and upheavals of huge magnitude. He derided John as a "mere sheepherder" and "ignoramus" and therefore unqualified to comment.

Clarence King, a geologist and mountaineer destined to become the first director of the United States Geological Survey, joined in and wrote that John was "an enthusiastic amateur" who should find other uses for his talents, such as tour guiding. If he persisted in his glacial explorations he would be floundering hopelessly amid those who knew far better. This tirade of stinging dismissal must have been dispiriting. Encouragement came from John D. Runkle, the president of the Massachusetts Institute of Technology, who urged John to present his work in more technical terms. Only science and logic would persuade his critics that the Sierras had been sculptured by ice.

John wrote to his brother, Daniel, "I have commenced the work of making a book for the Boston Academy of Science on the ancient glacial system of the Merced",[18] but if he was, yet again, after paternal approval, none was forthcoming. His father Daniel was vehemently opposed to these glacial fancies. They took him and the readers of his articles away from the one and only truth, the Bible. "You cannot warm the heart of the Saint of God with your cold icy topped mountains," he fumed. "Come away from them to the spirit of God and his holy word, and he will show our lovely Jesus unto you… the best and soonest way of getting quit of the writing and publishing of your book is to burn it, and then it will do no more harm either to you or others."[19]

The views of Whitney, King, and Daniel Muir typified the confused intermeshing of religion and science in the nineteenth century, particularly in the earth and life sciences. To dismiss cataclysmic events such as Whitney was proposing was to turn away from the tumultuous upheavals supported by the Bible narratives about the formation of the world. Belief in these was known as Catastrophism (the notion that the earth was the result of sudden and dramatic change), and Noah's flood was an example of such an event that rapidly changed the face of the earth. For Catastrophists the book of Genesis was a reliable guide to the creation of landscapes and the creatures that lived on them. It was therefore the role of the geologist to provide evidence that events happened quickly and ferociously, not gradually. Glaciers can never be fast agents of change as they take millions of years to grind away a mountain. To suggest that glaciers were responsible for altering the land was to suggest the earth is constantly subjected to slow but effective forces. In the nineteenth century this was anti-biblical and therefore unacceptable to the establishment.

John Muir, LeConte, and Agassiz were supporters of the opposite point of view, Uniformitarianism. This held that the processes acting on the earth at present also acted in the past. The present is the key to the past was their mantra. With this in mind it was inconceivable that valley bottoms could suddenly fall away, swallowing all the debris into the void underneath. Where was the evidence? Where could it be seen happening today? Earthquakes did happen in the Sierras (John had experienced them), but nothing on the scale required to open huge chasms. It was much more logical to look to the ice at work in the Alps or Alaska and accept that a valley was slowly but surely scraped into shape by a giant icy rasp working away for millennia.

To the uninformed amateur, both ideas required a lively imagination. To those who could read landscapes with an open mind, however, the scientific evidence for ice was clear and on display everywhere. Whitney saw those signs for himself on his mapping expeditions in the Sierras but chose to suppress them in his published work.

Charles Lyell, a contemporary of John, a fellow Scot, a friend of Darwin, and an eminent geologist, had popularized Uniformitarianism and dismissed those who held on to a catastrophic view of the world despite the evidence before their eyes: "Never was there a doctrine more calculated to foster indolence, and to blunt the keen edge of curiosity, than this assumption of the discordance between the former and the existing causes of change."[20] In an age when science was powering the Industrial Revolution and forging improvements in everything from medicine to farming to transport, it seems that otherwise scientific men put aside their rational minds when it came to the formation of the earth and its inhabitants. It would not be until the twentieth century that fundamental Christian teachings exited the corridors of university science departments.

Much the same battle was being fought over evolution. Charles Darwin's *On the Origin of Species*, which John read in 1871, also proposed a gradual mechanism for the diversification of species as opposed to the prevalent (and Genesis-friendly) consensus that species appeared on earth already formed. Darwin's detailed research and logical conclusion meant his treatise was rapidly gaining widespread acceptance, but it was causing great consternation too. Once again, traditional religious views were challenged and both earth and life sciences began to reel under the blows inflicted by these new ideas. It is understandable that the transition from the old world to the new was not easy. Nineteenth-century America was founded on fundamental Protestant theology and for established figures to venture too far away from that path was to elicit social and professional criticism. Whitney, King, and many others were the last vestiges of an old guard who were determined to stand firm, but the tide of change would prove to be unstoppable.

Jeanne too was not always so encouraging when it came to ice. Her lack of interest was not based on religion but on aesthetics. She had described glaciers as "pests" that lived in "horrible times". To a flowery, poetic soul, glaciers seemed hard, cold, and altogether too lifeless to be worth spending time exploring. John was disconcerted by her lack of interest and appealed to her love of plants as a route to understanding the importance of ice:

> Glaciers made the mountains and ground the corn for all the flowers, and the forests of silver fir, made smooth paths for human feet until the sacred Sierras have become the most approachable of mountains. Glaciers came down from heaven and they are angels with folded wings, white wings of snowy bloom.[21]

Without the work of glaciers, how could flowers live? They cracked the mountains so that Jeanne's beloved cassiope could make a home in the small crevasses. They provided the rough rock faces for mosses to smother and they broke the hard granite into crumbs so that the pines had food, just as the birds had crumbled bread. Come, he urged her, and see for yourself, "you will be iced"; but she refused: "My spirit was converted by your lovely sermon, but my flesh isn't, and when your track is from lands of snow to lands of sun, only then shall I be able to follow you."[22] She did, however, campaign for his ideas and enthused with the geologists Joseph LeConte and Louis Agassiz about John's theories and his discovery of an extant glacier high in the mountains.

Eventually the book on glaciation was completed but it was not successful. It was rejected by publishers and languished in his study, too much a mix of anecdote, poetry, and science. Glaciers would fill his life again later, but for the meantime success was found in newspaper and magazine articles.

As John's life retreated from the Yosemite and spread further afield he wrote a sad letter to Jeanne in 1874. He had returned to the valley in September and wandered around his old haunts refilling his soul with God and the beauty of nature, but something had changed: "No one of the rocks seems to call me now, nor any of the distant mountains. Surely this Merced and Tuolumne chapter of my life is done… I feel a stranger here."[23] Jeanne too began to recede and was less accessible. Gone were the cooing exchanges and intimate whisperings. Jeanne and Ezra were increasingly weighed down by their Californian life. "Where are you?" he wrote. "You always seem so inaccessible to me, as if you were in a crowd."[24]

If John's decade of writing led him on to ever-greater things, theirs was a time of failures and yet more tragedy. Ezra had fallen out with the University at Berkeley where he was a professor and had entered public life as California Superintendent of Public Instruction, which he found increasingly difficult to perform owing to rheumatoid arthritis. The family moved to Sacramento and became involved with setting up the Grange, an agricultural reform movement. It was hard work and absorbed all Jeanne's energy.

The hand of fate struck the Carr family once again. Their youngest son, John Henry Carr (Johnnie), had suffered from headaches and depression since being attacked in the street and in 1877 he booked into a hotel room in Sacramento and shot himself. A verdict of suicide was recorded, although some believe it was murder. Burdened with grief, Ezra found his arthritis intensifying, leaving him virtually crippled, and he gradually retreated into their home. "How great are your trials. I wish I could help you," wrote John.

Although Jeanne was increasingly distracted, she had already set important wheels in motion. Back in 1874 she had introduced John to the Strenzel family, who had a delightful, intelligent daughter, Louisa Wanda (Louie), who was then twenty-seven years old. A gifted pianist and horticulturalist, she seemed a good match. Touchingly, John took a piece of her lace with him when he travelled as a sign of his affection. Eventually, much to the family's delight, they were engaged in June 1879, the day before John left for a trip to Alaska. In April the next year they were married and settled on the fruit farm owned by Louie's parents in the Alhambra

Valley near Martinez. Jeanne was delighted. In a letter to Louie's mother she wrote, "Above fame and far stronger than my wish to see his genius acknowledged by his peers, I have desired for him the completeness which can only come in living for others, in perfected home relations."[25]

All this was in contrast to the marriage of John's parents. In 1873, as John was leaving his hermitage in the wilderness his father, Daniel was leaving the marital home, driven by an increasing desire to evangelize on the streets. He went to Canada to proclaim his version of God to those who needed salvation, leaving Ann for good. It was the end of their marriage and Ann stayed in the family home, which was now in Portage.

Although on the surface John and Daniel seemed poles apart, they were similar in more ways than John perhaps liked to admit. Both were driven by an evangelical zeal to proclaim the truth and convert the lost, and both dedicated their lives to that truth; it is just that their versions of truth were very different.

As his parents' marriage failed, so his own happy union began, and two children would follow. John had often lamented his lack of a home and family, believing his fate was to be alone. Now he had a beautiful house nestled in an orchard, a loving wife, and money flowed into his bank account. Stretching ahead was a career as a fruit farmer. For many it would have been enough to live off his already astonishing memories and to settle into domestic comfort and security. For John, however, it was far from over. Among the scent of oranges carried on the gentle Californian breeze, he could smell the sharp cold air of the far north and hear the creak of ice as it ground away granite. It was irresistible. As his mind worried about fruit; his heart yearned for Alaska.

Chapter 11

Alaskan Adventures

"Wanted – a man who, though he is dominated by a mighty purpose, will not permit one great faculty to dwarf, cripple, warp, or mutilate his manhood; who will not allow the over-development of one faculty to stunt or paralyze his other faculties."

Orison Swett Marden, *Pushing to the Front,* 1911

On 17 June 1879, the day after their engagement, John kissed his fiancée, Louie Strenzel, goodbye and boarded a steamer, the *Dakota*, heading north to deliver letters to the scarcely populated islands and settlements of the north-west coast. He had no particular plans; he was simply eager to pick up his glacial studies and find answers to the questions that had been haunting him for eleven years. Despite the rejection of his scientific book, John could not rest until he understood glaciers and "[t]he influence they exerted in sculpturing the rocks over which they passed with tremendous pressure, making new landscapes, scenery and beauty which so mysteriously influence every human being, and to some extent all of life".[1] The trip was to be financed by dispatches sent back about the trip.

The fresh sea air whipped the tops of the waves and the spouts of whales formed fountains in the ocean. The gulls, petrels and shearwaters, "strong, glad life in the midst of stormy beauty", gracefully skimmed the surface on stiff wings. He noted a full square mile of porpoises, "tossing themselves into the air with abounding strength and hilarity, adding foam to the waves and making all the wilderness wilder". The ship made a few stops, allowing some hours for exploring, and John's excitement increased the further north they travelled. The scenery was ever more glacial in character. Towns and villages sat directly on top of moraines that seemed as fresh as the day they were deposited. Gardens were planted around smooth, ice-polished boulders. Scratches on rocks from the sandpaper effect of stones embedded in ice were so fresh that it seemed the glacier had not long melted. Here was a landscape just breathing again after millennia entombed in ice.

The sea air blew away the constant tending of orchards and the dust, mire, and mugginess of city life, which he continued to despise: "The streets are barren and beeless and ineffably muddy and mean looking."[2] For weeks at a time he had been trapped inside, writing articles. Now stretched before him was nature untamed, and where people had settled their dwellings merged with the landscape.

For sheer beauty the hardest place to leave was Puget Sound in the state of Washington, famed for its gigantic coniferous forests that come down to the water's edge. They spoke of a wild interior, barely explored and full of delight. Sky, ocean, and land filled his heart with joy: "But when we contemplate the whole globe as one great dewdrop, striped and dotted with continents and islands, flying through space with other stars all singing and shining together as one, the whole universe appears as an infinite storm of beauty."[3]

The dismissal of his ideas on glaciation by academic geologists was still a disappointment. The only way to prove he was right was to become immersed in the reality of ice. He would climb into the heart of a glacier, trace its edges, stand at its snout, wade in the streams running out from the base, and clamber over the rock orphans it had transported from afar. He would study the rate at which glaciers moved and observe at first hand the process of shaping the land. Only by living with glaciers, he decided, could he uncover their secrets. Then he would have hard evidence to show that Alaska was a northern Yosemite in the making.

The steamer neared its journey's end, Fort Wrangell, by chugging its way around the islands and deep channels of south-eastern Alaska. The blasts of cold air and the smells and sounds of this sub-Arctic world awoke John's creative drive: "It seems as if surely we must at length reach the very paradise of the poets, the abode of the blessed." As the boat drew alongside the harbour wall a young minister waited on the quay to welcome three doctors of divinity, John's fellow passengers, to the Presbyterian mission house based in the old fort.

Samuel Hall Young was newly ordained and keen to begin his career converting the native Tlingit Indians. He spotted John standing on his own on deck, "his peering blue eyes already eagerly scanning the islands and mountains". His impression was of "a lean, sinewy man of forty, with waving reddish-brown hair and beard, and shoulders slightly stooped. He wore a Scotch cap and long, grey tweed ulster." John was introduced to Young as "Professor Muir, the Naturalist". As they shook hands Young was immediately captivated: "we seemed to coalesce at once in a friendship which, to me at least, has been one of the very best things I have known in a life full of blessings".[4] Young was also a keen naturalist, and here was a master.

First impressions of Fort Wrangell were not too good, however. Dismal rain fell as the steamer drifted away back to San Francisco, to his fiancée and their future marital home. The warmth of California seemed a vague dream as cold rain drenched the stumps of felled trees where once magnificent forests had grown. They stood jagged and proud above the bog surrounding the straggling huts and flimsy houses. Mist obscured most of the views. There were no taverns or lodgings of any kind and once again John faced the prospect of a wet and lonely night in the open. As many times before on his solitary journeys, he felt lonely. As evening fell he was fortunately offered a floor in a carpenter's workshop and then a bed in the house of a merchant, Mr Vanderbilt, and his family: "Here I found a real home, with freedom to go on all sorts of excursions as opportunity offered. Annie Vanderbilt, a little doctor of divinity two years old, ruled the household with love sermons and kept it warm."[5]

As often as he could John and some of the missionaries went on steamer trips down the Stickeen (Stikine) River while it remained free of ice. He saw the Great Glacier, the Dirt Glacier, and the Mud Glacier, great rivers of ice actively grinding away the mountains. They were tantalizingly close but there was no opportunity to leave the boat and explore. When they did make short stops he escaped to see as many mountain meadows and forests as he could reach before the ship's whistle called him back. He was intoxicated with Alaska and the stories he told around the table at Samuel Young's house lit up the evening meals:

> Although his books are all masterpieces of lucid and glowing English, Muir was one of those rare souls who talk better than they write; and he made the trees, the animals, and especially the glaciers, live before us. Somehow a glacier never seemed cold when John Muir was talking about it.[6]

These excursions bemused the locals, however; John was not like any other non-native that came to these remote places. Who was this man who seemed to have no interest in business deals, mining, hunting, or converting the Tlingits? Why did he spend hours on his knees peering at the stump of a tree as though expecting to find gold in it? Why were his pockets stuffed with flowers and mosses? What could possibly be so interesting about ice? "He seems to have no serious object whatever!" Young, however, was inspired and felt strangely unfulfilled and full of yearning, wishing he had spent more time looking for God in creation rather than in books. He accompanied John whenever he could.

To add even more mystery, at midnight on a wild rainy night an eerie red glow appeared above a forested hill near the town. It was terrible weather, rain lashed the windows, and a gale howled. The red light grew in intensity, lighting up the clouds. All the locals, Native Indians and whites, were afraid. No one could work out the cause. There was no gold there to attract prospectors and no one would be hunting so late in the night and in such foul weather.

When a group of panicked Tlingits banged on the door of Young's house demanding that he pray to God to get rid of the evil spirits,

Young was just as perplexed. Suddenly it dawned on him what was going on: "I shocked the Indians by bursting into a roar of laughter. In imagination I could see him so plainly – John Muir, wet but happy, feeding his fire with spruce sticks, studying and enjoying the storm!" And so he was. In the midst of a fierce storm, late at night, he had gone into the hills and lit a fire. "Of all the thousands of camp-fires I have elsewhere built none was just like this one, rejoicing in triumphant strength and beauty in the heart of the rain-laden gale."[7]

The first substantial expedition out of Fort Wrangell was in the spring with a group of missionaries, including Young, on a hired boat. They explored the waters around the Stickeen Glacier, a large sheet of ice fed by high mountains. It fans out of a narrow gap, producing a snout about six miles wide. John longed to leave the boat and take off into this wild region but he had to wait until the return leg when the captain decided to anchor for the afternoon at Glenora, an old trading post, informing the passengers they would return to Wrangell the next morning.

Young recounts that on hearing this news a "peculiar look" came into John's eyes and he fixed his stare on his eager missionary friend. Even though it was three o'clock in the afternoon John of the Mountains was determined to climb to the top of the nearest peak. It towered 8,000 feet above Glenora and was eight miles away over rough terrain. It was very late in the day to start such a long and difficult expedition but the star-struck reverend pleaded to go with him. He was in awe of this "poetico-trampo-geologist-bot and ornith-natural etc etc,"[8] as John described himself, and as Young was fit and able he reasoned that he would spend many years in the company of upstanding religious people, but how many opportunities would he have to be with an extraordinary man of the wild?

After three hours of tough scrambling they reached a high meadow, sparkling and vibrant with blooms. "Everything that was marvellous in form, fair of colour or sweet in fragrance seemed represented there," wrote Young. John naturally lost all control. In his 1915 book, *Alaska Days with John Muir*, Young gives us a wonderful and rare description of what it was like to watch John at work. Young tried to keep up and occasionally ask questions as John ran like a child "from cluster to cluster of flowers, babbling in unknown tongues, prattling a curious mixture of scientific lingo and baby talk, worshiping his little blue-and-pink goddesses". "Ah! My blue-eyed darlin', little did I think I'd see you here!" he would say to one flower. And to another: "Well, well! Who'd a thought that you'd have left that niche in the Merced Mountains to come here!" And to yet another: "And who might you be, now, with your wonder look?" And so on.

He constantly took specimens and stuffed them into his pockets and down the front of his shirt, "until he was bulbing and sprouting all over". And when his own clothes were full to bursting he started to fill Young's pockets too, but even the devoted reverend drew the line at prickly plants next to his skin.

Suddenly John realized they had little time left to reach the summit. Literally bounding up the mountain as though he had "Stockton's negative gravity machine attached to his back",[9] John led the way towards the higher land of rocks and cliffs. They crossed a large, crevassed glacier, which John navigated quickly and accurately. Exhausted but exhilarated, Young followed, gasping for breath.

As they scaled a sheer rock face just below the summit Young began to feel nervous. His legs and torso were strong and lean but his arms were weak. Years beforehand both his shoulders had been badly dislocated when breaking in horses and they were prone to slip out of joint, especially when bearing weight. This was uncomfortable and painful work. John on the other hand climbed like a spider, as though he were designed for scaling the steepest cliffs. "And such climbing!" enthused Young. "There was never an instant when both feet and hands were not in play, and often elbows, knees, thighs, upper arms and even chin must grip and hold… going up, up, no hesitation, no pause – that was Muir!"

Feeling weak and shaky, Young stood next to John on a narrow ledge, just fifty feet from the top, and admired the spectacular view.

Mountains stretched for hundreds of miles into the distance and a thousand feet below them was a sheer drop to the glacier. Within minutes John took off again, saying they had to reach the summit as the sun set. He raced around the narrow path to find a way to scale the last section of rock. Young tried to keep up, desperate not to lose his guide. As John rounded a steep curve he shouted something to Young, who couldn't make out what he said.

The shout had been a warning to take care on a fissured and unstable section. Too late. Young was tired and slipped as he tried to jump over the gap, and fell into it. He tried to grab the sides but his shoulders dislocated and he slid helplessly down the crack, landing on a narrow steep slope that led to the cliff, and a thousand-foot plunge to the glacier below. He came to a stop perilously close to the edge, his body flat against greasy, loose shingle, his feet sticking out over the side of the cliff.

John had heard Young cry out and when he realized the situation he shouted encouragement and whistled "The Blue Bells of Scotland" while he tried to find a route to a ledge just below Young. All the while the terrified missionary kept slipping an inch at a time further towards the drop, his arms in agony. It was a miracle that John managed to get Young next to him by grabbing his belt and trousers and swinging him out and back, Young's arms dangling uselessly by his side. They then had to climb back onto the original path above them, which they did with John partly holding the limp young man in his teeth.

Once they were in relative safety John reset one arm but the other was too dislocated and trapped. He therefore tore his own clothes and bound the badly damaged arm to Young's body, and they began a hazardous, desperately slow descent, working their way across a ridge above the ice. John held on to Young even when climbing down the vertical cliffs, where keeping his own footing was hard enough.

There was a long way to go and many dangers to overcome before they eventually reached the lower slopes. "All that night this man of steel and lightning worked, never resting a minute, doing the work of three men," wrote Young. Eventually they staggered up the gangplank at half past seven the next morning, just as a party was setting off to find them. It was a terrifying and desperate escapade. Some of the ministers were furious that Young had been so reckless; after all, he had responsibilities. After they had drunk coffee and eaten hot food, it took four men to yank Young's arm back into place.

This near-fatal incident had a profound effect. More than at any other time in his life so far, John was in the company of others when out in the wilds. As a solitary mountaineer in the Sierras he had only himself to consider and his scant regard for comfort and safety affected only himself. This incident was a salutary reminder that he could not act with others as he did when alone. From now on he would be exploring ever more remote mountains and glaciers in the company of less experienced people. Their loved ones waited nervously for them at home, as Louie did for him. It was also another strong reminder that nature was not always benign and giving. Human life was as nothing in the sharp, cold, craggy landscape of Alaska. As John had discovered in Florida and on Mount Shasta, the wilderness was not necessarily meant for humans to inhabit and they did so at their own risk.

The short cruises with the missionaries continued with John as on-board lecturer on natural history. The Indians were attentive and eager, "compared with the decent, death like apathy of weary civilized people, in whom natural curiosity has been quenched in toil and care and poor shallow comfort".[10]

On a trip in July the group were taken to a deserted Tlingit village with magnificently carved totem and ridge poles. John was astonished by the workmanship. As an accomplished carpenter himself he found it hard to believe the detail of the lifelike figures of people and animals: "With the same tools not one of our skilled mechanics could do as good a work."[11] The shape and form of the ravens, salmon, bears, wolves, and other animals were so true to life they could have been fashioned only by people who had spent years understanding them.

As he marvelled at this wonderful array of native skill, he heard a thudding sound and was outraged to see that one of the group, an archaeologist, had ordered deckhands to chop down a totem pole to take back to Europe. These beautiful artefacts were sacred to the Tlingits as shrines to their dead; they were believed to hold their souls. The Native Indians were furious, but to no avail. A few cheap trinkets seemed to calm the situation down but not before an old man had confronted the archaeologist asking him if he would be upset if they went to Europe to bring back gravestones.

At long last John and Young were able to organize their own trip in October to the Alexandrian Archipelago, a group of islands 300 miles long and mostly unmapped and unexplored. They hired a canoe that belonged to Chief Tow-a-att, a dignified and brave soul. They also took along another high-ranking Tlingit named Kadishan and two young men, Stickeen John and Stika Charley. John was to explore the glaciers and Young to make contact with distant Tlingit communities to lay plans for schools and churches.

Finally, the stifling "divines", who thwarted steamboat expeditions with their worries about value for money and cold weather, were left behind. There was not long to go before winter descended and there was a lot of Alaska to see. The canoe headed north towards the wilds of Glacier Bay, an area of the archipelago only recently freed by retreating ice. This was the perfect laboratory for John, fresh, untouched, and unexplored. Hoonah Native Indians, (a branch of the Tlingits) had also arrived there to hunt seals, providing new souls for Young. It was a match made in heaven.

The rowers, though perplexed by the ice mission, proved good companions. They were hardy and interested in seeing their land with new eyes. At last John was rowing into the heartland of ice. He often laboured long into the night on his notes and sketches. They camped on rock-strewn beaches, often in freezing rain, and when no level, stone-free ground could be found, "I learned from Muir", said Young, "the gentle art of sleeping on a rock, curled like a squirrel around a boulder."

Young also learned to see nature anew. Thoroughly grounded as he was in theological studies, he had never before seen God in such an expanded, all-encompassing way. From the patterns of the islands in the sounds to the way the branches of a tree balanced each other physically and aesthetically, or in the harmony of colours or the wonder of ice formation, God provided beauty in all things, from all angles and in all dimensions. Young felt as though he were relearning his faith. Here in John was a believer, but a different sort from his teachers in college. John Muir, he wrote, was "opening up to me new avenues of knowledge, delight and adoration. There was something so intimate in his theism that it purified, elevated and broadened mine."

Everywhere they went they found new earth in the making, brand new Yosemites in the process of formation. Mud made from the action of ice grinding up rock would one day be fertile soil. As the glaciers retreated, pioneering plants quickly began colonizing the new territory – the tentative beginnings of new life. When the ice finally melted, the U-shaped valleys with their steep walls and smooth surfaces, once filled to the brim with moving ice, would someday be clothed in lush meadows of grasses and flowers. The words of Louis Agassiz from 1875 must have revolved endlessly in John's brain: "One naturally asks, what was the use of this great engine set at work ages ago to grind, furrow, and knead over, as it were, the surface of the earth? We have our answer in the fertile soil which spreads over the temperate regions of the globe. The glacier was God's great plough."[12]

John was the first to write down any details about this intricate landscape of islands, ice, and forest. He suggested names such as the Geikie and Hugh Miller inlets to honour important Scottish geologists. One of the largest glaciers would be called Muir.

The religious mission was a success too, as Young held many meetings with various indigenous communities and the group were welcomed and treated as honoured guests. John was constantly impressed by the quiet dignity of the Native Indians in Alaska. They applied themselves with intelligence and patience to their work and treated their own kindly (though not necessarily other tribes). They rarely if ever scolded their children and he never witnessed any thrashings or harshness. How different it seemed from his Scottish upbringing. Once, though, they did encounter a "whisky howl" – a disconcerting mass moaning and screaming of a whole village, caused by alcohol.

After Young had preached, John was often invited to say a few words and he praised the people and the landscape they inhabited. The ice, the forests, and the wildlife lived in harmony with the tribes and all were a sign of the one great creator. Everything spoke of the divine and was therefore worthy of respect. One dignified old chief listened carefully. He then rose and spoke to the meeting:

> I am an old man... I remember the first white man I ever saw... but never until now have I felt a white man's heart. All white men I have hereto met wanted to get something from us... It has always seemed to me while trying to speak to traders and those seeking gold mines that it was like speaking to a person across a broad stream that was running fast over stones and making so loud a noise that scarce a single word could be heard. But now for the first time the Indian and the white man are on the same side of the river, eye to eye, heart to heart.[13]

A year later another chief was to give John a similar honour: "Your words are good, and they are strong words... and when storms come to try them they will stand the storms."[14]

After weeks of mountains, glaciers, crashing icebergs, and exhausting paddling, the expedition came to an end on 21 November 1879. The weather was now too severe to carry on further north and ice cut off the passages John most wanted to explore. The Tlingits were keen to get home to their families. Frustrated that he could not go as far as he would have liked, he was determined to return. First, however, he had to make his way back and marry the ever-patient Louie, who pined for him on the sun-soaked ranch in California. She could not really understand what drove him so far away from her, to a land famed for its savageness and deep cold. In her letters she pleaded with him to return.

John and Louie married on 14 April 1880. By June she was pregnant. In July John returned to Alaska to finish the journey, promising to be back for the birth of their baby. He went straight back to Fort Wrangell and, unannounced, marched into the house of an astonished Revd Young, who by then was also married. "When can you be ready?" were John's first words. "Get your crew and canoe and let's be off." Sadly, Chief Tow-a-att was not to join them; he had been killed in a senseless gun battle fuelled by alcohol. He had stood bravely, unarmed, refusing to leave the young men of his tribe as the shooting began. "Thus died for his people the noblest old Roman of them all," wrote John, who was deeply saddened.[15]

They left Fort Wrangell for the second trip on 16 August 1880 and headed for Glacier Bay. They were accompanied by three Tlingits, Captain Tyeen, Hunter Joe, and Smart Billy. The crew was completed by a small dog called Stickeen (after the tribe) that belonged to Young's wife. John objected, "The poor silly thing will be in rain and snow for weeks or months, and will require care like a baby." But Young insisted he would be no trouble and would even be a benefit. John thought him an odd-looking creature, "a funny, black, short-legged and bunchy-bodied, toy-dog", but he seemed so independent, wise, and peculiar that he couldn't help but like him. Stickeen was not easily won over and at first was aloof and uninterested in his human companions, although acutely aware of the surroundings:

> He sometimes reminded me of a small, squat, unshakable desert
> cactus. For he never displayed a single trace of the merry, tricksy,
> elfish fun of the terriers and collies that we all know … a true child
> of the wilderness, holding the even tenor of his hidden life with the
> silence and serenity of nature. His strength of character lay in his eyes.
> They looked as old as the hills, and as young, and as wild. I never tired
> of looking into them: it was like looking into a landscape.[16]

Over the weeks, however, Stickeen developed a devotion that was unerring. Perhaps it was the long walks into wild places or the way John talked to him as if to a friend that cemented their bond, but after a while he never left his side. In the wildest of storms he followed at his heels and seemed impervious to cold, rain, exertion, or fear. On one rough glacier the ice cut his paws so badly he left traces of blood all across the ice, but he never whined. John made him moccasins out of a handkerchief: "No superannuated mastiff or bulldog grown old in office surpassed this fluffy midget in stoic dignity."

It was on a stormy walk with Stickeen over the Brady Glacier (which is now in Glacier National Park) that John had one of his most famous adventures. His retelling of this terrifying crossing of a crevasse in 1897 (seventeen years after the event) in *The Century Magazine* became a bestseller. It can be read as a straightforward mountaineering escape but for John it was so much more. It was a direct lesson on the closeness of humanity to other life, "our fellow mortals", and the conclusions he drew coloured his thoughts for the rest of his life.

The day started before light as a wind howled over the camp. "Over the icy levels and over the woods, on the mountains, over the jagged rocks and spires and chasms of the glacier it boomed and moaned and roared, filling the fjord in even, grey, structureless gloom, inspiring and awful." As John climbed through the woods he noticed Stickeen close at heel. No matter how hard he tried to shoo him back to the safety and warmth of a tent, he would not obey, so the two of them faced the gale and headed out. They crossed the glacier where it was seven miles wide and explored the forest and smaller glaciers on the far side. By late afternoon the weather had closed in even more and the light was weakening in the sky. John, now soaked to the skin and getting cold, turned back for home across the glacier. Stickeen never flinched from leaping fissure to fissure no matter how deep and wide the gaps seemed to be for his short legs.

Despite the snow-laden wind and approaching dark they made good progress until they reached a large crevasse, which, at five feet wide, they only just managed to jump. It was a one-way move as the ice surface they had landed on was lower, making a return leap up to higher ground nigh impossible. They went on a little more and then John found to his horror that they had leaped onto an island of ice. Ahead was an uncrossable crevasse, a huge, forbidding chasm, forty feet wide. They were trapped, not able to go forwards or backwards. They ran up and down the edge trying to see if the gap narrowed but if anything it got wider as it merged with other crevasses. They were now blocked off from their route home, at least fifteen miles away.

Eventually John discovered a slight ray of hope in the form of a perilous ice bridge that hung like a frozen rope between the walls of the crevasse, fifteen feet below the surface. It stretched above utter blackness, a thin, badly weathered strip of ice. John could not be sure it would take his weight and a fall into the crevasse would be fatal. The pair now had two options: either spend the night on the glacier surface and "dance" to keep warm, in the hope that they could find a way off in the morning, or somehow cross the fragile ice bridge.

John lay down on the surface of the glacier and cut steps in the side of the crevasse with his axe. Stickeen stood by his shoulder, stared into the darkness and began to whimper, realizing what was happening.

This was the first time I had seen him gaze deliberately into a crevasse, or into my face with an eager, speaking, troubled look. That he should have recognized and appreciated the danger at the first glance showed wonderful sagacity. Never before had the daring midget seemed to know that ice was slippery or that there was any such thing as danger anywhere. His looks and tones of voice when he began to complain and speak his fears were so human that I unconsciously talked to him in sympathy as I would to a frightened boy, and in trying to calm his fears perhaps in some measure moderated my own. "Hush your fears, my boy," I said, "we will get across safe, though it is not going to be easy. No right way is easy in this rough world. We must risk our lives to save them. At the worst we can only slip, and then how grand a grave we will have, and by and by our nice bones will do good in the terminal moraine.

Stickeen only cried the more loudly. John slipped over the edge and reached the ice bridge. He then straddled it and shuffled across trying to smooth it as much as possible so that Stickeen would have a flat surface to walk over. It was only just wide enough and he would have to be very careful. The wind buffeted John dangerously hard. How could a small dog withstand this gale and not be blown off, or indeed slip, into the blackness below? "The tremendous abyss on either hand I studiously ignored. To me the edge of that blue sliver was then all the world."

When John reached the other side he faced the task of cutting holds in the ice back to the surface, the hardest part of the job. Standing on a tiny flake of ice looking up at a vertical wall and having to chip away small holds in rock-hard ice was one of the most testing things he had ever done. "Never before had I been so long under deadly strain. How I got up that cliff I never could tell." Stickeen looked across and howled piteously. He stared down into the crevasse and back at John and howled even more loudly.

The danger was enough to haunt anybody, but it seems wonderful that he should have been able to weight and appreciate it so justly. No mountaineer could have seen it more quickly or judged it more wisely, discriminating between real and apparent peril.

All John could do was shout encouragement over the ravine but Stickeen cried and whimpered and shook with fear. "His natural composure and courage had vanished utterly in a tumultuous storm of fear. Had the danger been less, his distress would have seemed ridiculous. But in this dismal, merciless abyss lay the shadow of death, and his heart-rending cries might well have called Heaven to his help."

Perhaps heaven did hear because, just as John was giving up hope that he would ever be able to coax him across, Stickeen suddenly began to slither down the ice steps and very slowly and tentatively walk over the bridge. John's heart was in his mouth as the courageous little dog kept his eyes fixed on the other side and stood firm every time the wind threatened to blow him off or his paws slithered on the ice. He reached the other side and, before John could reach down to help him, Stickeen scrabbled up the slippery steps and leaped past John.

> And now came a scene! "Well done, well done, little boy! Brave boy!" I cried, trying to catch and caress him; but he would not be caught. Never before or since have I seen anything like so passionate a revulsion from the depths of despair to exultant, triumphant, uncontrollable joy. He flashed and darted hither and thither as if fairly demented, screaming and shouting, swirling round and round in giddy loops and circles like a leaf in a whirlwind, lying down, and rolling over and over, sidewise and heels over head, and pouring forth a tumultuous flood of hysterical cries and sobs and gasping mutterings. When I ran up to him to shake him, fearing he might die of joy, he flashed off two or three hundred yards, his feet in a mist of motion; then, turning suddenly, came back in a wild rush and launched himself at my face, almost knocking me down, all the while screeching and screaming and shouting as if saying, "Saved! saved! saved!" … Nobody could have helped crying with him!

John and Stickeen made it back to camp well after dark, trembling and overcome with relief, hunger, and cold. Nevertheless, recalls Young, after this terrifying adventure, which had lasted for seventeen hours with almost no food and involving extreme danger, John was up at dawn the next day to climb a mountain and returned after nightfall, spending a few hours before sleeping working on notes. He does not record whether Stickeen joined him but this fluffy midget had imprinted himself into John's heart.

> I have known many dogs, and many a story I could tell of their wisdom and devotion; but to none do I owe so much as to Stickeen.

At first the least promising and least known of my dog-friends, he suddenly became the best known of them all. Our storm-battle for life brought him to light, and through him as through a window I have ever since been looking with deeper sympathy into all my fellow mortals.

These early Alaskan adventures with Samuel Young and Stickeen highlight a John Muir further down a path of self-discovery. He developed and refined his theories on glaciation certainly, but he was forced to accept responsibility for others in a hostile environment. The natural world was indeed undiscerning when it came to human life and, when faced with death, a small dog could demonstrate fear seemingly as acute as that of any person. With Stickeen firmly grafted onto his soul, the next trip to Alaska on board a government ship in May 1881 was particularly galling.

John was invited to join an ornithologist, E. W. Nelson, and an anthropologist, Irving Rosse, to explore the Aleutians to see if any trace could be found of ships that had gone missing in the area two years earlier. It was a long voyage, which took him away from his new wife and two-month-old daughter for half a year. Here he would observe the callousness that characterized Western attitudes to wildlife and also towards the culture and history of the Native Indian communities. Standing on deck he watched a small boat, dispatched from a schooner, sail alongside pack ice covered in walruses. The men on board were killing these huge animals for their tusks.

A puff of smoke now and then, a dull report, and a huge animal rears and falls – another and another, as they lie on the ice without showing any alarm, waiting to be killed, like cattle lying in a barnyard!... In nothing does man, with his grand notions of heaven and charity, show forth his innate, low-bred, wild animalism more clearly than in his treatment of his fellow beasts. From the shepherd with his lambs to the red-handed hunter, it is the same; no recognition of rights – only murder in one form or another.[17]

Slaughter for tusks was one thing, killing for pure pleasure another. On his own ship the captain, along with others on board, took great delight in shooting any polar bears they saw for no other reason than that they could.

> How civilized people, seeking for heavens and angels and millenniums, and the reign of universal peace and love, can enjoy this red, brutal amusement, is not so easily accounted for… the frame of mind that can reap giggling, jolly pleasure from the blood and agony of these fine animals, with their humanlike groans, are too devilish for anything but hell. Of all the animals man is at once the worst and the best.[18]

He had already witnessed an archaeologist chopping down a totem pole without permission; now worse was to come. On St Lawrence Island they found utter oblivion:

> We found twelve desolate huts close to the beach with about two hundred skeletons in them or strewn about on the rocks and rubbish heaps within a few yards of the doors. The scene was indescribably ghastly and desolate… The shrunken bodies, with rotting furs on them, or white, bleaching skeletons, picked bare by the crows, were lying mixed with kitchen-midden rubbish where they had been cast out by surviving relatives while they yet had strength to carry them.[19]

Men, women, and children had all died of starvation. There seemed to be no single cause, but the extreme cold of the winter of 1878-79 was certainly an important factor. The native people didn't normally freeze, however; there were plenty of skins in the houses. John's conclusion was that trading with Westerners was "a degrading influence, making them less self-reliant, and less skilful as hunters. They seem easily susceptible of civilization." That and a fall in the walrus population due to intense harvesting by the commercial hunters combined to bring a slow and agonizing death to a whole community. Bodies were piled "like firewood" in the corners of huts, or found side by side on beds or on the floor, meeting their fate with "tranquil apathy". The last few were too weak to remove bodies and simply lay down beside them on the floor.

It was a heart-rending scene and John wrote that the government had a moral duty to help, as "unless some aid be extended by our government which claims these people, in a few years at most every soul of them will have vanished from the face of the earth".

This grisly scene, however, was met with enthusiasm by Mr Nelson, who busied himself collecting for the Smithsonian and other museums, "gathering the fine white harvest of skulls spread before him, and throwing them in heaps like a boy gathering pumpkins". This aggressive acquisitiveness on the part of Western collectors and rich travellers devastated native community culture. By 1895 American naturalist and Alaskan expert William Dall wrote, "The day of the ethnological collector is past. South-eastern Alaska is swept clean of relics, hardly a shaman's grave remains inviolate."[20]

In John's opinion, the upstanding citizens who brought their way of life to the northern territories were often too pious to be kind and too religious to see God beyond their own culture. But these examples give us a glimpse of the pressures bearing down on this last wild frontier of North America at the end of the nineteenth century. Gold prospectors had arrived with their single-minded desire to make themselves rich. Fur traders set their sights and guns on the otters, seals, wolves, and beavers. Ivory hunters took more than their share of walrus, narwhals, and elephant seals. Whisky and firearms entered the Native Indian communities, with devastating consequences. Christian missionaries overlaid and profoundly altered native spirituality. By the time John explored Alaska, this changeover from a hunter/gatherer way of life to commercialism and Western culture was almost complete and he found himself amid the last vestiges of non-Westernized Alaska as it teetered on the brink of oblivion.

At the same time as John was roaming the glaciers of the American Arctic, Mark Twain was discovering the wildness of ice in the Alps in Europe. He found, just like John Muir, that being in such cold, unrelenting harshness and stark beauty had a profound effect on his soul. In his 1880 book *A Tramp Abroad* he wrote that "A man who keeps company with glaciers comes to feel tolerably insignificant by and by. The Alps and the glaciers together are able to take every bit of conceit out of a man and reduce his self-importance to zero if he will only remain within the influence of their sublime presence long enough to give it a fair and reasonable chance to do its work." But the humility brought on by ice in the Alps didn't affect everyone, it seems. In Alaska it often brought about a freezing of the heart towards wildlife and native human life that John found hard to bear.

The Alaskan adventures, and there were seven trips in all, take us to the heart of John Muir. They show us who the man really was when tested to the limit. He was supremely fit and able to withstand intense cold, hardship, and hunger without ever losing his humanity. He faced death on many occasions and carried on as though it were simply part of what he had to do. He would spend a day climbing a mountain or a day talking to flowers. He spent hours "playing with the pines" and then days recording scientific data. He worked long hours from before light to late into the night. He was at once a child and a scientist, a mystic and a rationalist. He defied all boundaries.

His Alaskan travels also show us a side that is rarely discussed, his compassion and sensitivity to other human cultures. Exploitation and subjugation of the natural world, so powerfully illustrated in Alaska, proved once again that the destruction of nature was at the centre of American industrial and commercial development. John Muir made further connections in Alaska, realizing just how far the drive for money ruled all things. He was appalled by what he saw. When viewed together with his other experiences in forests and mountains he knew he had no choice but to launch himself into political activism, a battle that would preoccupy him for the rest of his life. For a man of the wilderness the journey into the halls of power proved to be the most arduous of all, but before he wrestled with presidents he had a home to make among the balmy, fruit-laden trees of California.

Chapter 12

Preparing for the Fight

"The price of greatness is responsibility."

Winston Churchill

John returned to Alhambra and his heavily pregnant wife at the end of his third Alaskan trip in 1881. The great wilderness sprite who took to the mountains to face tempest, extreme danger, the heights of wild bliss, and bone-snapping cold now turned his formidable energy to soft fruit. Just as John's standing as a writer and spokesman for nature was being recognized from coast to coast, he settled abruptly into a lowland life of commercial horticulture for nearly a decade. His task now was to be as dutiful a husband and father as he had been an enthusiastic mountaineer, and that meant providing for his family through hard work in business. Writing brought in some money and plenty of opportunity for travel, but it didn't keep Louie and baby Wanda, plus his own extended family, in financial security and comfort.

A thriving fruit-growing business was John Strenzel's gift to his son-in-law. In 1880, the year John and Louie were married, the state of California produced 3 million pounds of fresh fruit, comprising grapes, cherries, apples, pears, and peaches, and 400,000 pounds of dried fruit. Over the next 5 years, as markets grew, that output would increase to 45 million pounds of fresh fruit, 6 million pounds of dried, and 17 million gallons of wine. John stepped into a business that was literally blossoming.[1]

The orchards and vineyards nestled in the beautiful Alhambra Valley, an area of rich soils and undulating hills watered by the Alhambra Creek. Along the river grew willows, cottonwoods, sycamores, big-leaf maples, and valley oaks. The understorey of California blackberry and California rose provided a habitat for many songbirds and woodpeckers. Herons fished from the riverbanks, competing with otters and mink, which were so common they were killed by the thousand for their skins. Salmon swam in such profusion that the Martinez Packing Company was established in 1882 and canned and shipped about 350 cases of salmon per day.[2] Warm, sun-kissed, and filled with wildlife and cultivated fruit trees buzzing with bees, this valley was a gentle paradise after so much rock and ice.

Although he had grown up on a farm, growing fruit was a new trade and there was a lot to learn. Unlike Daniel's gritty, family-run homestead, this amount of land and production required a team of workers, mainly Chinese immigrants, who needed to be managed. Negotiations had to be made with distributors, agricultural pests had to be controlled, and new growing techniques and varieties had to be experimented with.

It was all-consuming and left very little time for anything else. John Muir's biographer Linnie Marsh Wolfe referred to the time between 1882 and 1888 as "the lost years". Despite his conviction that the natural world was under increasing threat, John virtually ceased submitting articles for newspapers and no books were in the pipeline. Even his prolific letter writing dropped away. He never wrote publicly about this time. Steeped in Scottish industriousness and with a keen sense of efficiency, John took his role as husband and land manager seriously, but this period was always tinged with dissatisfaction and yearning.

The dissatisfaction came from buying into a way of life that manipulated the natural world to meet only human needs. John was no idealist – he knew people needed food – but he questioned the techniques and principles by which it was obtained. Far from working with nature and learning lessons from wild animals, fruits, and cereals, farmers seemed to want to eradicate any vestiges of wildness. His experiences with Billy and the half-manufactured "silly sheep" in the mountains over a decade before had cured him of any notions that what people create is better than what nature has evolved over countless millennia.

He worried about the resilience of intensively farmed fruits compared with wild varieties; how they must be constantly protected, nurtured, and fussed over like a house plants rather than able to withstand storms, insects, birds, and heat and cold as their wild cousins do. This meant mass killing of everything that posed a threat, from the smallest insects to the ground squirrels growing fat on the produce. More than ever he saw people attempting to play God and getting it wrong. By manipulating species to suit only human needs, they created distortions, not perfection. Perhaps the manicured gardens of the hotel by Mammoth Cave in Kentucky came back to mind: "Many a beautiful plant cultivated to deformity… the whole affair a laborious failure side by side with Divine beauty."

In the beautifully written article "The Bee Pastures of California", published in *The Century Magazine* in 1882, John extols the wonders of the still-wild San Joaquin Valley he had explored fourteen years earlier: "it was one sweet bee-garden throughout its entire length, north and south, and all the way across from the snowy Sierra to the ocean". In describing the brambles that grew along the river's edge he makes a pointed comment about wild versus mass-produced fruit:

And in midsummer, when the blackberries were ripe, the Indians came from the mountains to feast – men, women, and babies in long, noisy trains, often joined by the farmers of the neighborhood, who gathered this wild fruit with commendable appreciation of its superior flavor, while their home orchards were full of ripe peaches, apricots, nectarines, and figs, and their vineyards were laden with grapes.

Californian fruit growing, however, was more than a business to John's father-in-law John Strenzel; it was the realization of an ideal. Both the Strenzels and the Carrs were supporters of the Granger movement, a coalition of American farmers separated into local Granges throughout the country. It had begun in the 1860s and was growing in popularity. The Granger movement urged local farmers to work together to create a society of like-minded producers. Together their gentle, deeply earthed way of living could defy the unreasonable demands of big business, namely the railways that charged exorbitant prices for transportation. By cooperating they believed they could create a just society that was both peaceful and nurturing. It would not only encourage fair-minded business but also provide the right setting for the exploration of ideas that were pure in heart and mind.

John was not so sure. Nothing about farmers and the way they lived suggested to him a vision of harmony between farming and the natural world. He found the Grange too focused on the needs of people and unaware of the wilder world: "The astronomer looks high, the geologist low. Who looks between on the surface of the earth? The farmer I suppose, but too often he sees only grain, and of that only the mere bread-bushel-and-price of it."[3] Visions of dollars still flashed in farmers' eyes rather than a Garden of Eden.

Growing fruit was better than digging for gold, with all the destruction that entailed, but, for John, farming was like most of American life: its purpose was creating wealth and nothing to do with establishing harmony among life on earth. Nevertheless, he did his duty and he did it very well. Under his keen eye the business grew and thrived.

The deep yearning he felt daily was for the cold blasts of air he had left behind in Alaska and the range of light-filled Sierra Mountains only 150 miles away – tantalizingly close. Still in his forties and full of curiosity, he wanted to carry on exploring the earth for beauty in its wild and untouched state. He longed for the days of wandering at will, untroubled by responsibility and led only by instinct. The genteel, indulgent life of California stifled his mind and soul. He worked too hard, ate too little, and began to shrink mentally and physically. Louie worried that he was overdoing it and tried to support him in every way she could, but there was no getting away from the fact that John felt trapped. Much as he loved Louie and adored Wanda, and then in 1886 also baby Helen, we get a glimpse of this frustration from correspondence with Revd Samuel Young: "I am losing precious days. I am degenerating into a machine for making money. I am learning nothing in this trivial world of men. I must break away and get out into the mountains to learn the news."[4]

In 1888 Samuel Young made an unannounced visit to the Martinez ranch and found John at cherry-picking time with a large group of Chinese workmen:

> He saw me as soon as I discovered him, and dropping the basket he was carrying came running to greet me with both hands outstretched. "Ah my friend," he cried, "I have been longing mightily for you. You have come to take me on a canoe trip to the countries beyond – to Lituya and Yakutat Bays and Prince William Sound; have you not? My weariness of this hum-drum, work-a-day life has grown so heavy it is like to crush me. I'm ready to break away and go with you whenever you say… I, who have breathed the mountain air – who have really lived a life of freedom – condemned to penal servitude with these miserable little bald-heads!" (holding up a bunch of cherries). "Gin it were na for my bairnies I'd rin awa' frae a' this tribble an' hale ye back north wi' me." So Muir would run on, now in English, now in broad Scotch; but through all his raillery there ran a note of longing for the wilderness.[5]

Although John mainly threw himself into fruit growing for eight years, there were occasional ventures beyond the ranch in an attempt to satisfy his wilderness yearnings. In 1884 John and Louie left Wanda with the Strenzels and went to the Yosemite Valley, the only holiday they had together. It was not an overwhelming success. Louie was plump and unfit for mountain walking and constantly worried about bears. Both of them fretted about the baby. John sent home an amusing drawing of Louie struggling up a path with John pushing her from behind with a stick. Louie was as hopelessly and forever a home bird as John was a wanderer, but she understood John's need to escape and loved him enough to endure long periods apart.

In the summer of 1885 John left Louie pregnant with Helen and went on a trip to see his family in Portage, acting on a premonition that his father was nearing the end of his life. These moments of intense sensitivity to events occurred just a handful of times in his life, but when they came they were overwhelming. In 1869 he had had a similar intuition about Professor Butler arriving in the Yosemite Valley, which had caused him to race down a mountain to find him by a river. This time, without any concrete intelligence that his father was failing, he packed his bags and went to gather his siblings to be at Daniel's bedside.

Not, however, without taking in Yellowstone National Park en route. Despite feeling unwell and camping there for only a week, he found it an astonishing natural cooking pot full of bubbling, spitting mud and water and wrote effusively about it for the *Evening Bulletin*: "The park is full of exciting wonders. The wildest geysers in the world, in bright, triumphant bands, are dancing and singing in it amid thousands of boiling springs... and hot-paint pots, mud springs, mud volcanoes, mush and broth caldrons."[6]

In Portage he generously sorted out his brother David's failing finances, reminisced over the old days with his beloved mother (who lived until 1896), rounded up his other siblings and then, with a deep breath, went to Kansas City to see his father, who was living with his youngest sister, Joanna. They had last met eighteen years ago and it had been an unpleasant and painful visit. The exchange of letters ever since had been testy, with Daniel repeatedly disapproving of John's life and beliefs. John was therefore prepared for a difficult reunion. But instead of a raging and dogmatic fanatic he found a weak and frail old man, bedridden and suffering from advanced dementia.

Only when John spoke in broad Scotch did he show any

recognition, eventually nodding when John said he was his son. He muttered, "Oh yes, my dear wanderer." Daniel had softened before his end, telling Joanna he had made many mistakes and particularly regretted the "cruel things" he had said to John. In a rare moment of self-doubt he urged her to treat her own children with kindness. John lay on the bed next to his dying father and held his hand. When he passed away in early October, John cried tears of true grief, perhaps in recognition of just how much this austere and driven man had shaped his life. His obituary for Daniel was full of reconciliation:

> Few lives were more restless and eventful than his, few more steadily toilsome and full of enthusiastic endeavor, ever fighting his way onward unwearied toward light and truth and eternal love…
>
> His life was singularly clean and pure. He never had a single vice excepting perhaps the vices of over-industry and over-giving. Good scripture measure "heaped up shaken together and running over" he meted out to all.[7]

He did, however, add privately to Louie that Daniel's passionately religious life had taken its toll on those around him.

Helen Muir was born shortly after his return to Martinez on 23 January 1886. Unlike Wanda she was small and sickly, compounding John's responsibilities. He adored his children and was determined to see that they would always be secure. His own siblings increasingly looked to him for cash, advice, and comfort as they struggled with business failures and illness. He found himself the pillar of support for many people he loved. Far from releasing himself from obligations, he gained more by the day.

In 1887 he took on the task of editing a popular magazine of engravings and essays called *Picturesque California*, probably as a result of friends urging him not to abandon the writing altogether. He contributed six essays of his own on the glaciers and passes of the High Sierra, the Yosemite, Mount Shasta, Washington and the Puget Sound, and the Columbia River. This popular journal aimed to bring the delights of Californian living to a wide audience, showing there was more to this far-western outpost than gold and sheep. Contributors ranged from the poet Joaquin Miller, "the poet of the Sierras", and the fiery politician John Irish, to the gentle-minded Jeanne Carr. John's friend William Keith provided illustrations. Apart from raising his horizons above the level of hanging fruit, it allowed John to get away from the ranch. In 1888 he at last organized time off and packed his bags for a trip to gather material for his essays.

Mount Rainier, Puget Sound, Lake Tahoe, and Mount Shasta were all on the itinerary. Although tired by too much ranch work he wrote to Louie from Mount Rainier, "Did not mean to climb it, but got excited, and soon was on top."[8]

All these places provided more thoughts and evidence for his glacial work, but, as in Alaska, among the effusive words of beauty and sound science, there crept a tone of concern, a recognition that all was not well in the wild, as in the article on Mount Shasta:

> The great wilds of our country once held to be boundless and inexhaustible are being rapidly invaded and overrun in every direction, and everything destructible in them is being destroyed. How far can destruction go is not easy to guess. Every landscape low and high seems doomed to be trampled and harried.[9]

And in the "Washington and Puget Sound" article in *Picturesque California*:

> The wedges of development are being driven hard and none of the obstacles or defences of nature can long withstand the onset of this immeasurable industry.[10]

What John saw was the relentless growth of the biggest economy on earth: a ravenous beast that devoured everything in its path. This was the Gilded Age, forty years of unsurpassed growth and industrialization at the end of the nineteenth century, and the natural world was feeling the effects in every state.

A booming population drove the demand for goods and services. By 1880 it had reached 50 million, having doubled since the Muir family arrived in Wisconsin thirty years earlier. Railway lines tripled between 1860 and 1880. These opened up markets and allowed for the burgeoning of commercial farming, ranching, and mining. Between 1865 and 1900 the output of wheat and corn increased by 250 per cent and coal by 800 per cent. American steel production rose to exceed the combined total of Britain, Germany, and France. The number of farms tripled from 2 million in 1860 to 6 million in 1900.[11] Even wildlife, such as salmon, was a commodity: "Used, wasted, canned and sent in shiploads to all the world, a grand harvest was reaped every year while nobody sowed," wrote John despairingly.[12] During the 1870s and 1880s, the US economy rose at the fastest rate in its history.

All this industry brought wealth. Although many ordinary factory workers lived in poverty, the growing number of middle-class people increasingly used their cash to escape the grit and smog of the major cities. The glorious wilderness of America was the perfect tonic for the overworked and overburdened. John welcomed the increase in interest, and indeed encouraged people as much as possible to taste and see for themselves, though he was not convinced that most were getting much benefit. Going to mountains and rivers and forests in a train and staying for just a few hours or days might be an efficient use of time, "yet a pity to go so fast in a blur where so much might be seen and enjoyed". He tried to soothe people's nerves by assuring them that savage beasts and murderous Indians were figments of imagination and not a reality. They would find peace only if they left the well-worn trail and headed into the wilds. But most people stuck to the "battered highways like a drowning sailor to a life-raft".[13] The wilderness was becoming packaged and presented in comfortable and easy-to-grab sight-bites, rather than savoured lovingly and longingly.

John must have understood the pressures many people were under, though; he was certainly suffering from over-industriousness and lack of time himself. His articles were speaking of his own life as well as to others:

> Perhaps the profession of doing good may be full, but everybody should be kind at least to himself. Take a course in good water and air, and in the eternal youth of nature you may renew your own. Go quietly, alone, no harm will befall you.[14]

His concern for the wilderness appeared increasingly in his writing, something not unnoticed by the next great figure to appear in John's life. As Daniel Muir had fashioned his fortitude and Jeanne Carr had encouraged his poetry, so Robert Underwood Johnson, the editor of an influential magazine, fired up this mystical mountain man into a powerhouse of activism. In May 1889, John was summoned to San Francisco's Palace Hotel. Johnson was late for dinner and asked John to go to his room while he carried on preparing for a night out. John, however, took a long time in arriving.

> I can remember, as if it were yesterday, hearing him call down the corridor, "Johnson, Johnson! where are you? I can't get the hang of these artificial canyons," and before he had made any of the conventional greetings or inquiries, he added, "Up in the Sierra, all along the gorges, the glaciers have put up natural sign-posts, and you can't miss your way, but here - there's nothing to tell you where to go."[15]

And thus met two men who, together, would lay plans for saving America's wild places. One was a savvy, intelligent journalist aged thirty-six: the other was fifty-one and looked like a biblical prophet. Johnson described John as "spare of frame, hardy, keen of eye and visage, and on the march eager of movement". He noted John's long shaggy hair and beard just turning grey, and the kindliest look in his eyes. Here was a wilderness sage for the people, concluded Johnson, a charismatic writer and the "real thing". Johnson would be his agent.

The Century Magazine had a million readers and espoused values for America that were higher than pure money-making. It campaigned for social justice, aesthetics, social reform, and nature – in other words a perfect outlet for John's message. The two men went to the Yosemite and then up into the Tuolumne meadows, where they camped out under the stars and dreamed of a nation that protected its spectacular wilderness. The increasingly gaudy tourism of the valley bottom sported smart hotels, pig farms, ploughed-up meadows, and acres of tree stumps. It was transformed from the days when John had arrived twenty years earlier. Despite the Yosemite Valley having come under the protection of the state-appointed Yosemite Commission it had been allowed to develop in a ramshackle, unthought-out way and had deteriorated into a sorry state. Even the high meadows and mountainsides where tourists seldom ventured were damaged by decades of sheep grazing.

Johnson knew John was overburdened with ranch work, and that he was not naturally a political animal, but he also knew there was no one better to galvanize opinion towards establishing what could be America's second national park. They doubted that the valley bottom itself could be wrested away from state control, but it might be possible to protect the surrounding land and put it under federal control, including the "other Yosemite", Hetch Hetchy. John was unsure whether he wanted to step into the fray and take on more work. It was Louie who helped release her overworked husband. More than anyone she saw what her preferred way of life was doing to his spirit and she understood the role he could play. In a letter to him in 1888 she gave her blessing:

> Dear John, A ranch that needs and takes the sacrifice of a noble life, or work, ought to be flung away beyond all reach... The Alaska book and the Yosemite book, dear John, must be written, and you need to be your own self, well and strong to make them worthy of you. Ever your wife, Louie.[16]

It was a noble, selfless gesture of support and she looked for ways to lessen the burden. John struggled to release his creative juices, however. He felt like a mountain stream that had been dammed by the silt of industry and was unable to flow freely. As he fussed and fretted over the ranch and his writer's block, other influential voices from all walks of life were beginning to be heard in letters and articles and they piqued John's conscience. Many who put pen to paper may have done so because of their own vested interests, holding stakes in tourism or water resources, for example, but nevertheless they made the effort to write, leaving the acclaimed prophet of the Yosemite silently pruning his trees.

Johnson was not a man to allow this opportunity to pass by and he harried and hassled John for articles for *The Century Magazine*, and also urged him to set up an association for preserving California's natural monuments. Surely, he demanded, John knew enough influential people to form a society that could exercise real influence; this must be within his powers?

Shamed by the work of others and to keep Johnson from pestering him, John eventually produced two outstanding articles, the first in August 1890 called "The Treasures of the Yosemite" and the second a month later, "Features of the Proposed Yosemite National Park". They were worth the wait. Beautiful, evocative, lyrical, and straight from the heart, they led the reader to the very core of the Sierra Range. "The Treasures of the Yosemite" begins with John remembering his first glimpse of them far away, towering above the golden San Joaquin Valley:

> so gloriously colored and so radiant that it seemed not clothed with
> light, but wholly composed of it, like the wall of some celestial city…
> Then it seemed to me the Sierra should be called, not the Nevada
> or Snowy Range, but the Range of Light. And after ten years in the
> midst of it, rejoicing and wondering, seeing the glorious floods of
> light that fill it, the sunbursts of morning among the mountain-peaks,
> the broad noonday radiance on the crystal rocks, the flush of the
> alpenglow, and the thousand dashing waterfalls with their marvellous

abundance of irised spray, it still seems to me a range of light. But no terrestrial beauty may endure forever. The glory of wildness has already departed from the great central plain. Its bloom is shed, and so in part is the bloom of the mountains. In Yosemite, even under the protection of the Government, all that is perishable is vanishing apace.[17]

No one else could have written so authentically and so passionately. Every sequoia grove, waterfall, bird, rock fall, flood, storm, and canyon is described with pure love. Wilderness pumped through John's veins. As soon as he began to write, love poured onto the paper. When that love cast down its eyes in sorrow at the desecration of such magnificent temples the reader was disturbed too. The damage being imposed was held out like a sullied cloth. See what is happening? See what we are doing in the name of industry and money? Let us save our wilderness! was the underscore to a magnificent chorus of Yosemite delights.

The end of the second article forms a plea for "right relationship" with the Yosemite, Hetch Hetchy, the meadows, and the sequoia groves before it was too late and all fall beneath the trampling feet of dollar seekers.

Ax and plow, hogs and horses, have long been and are still busy in Yosemite's gardens and groves. All that is accessible and destructible is being rapidly destroyed – more rapidly than in any other Yosemite in the Sierra, though this is the only one that is under the special protection of the Government. And by far the greater part of this destruction of the fineness of wildness is of a kind that can claim no right relationship with that which necessarily follows use.[18]

His articles written and posted to the impatient Johnson, John then packed his Arctic clothes and headed to Glacier Bay. Departing on 14 June 1890, he would not return until September, giving him a summer of ice and wilderness in abundance. As Johnson lobbied Congress and other campaigners stoked up the fires of change,

John luxuriated in the harshest of conditions. He undertook a solo, ten-day trip across the Muir Glacier, pulling a wooden sled and sleeping out on the ice. At first his body shook with severe bronchitis, which he was harbouring from the lowlands. But, as the wolves howled through the night and the ice crystals twinkled like stars, his lungs began to breathe freely again. His only food was hardtack biscuits, sweet tea, and water. He pushed his body to the limits yet again.

The soles of his shoes wore out on the ice and he replaced them with wood. He was forced to make small fires by shaving wood from his sled. He shuffled over thin ice bridges, similar to the one he had crossed with Stickeen, pushing the sled ahead of him. Vast, black caverns plunged on either side. On one occasion he slipped on a patch of smooth ice and slithered down the glacier onto a pile of rocks. Delighted ravens cawed above him, hoping for a body to scavenge, but John shouted at them, "Not yet!" His snow blindness was so severe he could barely see, staggering with double vision and unable to locate his route home.

Eventually he succeeded in crossing this hummocky, deeply fissured and dangerous glacier, fifteen miles wide, dragging a sled weighing 100 pounds. It was just what he needed. Back on shore he took to a canoe and explored the iceberg-filled sounds alone. When trying to paddle between two huge blocks of ice, his luck almost ran out:

> When I got about a third of the way in, I suddenly discovered that the smooth-walled ice-lane was growing narrower and with desperate haste backed out. Just as the bow of the canoe cleared the sheer walls they came together with a growling crunch. Terror-stricken I turned back.[19]

Just as the canoe cleared the channel the icebergs crashed together.

After years of orchards John Muir had returned to form. "I know that our bodies were made to thrive only in pure air, and the scenes in which pure air is found," he had written in a journal.[20]

This Arctic wilderness was the only medicine his body and soul needed and he arrived home ready for the fight.

John was convinced that all people possess a love of nature. It may be buried under cares and duty, but if people only take time to be in the wilderness, their true "ancient mother-love" will once again surface. This is what he appealed to in his articles, urging all to go and see. Many did, fired by John's pure enthusiasm, which made the magazines he wrote for glow with irresistible warmth and light.

> Thousands of tired, nerve-shaken, over-civilized people are
> beginning to find out that going to the mountains is going home; that
> wildness is a necessity; and that mountain parks and reservations are
> useful not only as fountains of timber and irrigating rivers, but as
> fountains of life.[21]

As John returned to Martinez in time for the grape harvest, renewed and refreshed, he joined an America undergoing a profound change. In September, Congress established two new national parks, both in California. Yellowstone held the crown as the first, designated in 1872 as a place "set apart as a public park or pleasuring ground for the benefit and enjoyment of the people". Now in quick succession Sequoia, including the General Grant Grove of sequoias, and Yosemite joined the list (although the valley bottom stayed under state control as predicted).

The establishment of national parks was unprecedented in the world. The United States had suddenly woken from its slumbers and decided to act to protect at least some of the magnificence of its natural treasures. John's voice was not the only one that had long stirred the public imagination, but his was the most eloquent and best known. His words had a unique ability to go straight to the heart and when those hearts beat together they created change. From his adoration of giant sequoias to the descriptions of the overpowering Sierra domes to the bright water ouzel singing its praises in fast mountain streams, all contributed to a national change

231

of heart. The lines of the Yosemite National Park were exactly those that John had suggested in his *Century* article, "Features of the Proposed Yosemite National Park".

Johnson was delighted. He had played a major role in lobbying politicians, but he was in no doubt that John's influence had been vital. He wrote him a letter praising his "very outspoken reference to the depredations of that region, and practically to your sketch of the limits, which I think are identical with those of the bill". John was natually thrilled.

> Happy will be the men who, having the power and the love and the benevolent forecast to [create a park], will do it. They will not be forgotten. The trees and their lovers will sing their praises, and generations yet unborn will rise up and call them blessed.[22]

It was not only national parks that were created. The Forest Reserve Act of 1891 allowed the incumbent president of the United States to protect some areas of forest from private exploitation. Benjamin Harrison's administration (1889–93) put 20,460 square miles into national forests, Grover Cleveland (1893–97) designated 38,600 square miles, and William McKinley (1897–1901) set aside 10,800 square miles. The forest reserves had less protection than national parks, and allowed some use of resources, but they banned privatization of land and private commercial interests. Battles immediately commenced to lessen the protection. Vested interests reared and snarled at this raft of successes, their means of making money severely limited. There was no time for resting on laurels.

Johnson was determined to see another national park created, this one around the spectacular Kings Canyon, also in the southern Sierra but left out of the Sequoia National Park. As early as 1873, John had been enchanted by this area, home to some of the largest trees in the world. This dramatic valley, carved out by glaciers and cloaked in forests, had prompted John to write "In every walk with Nature one receives far more than he seeks." But this time protection would not be so easy. Great counterforces were mobilizing that would prevent the securing of Kings Canyon until 1940. These forces began to square up to the environmentalists, forcing decades of hard, bruising, and life-sapping confrontation, which would take its toll.

The flush of first success was sweet, but it was to turn bitter over the coming years. Huge changes were afoot and John found himself in the middle of a cacophony of voices from many camps. Loggers, sheepherders, and miners campaigned for the freedom to exploit resources to fuel the burgeoning economy. Others suggested more restrained use, based on providing goods that would enhance society and create the greatest good for the greatest number of people, the so-called "wise use" camp.

Still others, like John, wanted to set areas aside simply for their own sake, to be left wild and true to themselves. These preservationists wanted no logging, no grazing, and no mining within park boundaries at all. Nature was to be cherished for the spiritual and nurturing qualities it gave to humanity, and money had to be excluded from the equation. "In God's wilderness lies the hope of the world – the great fresh unblighted, unredeemed wilderness," wrote John.[23] It was not a message many people in industry wanted to hear.

Nature now relied on John Muir, and turned to him for his powers of persuasion. From the smallest flower to the highest mountain, he seemed to give voice to the voiceless in passionate tones that directly joined us all together:

> How many hearts with warm red blood in them are beating under cover of the woods, and how many teeth and eyes are shining! A multitude of animal people, intimately related to us, but of whose lives we know almost nothing, are as busy about their own affairs as we are about ours.[24]

John was also, however, a businessman, husband, father, and brother. Human ties tugged at his heart and relied on him for stability and succour; there were many forces pulling him in many directions.

He stood tall and spoke out for the natural world but he would take many body blows on its behalf. By the end of 1890, he was fifty-two. That same year his father-in-law, John Strenzel, died and Louie, John, and the girls moved out of their small Dutch-style house on the estate to live in the large manse with Mrs Strenzel. Now he had a house of many rooms and servants. He was the official head of the household and the recognized head of a growing movement for the preservation of nature. Suddenly life got tougher and more complicated. On the horizon, dark clouds were gathering as the rich and powerful prepared to win back the wilderness. Natural storms he knew he could weather; political ones were in an entirely different league.

Chapter 13

The Last Battles

"Everybody needs beauty as well as bread, places to play in and pray in, where nature may heal and give strength to body and soul alike."

John Muir[1]

This most famous of John Muir quotes could serve as his strapline. He wrote it in 1908, in defence of the Hetch Hetchy Valley, the magnificent and inaccessible "other Yosemite" high in the Sierra. It had been earmarked as a perfect location for a reservoir to supply San Francisco. No one believed more passionately than John that nature had a practical as well as a spiritual role in the life of every human being. But some places, he argued, were simply too extraordinary to be harnessed to human needs. Places that ignited our ancient mother-love of the wild had to remain unsullied for all generations. If all of "God's temples" were utilized, then humanity would slip ever further away from the source of what makes us fully human.

We were nurtured, he felt, from our first appearance on earth as hunter-gatherers, in the bosom of Mother Nature, surrounded by a harmonious blend of colour and physical form. Our ears were filled with a breathtaking array of natural music. The beauty of nature instilled peace and joy in our developing hearts, giving us all an inbuilt love of the wild. Dangers didn't diminish that joy: they served to sharpen our senses and make the world a stage of drama and delight. Nature hasn't changed, insisted John; it still performs this vital service as well as it ever did, but humanity is less inclined to accept it.

Not it seemed that only money, not beauty, filled the thoughts of most Americans, removing the nation further from a sense of reverence for what sustains humanity's soul. The blame for some of that change he laid at the feet of the type of fundamentalist Christianity he had been taught as a child, as it put man not only in the centre of creation but also above, removed from it. Accepting without humility the command to subdue the earth and fill it resulted in the devastation of the Gilded Age. Other forces aided the break from nature, such as a growing secularism that valued money over spirituality and viewed any emotional attachment to nature as weakness. As early as 1871 he had written to his Oakland friend J.B. McChesney:

> Man as he came from the hand of his Maker was poetic in both
> mind and body, but the gross heathenism of civilization has generally
> destroyed Nature, and poetry, and all that is spiritual.[2]

John's opinion was not kind to those he saw as hypocrites either, such as the loggers, miners, and trappers who inflicted terrible damage but who wore a cloak of morality in church on Sunday. He derided those who blasted passenger pigeons from the skies and bison from the plains, those who enjoyed inflicting pain and death on defenceless creatures for no practical reason, those who looked to the wilderness and saw only dollars, yet still pronounced themselves good Christians. In "Among the Birds of the Yosemite" published in *Atlantic Monthly* in 1898, he turned his glare towards the killers of migrating birds:

> many of the wanderers are shot for sport and the morsel of meat
> on their breasts. Man then seems a beast of prey. Not even genuine
> piety can make the robin-killer quite respectable. Saturday is the
> great slaughter day in the bay region. Then the city pot-hunters,
> with a rag-tag of boys, go forth to kill, kept in countenance by a
> sprinkling of regular sportsmen arrayed in self-conscious majesty
> and leggins, leading dogs and carrying hammerless, breech-loading

guns of famous makers. Over the fine landscapes the killing goes forward with shameful enthusiasm. After escaping countless dangers, thousands fall, big bagfuls are gathered, many are left wounded to die slowly, no Red Cross Society to help them. Next day, Sunday, the blood and leggins vanish from the most devout of the bird-butchers, who go to church, carrying gold-headed canes instead of guns. After hymns, prayers, and sermon they go home to feast, to put God's song birds to use, put them in their dinners instead of in their hearts, eat them, and suck the pitiful little drumsticks. It is only race living on race, to be sure, but Christians singing Divine Love need not be driven to such straits while wheat and apples grow and the shops are full of dead cattle. Song birds for food! Compared with this, making kindlings of pianos and violins would be pious economy.

The Gilded Age, with all its extravagance, wastefulness, disrespect, and adoration of money was to John's mind the sorry manifestation of a damaged spiritual life. Gilded was a good term: a thin layer of gold over a much baser substrate. Scratch away the thin, shiny paint and dullness broods beneath, stifling the soul, making us barely able to reflect back the divine light pouring down on the earth.

The publications that emerged in the final years of John's life were in many ways his most elegant and his most direct. Taken from notes and journals from the past, as well as from new insights, he captured the winds of change blowing through society. Ever stronger stirrings were showing signs that people were growing tired of nothing but creating money. More people were visiting nature and politicians were realizing they needed to connect with the zeitgeist if they were to stay in power. Now was the time to build on success before more precious landscapes and species were eradicated from the earth. All that solitude, hunger, exhaustion, ecstasy, divine insight, joy, and love were to come to fruition.

Robert Underwood Johnson had long been urging John to gather a group of influential people to speak out for the Sierra, and at last that became a reality in 1892. The Sierra Club was established on 28 May, not because John organized it but because of the energy and drive of some Californian academics. Its brief was "to explore, enjoy, and render accessible the mountain regions of the Pacific Coast; to publish authentic information concerning them", and "to enlist the support and cooperation of the people and government in preserving the forests and other natural features of the Sierra Nevada".

John was the overwhelming choice for leader, a position he occupied for the rest of his life. Over the years the membership grew from mainly dons to include businessmen, artists, writers, and other movers and shakers. John Muir was an intelligent choice as leader. He was a wilderness-loving American-Scotsman who looked like a prophet but dressed in a suit. He knew what it was like to do physical work for a living but was a successful businessman who lived in elegant luxury. He had an endearing, self-effacing manner and a keen way with words, both spoken and written. He was a tough mountaineer who had survived against the odds some of the most testing circumstances, and was therefore safely a man's man, yet he counted many women among his best friends. In fact, his women friends, both humble and prominent, had been a major influence throughout his life and he treasured their counsel. He seemed to be a walking representative of most sectors of society, speaking to all without alienating any particular group. His ability to make friends without compromising his beliefs spread firm glue over a varied membership.

The Sierra Club was not about keeping people out of the Sierra; only destructive industry. They actively encouraged day-trippers, naturalists, mountaineers, scientists, artists: indeed, anyone who wanted to experience unadulterated nature. But no sooner had the national parks been created than they came under threat from those dismayed that their commercial activities were being halted. Even a Californian Congressman, Camonetti, who had cattle ranchers in his constituency, tried to force a bill halving the size of the Yosemite Park. John's pen virtually spat out ink, as in "Forests of the Sierra" in 1889:

> If possible and profitable every tree, bush and leaf, with the soil they are growing on, and the whole solid uplift of the mountains

would be cut, blasted, scraped and shovelled and shipped away to any market home or foreign. Everything without exception, even to souls and geography, would be sold for money could a market be found for such articles.

Criticism is hard to take, especially when made publicly. John Irish, who had written for *Picturesque California*, which John edited, was also the secretary/treasurer of the Yosemite Commission, the body that had allowed the valley floor to be so badly abused. Stung by John's condemnation, he released a tirade of public abuse, calling John a liar, a libeller, and a hypocrite. He accused John of being part of the destruction when he worked for Hutchings' sawmill:

Muir logged and sawed the trees of the valley for commercial purposes, and the mill was finally suppressed by the State, which he now falsely accuses of "rapidly destroying all that is accessible and destructible in the valley."[3]

In fact, the only logs sawed at the mill were from trees that had come down in storms; not one was hand-felled. Although John refuted the allegations, they stuck around for years. A prominent figurehead is an easy target to shoot at, and John and the Sierra Club found themselves fighting battles on all fronts. They were cast wholesale into the rough world of politics and personal agendas.

Much as Robert Underwood Johnson supported John in these public spats, he had a bigger plan in mind; he wanted to expand protection to far more of America's wilderness. In 1893 he set about introducing John to some of the most important figures of the time. Through him John met the other nature-championing "Jonnie", the famed essayist and naturalist John Burroughs (often called "John of the Birds" while John Muir was referred to as "John of the Mountains"). They were virtually the same age and both passionate advocates of wilderness protection, but they were very different characters. Burroughs was quiet and retiring and eschewed company. His heart and feet were deeply rooted in the

Catskill Mountains in New York State and his pen urged people to find their joy in the normal and everyday life surrounding them. Why travel when there is so much to explore around you?

John Muir was almost the polar opposite. He was gregarious chatterer who sought solitude but felt lonely in it. He loved holding court, delighting everyone with his tales of adventures laced with fun and mimicry. Many recorded John as a better talker than writer and Burroughs as the opposite. Upon meeting, however, they bonded for life, but they didn't always get along. Burroughs sometimes found John's incessant talking and enthusiasm too much.

On one occasion, when John tried to convince Burroughs about his theories of glaciation, using his "contumacious quibbling" to argue every point, Burroughs despaired, "I love you, though at times I want to punch you or thrash the ground with you." Nevertheless, he held a lifelong admiration for John of the Mountains:

> He is a poet and almost a Seer. Something ancient and far-away in the look of his eyes. He could not sit down in the corner of the landscape, as Thoreau did, he must have a continent for his playground... Probably the truest lover of Nature... we have yet had... [But he is] a little prolix... Ask him to tell you his famous dog story and you will get the whole theory of glaciation thrown in.[4]

He was right. John was a true lover of nature, and talkative with it, but he was wrong about the continent. John needed a whole globe. As farm management was taken over by his brother David, his brother-in-law, John Reid, and his sisters, whom he had invited to live in Martinez, he took the opportunity to travel as well as write. In an extraordinary decade between 1893 and 1903 he was rarely at home. He made many trips that covered the breadth of America, gathering information for articles. He went to the forests of Yellowstone, the Black Hills, Idaho, Oregon, and Washington, to the Cascades, Santa Lucia, the Grand Canyon, Alaska, North Carolina, Tennessee, Alabama, the Canadian Rockies, Banff, Maine, and the St Lawrence River, to name but a few, as well as revisiting old haunts in the Sierra Mountains. His articles continued to combine enthusiasm with protection. Through his writing, he campaigned to make Mount Rainier a national park, and in 1899 it became a reality.

In Concord, Massachusetts, as part of Johnson's great east-coast trip, John finally managed to visit Emerson, as he had long hoped to do, but only to stand at his grave in Sleepy Hollow Cemetery: "It was seventeen years after our parting on Wawona ridge that I stood beside his grave under a pine tree on the hill above Sleepy Hollow. He had gone to higher Sierras, and, as I fancied, was again waving his hand in friendly recognition."[5]

Thoreau's grave, in the same place, also provided a time of deep reflection. John and Thoreau had shared the belief that "in wildness lies the hope of the world",[6] and many of John's words show how familiar he was with Thoreau's writing. Emerson and Thoreau, the two great Transcendentalists who had done so much to shape his thoughts, now lay together in peace and from across the divide seemed to send him their blessings. John was, however, surprised at the closeness of Walden Pond to civilization. The popular image of Thoreau was that of a hermit living in a rustic cabin by a lake, relying purely on his skill and love of the wild to survive. Bemused by this reputation he wrote, "It is only about one and a half or two miles from Concord, a mere saunter, and how people should regard Thoreau as a hermit on account of his little delightful stay here I cannot guess".[7]

The year 1893 also saw John take on a grand tour of Europe, partly for his own interest but also to expand his writing. He at last made it back to Scotland, including Edinburgh and his home town of Dunbar, and then went to England, Ireland, Norway, Switzerland, France, and Italy. In Dumfries he paid homage to his mentor and inspiration, Robert Burns. A few years later he wrote:

> Wherever a Scotsman goes, there goes Burns. His grand whole, Catholic soul squares with the good of all; therefore we find him in everything, everywhere. Throughout these last hundred and ten years, thousands of good men have been telling God's love; but the man

who has done most to warm human hearts and bring to light the kinship of the world, is Burns, Robert Burns, the Scotsman.[8]

In the Lake District, he paid an emotional visit to the grave of yet another giant figure in his life, William Wordsworth. He stood in silent contemplation, moved beyond words by the spirit of this giant drifting among the glacial lakes and rugged hills surrounding Grasmere. John had stood on Wordsworth's powerful shoulders and glimpsed great beauty. His poems were shot through with divine presence, as well as with ideals of an egalitarian society founded in nature, and they had brought light to many hours of solitude in John's early years. In a letter to Louie, he wrote, "I never before saw a place where I was so anxious to have you with me to enjoy it… Here are some leaves I picked for you from the branches leaning over Wordsworth's grave."[9]

So much time away meant that Louie and the girls must have struggled to remember what he looked like. Some of John's family, who were helping to run the farm, provided company for Louie in the large house, particularly after Mrs Strenzel died in 1895, but there is no arguing that John missed many birthdays and special celebrations and that he was largely an absent father once his intensive fruit-growing years were over. In fact we get an insight into what the local people thought of John Muir and his extensive peripatetic wanderings, in a rare note of criticism from a letter written in 1984 by Myra Honneger, who was a neighbour of the Muirs:

Dr and Mrs Strenzel had built a lovely big home on a small knoll on the outskirts of Martinez – the building which now is a shrine to John Muir – and there the Muirs lived. Two daughters were born of this union, Helen and Wanda. They saw very little of their father for the "Call of the Great Outdoors" was in John Muir's blood and he would suddenly disappear to be gone for many months at a time, to return unannounced when he had completed his expedition. Louise loved as always, by her friends, but the local people looked upon John Muir as a ne'er-do-well who neglected his family.[10]

Even when he was at home, he was locked in his "scribbling den", as he called his study. All his notes and journals ended up on the floor, providing a growing pile of chaos that he likened to glacial debris, which he hoped would be sifted and winnowed by some unknown force into a useable array of data. Eventually that force would take the form of Marion Parsons, a friend and assistant, but until then papers lay scattered everywhere.

Somehow, after much haranguing and harassing by Johnson and others, *The Mountains of California* was published in 1894. This collection of essays stands as a classic example of nature writing where science and passion sit alongside delightful portraits of animals. It set a bright tone that rang through the corridors of power.

John's vision of harmony with nature remained elusive, however. Forestry became a major cause of contention. At first, he was convinced that the innate love of the wild could be ignited in anyone, given time and a visit to the trees he loved most. In a *Sierra Club Bulletin*, John wrote:

> Few are altogether deaf to the preaching of pine trees. Their
> sermons on the mountains go to our hearts; and if people in general
> could be got into the woods, even for once, to hear the trees speak
> for themselves, all difficulties in the way of forest preservation would
> vanish.[11]

The first forest reserves were signed into law by the outgoing president, Grover Cleveland, in 1896. He suggested thirteen sites totalling 21 million acres, on the recommendation of a report that John had helped create. The laws governing the reserves forbade grazing and logging. The Chief Forester at the time, Gifford Pinchot, disagreed with this ruling, and so did many graziers, landowners, and businesses – so much so that the reserves would not be created for two years while a vicious storm raged. Pinchot had camped with Muir in the Grand Canyon back in 1896 and the two men had been good friends. When Pinchot wrote against the reserves, however, saying sheep did not damage forests, John and he fell out. Pinchot was a "wise use" supporter, believing all of nature was at our disposal to use carefully for our own good. His statement on forests summarized his ideology:

The object of our forest policy is not to preserve the forests because they are beautiful or wild or the habitat of wild animals, it is to ensure a steady supply of timber for human prosperity. Every other consideration is secondary.[12]

John was furious. In 1630, at the beginning of the European settlement of America, forests covered almost 50 per cent of the land. By the end of the nineteenth century that had been reduced to 34 per cent, and most of that deforestation had occurred in John's lifetime. Enough, he cried; we have destroyed too much. Articles such as "The American Forests", published in 1897, contain a tirade of despair and downright anger:

Any fool can destroy trees. They cannot run away; and if they could, they would still be destroyed, chased and hunted down as long as fun or a dollar could be got out of their bark hides, branching horns or magnificent bole backbones.[13]

John urged the government to take responsibility and go ahead with the reserves because, without laws and enforceable penalties, nothing would stop the destruction:

Few that fell trees plant them; nor would planting avail much towards getting back anything like the noble primeval forests... It took more than three thousand years to make some of the trees in these Western woods — trees that are still standing in perfect strength and beauty, waving and singing in the mighty forests of the Sierra. Through all the wonderful, eventful centuries ... God has cared for these trees, saved them from drought, disease, avalanches, and a thousand straining, levelling tempests and floods; but he cannot save them from fools — only Uncle Sam can do that.[14]

To those, like Pinchot, who would use the argument that forests provided a uniquely useful resource that was needed not only for America's benefit but also for export, he retorted:

> No doubt these trees would make good lumber after passing through a sawmill, as George Washington after passing through the hands of a French cook would have made good food.[15]

In 1897 articles in *Harper's Weekly* and *Atlantic Monthly* created yet more popular support for wilderness preservation. When a collection of articles was published as *Our National Parks* in 1901, America was in no doubt that wild places, particularly forests, needed ever more protection:

> Thoreau, when contemplating the destruction of the forests on the east side of the continent, said that soon the country would be so bald every man would have to grow whiskers to hide its nakedness, but he thanked God that at least the sky was safe. Had he gone West he would have found out that the sky was not safe; for all through the summer months, over most of the mountain regions, the smoke of mill and forest fires is so thick and black that no sunbeam can pierce it. The whole sky, with clouds, sun, moon and stars, is simply blotted out.[16]

Sometimes fate is kind. Concerned words and voices reach those who have not only sympathy but also power. Seeds scattered by a variety of sowers just occasionally land on fertile ground and take root. It is a testament to the status of John Muir that the president of the United States, Theodore Roosevelt, chose him in 1903 to be his guide in the Yosemite: "I do not want anyone with me but you, and I want to drop politics absolutely for four days and just be out in the open with you."[17]

The timing meant John had to reorganize the start of a world tour, but it was an invitation he could not refuse. This was a chance to brush with real power and effect change. As they rode off the beaten track, both men wanted to dominate the conversation and both wanted to show how much they knew about nature. Roosevelt was surprised that John couldn't name as many birds as he could. John, however, waxed lyrical about plants. Sleeping outside and waking up covered in a dusting of snow added natural authenticity to a highly political meeting. Roosevelt remembered the trip as a delight and described John as "second only to John Burroughs and in some respects ahead".[18] John also wrote to Louie that he had thoroughly enjoyed his "hearty and manly" company.[19]

Roosevelt was in many ways the right man at the right time as far as nature was concerned. He was a passionate bird lover and needed no convincing that humanity could flourish and prosper only on a vibrant planet. To degrade the earth was pure foolishness. In his inaugural address to Congress in 1901 he wrote, "There can be no greater issue than that of conservation in this country. Just as we must conserve our men, women and children, so we must conserve the resources of the land on which they live."

That's not to say that this savvy politician, who had risen to the heights of the presidency, didn't understand the public value of standing on Glacier Point with the nation's favourite wilderness prophet. For the same reason he had met with Burroughs too. Nevertheless, the Roosevelt–Muir camping trip has been heralded as the most important conservation meeting in American history. John showered the president with urgent and eloquent words about protecting many of America's wildernesses. Set against a backdrop of a sublime landscape and its wildlife, this heady combination galvanized Roosevelt into action. During his presidency Roosevelt established five national parks, fifteen national nature reserves, fifty-five national bird sanctuaries and wildlife refuges, and one hundred and fifty national forests.

After the trip John kept up the pressure, lobbying whenever and wherever he could for the Yosemite Valley to be given over to federal control and absorbed into the national park. In 1905 John, the Sierra Club, Johnson, and many others celebrated the enlarged

Yosemite National Park.

Roosevelt was the president who is acclaimed for his love of nature, especially birds. He declared that:

> [b]irds should be saved for utilitarian reasons; and, moreover, they should be saved because of reasons unconnected with dollars and cents. A grove of giant redwoods or sequoias should be kept just as we keep a great and beautiful cathedral. The extermination of the passenger pigeon meant that mankind was just so much poorer...
> And to lose the chance to see frigate-birds soaring in circles above the storm, or a file of pelicans winging their way homeward across the crimson afterglow of the sunset, or a myriad of terns flashing in the bright light of midday as they hover in a shifting maze above the beach – why, the loss is like the loss of a gallery of the masterpieces of the artists of old time.[20]

Roosevelt was so appalled by the obliteration of the Plains bison that he assisted in its rehabilitation by co-founding the American Bison Society in 1905. And in 1908 he signed into law the Antiquities Act, which protected archaeological sites, including Native American sites, all over the continent. During his presidency he protected 230 million acres of public land and there is no doubt that, as the leading voice for nature conservation in the country at that time, John helped create the milieu to make this possible.

Roosevelt differed from John, however, in his love of hunting. He had caught and killed animals from boyhood and believed that strenuous, masculine pursuits made men strong physically and mentally. In 1909, just after his presidency ended, he travelled through Africa and his party shot and trapped 11,400 animals, 1,000 of which were large game, including six rare white rhinos. Most were transported back to America and ended up as specimens in the Smithsonian and other museums. "I can be condemned only if the existence of the National Museum, the American Museum of Natural History, and all similar zoological institutions are to be condemned," he wrote in his defence.[21]

After the auspicious camping trip with Roosevelt, John left on an exhausting world tour with the hope of writing more articles and books. He visited London, Paris, Berlin, Russia, Finland, Siberia, Korea, Japan, China, Egypt, Ceylon, Australia, New Zealand, Malaysia, Indonesia, the Philippines, Hong Kong, and Hawaii. Such a schedule took its toll on his health and endurance, but he still managed to climb the Mueller Glacier on Mount Cook in New Zealand at the age of sixty-five.

For all John's despair at the rapidity with which tourists went to the Yosemite and other natural treasures in America, he himself sped over continents at an astonishing rate. Apart from some glacial observations in the Alps, disappointingly little writing came out of the trips. There is no doubt that he found many places simply overwhelming, but everything went by too fast to be absorbed and processed into crafted words. It made him, however, one of the best-travelled men of his generation.

Constant travelling removed John from political fights, but it also meant he was thousands of miles away when his lifelong friend Jeanne Carr died in December 1903. She had been suffering from dementia. Her brother-in-law, Elijah Melanthon Carr, wrote, "Her last days were peaceful, she gradually sank to her rest and did not seem to suffer much pain."[22]

By 1905 John was lacking his youthful robustness. He was now sixty-seven years old and through the winter suffered from flu and bronchitis. His younger daughter, Helen, too was seriously ill with an inflamed lung. To help them both, John, Helen, and Wanda left Louie at home and travelled to Arizona to benefit from the healing powers of desert air. As their lungs began to dry out word came from home that Louie was seriously ill with pneumonia. John and Wanda left Helen, who was still far from well, and found Louie nearing death. In fact it was a tumour that was affecting her breathing. After six painful weeks she died, aged fifty-eight, with John at her bedside.

The marriage of Louie and John had been strong and devoted, despite many long absences on John's part. Helen wrote a tribute to her mother saying it would be wrong to consider her a martyr in any way to her famous, peripatetic husband. She willingly and gladly made his success her goal and much preferred to stay at home where she could delight in flowers, poetry, and music rather than endure rough travel. She was an accomplished pianist and horticulturalist and competent at running the estate. She thrived when surrounded by beauty and created delightful and fragrant gardens. She was a trusted critic when John sent her draft manuscripts. The passing of this bright, intelligent, and supportive soul left a raw hole in John's life.

The rambling manse now seemed empty and lonely. He felt guilty at leaving her for so long, unaware of how ill she had become. He had written in 1872 that "Earth has no sorrow that earth cannot heal;"[23] it was a direct reference to the 1816 hymn by Thomas Moore, "Come Ye Disconsolate". But instead of heading to the mountains for solace, as Roosevelt recommended, John returned to Arizona to be with his daughters.

In eastern Arizona he distracted himself by studying the Petrified Forest, an area of extraordinary fossilized tree stumps dating back 225 million years to when Arizona was an area of wet subtropical forest. In 1906 Roosevelt made the Petrified Forest a national monument, and John provided maps of the possible boundaries.

The loss of Louie shook John's life to its foundation and once back in Martinez he slowly tried to rebuild. His world had changed forever now that his wife was dead and his daughters grown up. Helen stayed in Arizona for the rest of her life, eventually marrying there, and Wanda married in June 1906 and moved out to live in a house nearby with her husband. John was left alone with Ah Wong, the houseman and cook.

On 18 April 1906, at just after 5 a.m., he was woken by another earth-shattering event described by his friend Charles Keeler:

> The earth tremors increased in violence, and rose and took
> possession of the walls, shaking them so that masonry and timbers
> crunched and creaked and groaned. There was a sickening sensation
> as if everything was toppling… After forty-eight tumultuous

seconds, every one of which was packed with sensations of destruction, followed a bewildering calm.[24]

The earthquake was not only a terrible tragedy, killing 3,000 people and destroying over 80 per cent of San Francisco, but it sealed the fate of the place John had termed the Sierra's "other Yosemite", the Hetch Hetchy Valley. The valley sat securely inside the national park boundary, supposedly safe from exploitation. As the population of San Francisco grew, however, so did their demands for water, and planners repeatedly turned their eyes to the valley as a perfect site for a reservoir. By damming the Tuolumne River running through it, plenty of water could be accumulated to provide for the city's needs.

The city repeatedly tried to force the legislation through but was rebuffed time and again by farmers, who relied on the river to irrigate the land downstream, and because of its status as a protected area. The earthquake, however, revealed just how old and inadequate the water supply to the city was. Many pipes had been damaged and water became a priority. Just six weeks after the earthquake, John's nemesis, the nation's Chief Forester Gifford Pinchot, started his campaign to make Hetch Hetchy the reservoir to supply San Francisco.

As a practical forester and a canny politician, Pinchot saw utility before beauty, and in Hetch Hetchy he saw a well-placed reservoir rather than a temple to God's glory. This was the start of a seven-year battle that was full of rage and unbridled aggression. In 1908 in a *Sierra Club Bulletin* John wrote:

> These temple destroyers, devotees of ravaging commercialism, seem to have a perfect contempt for Nature, and, instead of lifting their eyes to the God of the mountains, lift them to the Almighty Dollar.
>
> Dam Hetch Hetchy! As well dam for water-tanks the people's cathedrals and churches, for no holier temple has ever been consecrated by the heart of man.[25]

Pinchot, advocating his "wise use" principles, believed, however, that "the highest possible use which could be made of it would be to supply pure water to a great centre of population".[26]

Andrew Carnegie, the immensely wealthy and successful industrialist who had met Muir and occasionally corresponded with him, sided with Pinchot:

> John Muir is a fine Scotchman, like my friend John Burroughs; but for all that it is too foolish to say that the imperative needs of a city to a full and pure water supply should be thwarted for the sake of a few trees or for scenery, no matter how beautiful it might be.[27]

Insults poured in against John, the Sierra Club, and all those who were opposed to the dam. Congressman William Kent called Muir "a man entirely without social sense. With him, it is me and God and the rock where God put it, and that is the end of the story."[28] San Francisco's city engineer, Marsden Manson, called the preservationists "short-haired women and long-haired men".[29] *The San Francisco Chronicle* called John's camp "hoggish and mushy aesthetes".[30]

Many bitter and personal fights soured John's last years. Some people whom John had thought of as friends and colleagues also failed to support him, either because, like Carnegie, they agreed with Pinchot's ideas, or because they wanted to stay on the right side of officialdom. Prominent members of the Sierra Club also decided to support the dam, afraid of being identified as effeminate and flower-loving. In one spiteful cartoon John was portrayed as a fussy old woman in a black dress and bonnet, sweeping the floor but failing to hold back the tide of progress, represented by a giant waterfall in the background, about to engulf him. "All these long-haired sentimentalists will be swept away by the forces sweeping modern America", was the message. It was a cruel depiction; John was as far from a weak old lady as it was possible to get. Few if any of John's detractors could have matched him for sheer ruggedness.

It was also unfair. John was not opposed to progress; he had welcomed a railway line through his land and he understood that society needed to evolve and adapt – after all, he had been part of the industrial progress in his days as an inventor. He was under no illusion that some of nature had to be used to provide that development. What he was not prepared to relinquish was the belief that national parks like Yosemite could suddenly be considered fair game.

John worked at finding a compromise. He was prepared to see a road built to carry tourists to Hetch Hetchy so that more could benefit from its beauty. He even proposed a "grand circular drive" so that most people could see both valleys from a car. The dam supporters argued that a reservoir would actually improve Hetch Hetchy, by providing a glorious and sparkling lake. Even Roosevelt wavered, saying it could be saved only if the people of California wanted it left untouched. Leafleting and campaigns in newspapers raged on, leaving John's party at a disadvantage, as their funds could not match those of the pro-dam lobbyists. At last the fate of the valley was debated in Congress in 1913 and the dam was approved by forty-three votes to twenty-five, with twenty-nine abstentions. Woodrow Wilson's administration then paved the way for the O'Shaughnessy dam to be built, and work began in 1919.

The loss of Hetch Hetchy was a severe blow to a man already laid low by grief and bouts of illness. It left John with immense questions about what he had actually achieved, if such a jewel in nature's crown could be betrayed so easily. Was nature to be protected only as long as people could not see a use for it? Was commitment to the preservation of the wilderness really a shallow sham when put to the test? Forever the optimist who looked for good in all situations, he comforted himself that at least this fiasco had put the case for protecting the wild out into an even wider domain. Now more people were aware of the arguments and must surely put that to some good in the future. He then tried to put it all behind him.

The final years of John's life were marred by loss of all kinds. Joseph LeConte, the famed geologist and supporter of John's theories on glaciation, died in the Yosemite on the eve of a Sierra Club outing in 1901. As we have seen, Jeanne Carr died in 1903, the same year as John's sister Annie. The great botanist and friend J. D. Hooker and the artist William Keith both died in 1911. Other close friends, some of whom he had known since he was a young man, passed away one after the other. He wrote to Helen, "I wonder if leaves feel lonely when they see their neighbours falling."[31]

Worried that time was passing and that since 1901 John had written nothing but campaign leaflets, in 1908 friends persuaded him to finish his books and write his memoirs. He found it hard to do; there was so much to be assembled from piles of notes and illegible scraps that he was overwhelmed. Eventually a friend, the railway magnate E. H. Harriman, who had funded one of the Alaska trips in 1899, invited John to stay at his summer home in the Upper Klamath Lake region of Oregon, a beautiful, rural idyll free from distractions. He also provided John with a male secretary to follow him around and jot down everything he remembered about his childhood and youth. Wherever John went, he was pursued with pen and paper. He drove John relentlessly, applying his mantra, "Much good work is lost for the lack of a little more", to his ageing, reluctant house guest. "I don't know when I'll get away and get free from this beneficent bondage," he complained to Helen.[32] The hard task-mastering worked, however, as John delivered over 1,000 pages of manuscript of memories of Scotland and early days in Wisconsin, which would eventually end up as *My Boyhood and Youth*, published in 1913.

In the midst of all the political wrangling, John knew he had to finish the books he so wanted to leave as his legacy. In 1910, he wrote to his friend Mrs Hooker, "As for myself I have been reading through old musty dusty Yosemite notes until I'm tired and blinky blind, trying to arrange them into something like lateral, medial and terminal moraines on my den floor."[33] He managed it, though, and in 1911 *My First Summer in Sierra* appeared and then in 1912 *The Yosemite* was published.

In 1911, John also realized the dream he had been cherishing since he was a boy. On 12 August he left New York for South

America. He travelled up the Amazon River and explored the rainforests of Brazil and Chile. Over the following months he also went to South Africa, East Africa, Egypt, and Italy.

On 21 April 1914 John became seventy-six years old. That year he received his third honorary degree, this one a Doctor of Laws from the University of California. In 1896 he had been given a University Diploma from Harvard and in 1911 a Doctorate of Letters from Yale. Over the decades he had influenced Americans from all walks of life, from three presidents to workers in the cities. He had introduced a fresh, inspiring take on the presence of God in nature and had presented the wilderness as a welcoming, delightful grove for play and prayer for all. Here everyone could experience divine love and hear the earth sing constant praise. He had survived wild adventures on glaciers, mountain tops, and deserts. He had wandered for months on end in solitude, eating little and drinking river water, just like a true prophet. In the mountains he had met American wildlife face to face and loved it all. Birds, beasts, flowers, and giant trees he had absorbed into his heart. He had encountered his Maker in the blissful landscapes of an astonishingly beautiful and varied continent and had taken every challenge with a good heart. He had fashioned personal pain into joy. He had also contributed unprecedented evidence for the power of glaciers in shaping the land which was increasingly gaining acceptance. Now he was very tired.

The year 1914 was auspicious on many accounts. On 28 July the world went to war with itself. Over 17 million people died; 10 million soldiers and 7 million civilians. It was the bloodiest conflict in human history. In September the last passenger pigeon, the only survivor of the most numerous bird on the planet, died in Cincinnati Zoo. She was named Martha and was viewed as the embodiment of extinction caused by mankind. In December John left his home in the Alhambra Valley to see his daughter Helen in the southern part of California. He had been invited to lead a Sierra Club trip and longed to go, but yet again his lungs were suffering badly. He was keen to heal his relationship with Helen, which had become frayed as she had married without his knowledge and led a life far removed from his own in ideals and aspiration.

Helen was so alarmed by his condition that she immediately sent him to Los Angeles hospital. Early in the morning on Christmas Eve he died alone in his room, unable to breathe as his lungs filled with fluid. There was no one there to hold his hand or record his last words, but his bed was covered in notes on Alaska. Perhaps, as he slipped away, he was once more breathing deeply the blasts of Arctic air that blew off the "ice fountains" in those high, cold valleys.

His funeral, held on 28 December 1914, was beautiful and simple. It was a calm sunny day and he was laid to rest next to Louie. Friends and neighbours gathered and eulogies poured in, many deeply moving. Perhaps the grief of Ah Wong sums up what many felt that day. *The San Francisco Chronicle* published a description of the mourners standing by John's grave:

> Nearby, his hat in his hand, and sad-faced, waited Wong, for twenty-five years the faithful servant of Muir. He stood a little apart from the others. He was motionless, but there was that in his eyes that made you turn away from the sight of him with a strange something gripping at your throat.[34]

The great and the good wrote their memories of John, including Robert Underwood Johnson: "To some, beauty seems but an accident of creation: to Muir it was the very smile of God. He sung the glory of nature like another Psalmist, and, as a true artist, was unashamed of his emotions."[35] William Frederic Badè, whom Wanda and Helen had asked to be the literary executor of John's writings, wrote:

> To all who knew John Muir intimately, his gentleness and humaneness toward all creatures that shared the world with him was one of the finest attributes of his character. He was ever looking

forward to the time when our wild fellow creatures would be granted
their indisputable right to a place in the sun. The shy creatures of
forest and plain have lost in him an incomparable lover, biographer,
and defender.[36]

Reverend Samuel Young felt keenly the loss of this giant of a
man who had saved his life and caused him to redefine his own
spirituality amid the ice of Alaska:

> I cannot think of John Muir as dead, or as much changed from the
> man with whom I canoed and camped. He was too much a part of
> nature – too natural – to be separated from his mountains, trees and
> glaciers. I am sure he is making other explorations, solving other natural
> problems, using that brilliant inventive genius to good effect; and
> sometime again I shall hear him unfold anew, with still clearer insight
> and more eloquent words, fresh secrets of his "mountains of God".[37]

John left behind a world in transition. He had lived through a time
of immense change in North America and that continued apace.
Throughout the twentieth century it became the most powerful
nation on earth. The battles continue over nature's role in American
society, but today there are 58 national parks, 108 national
monuments, 155 national forests, 14 marine protected areas, and
many other refuges, wilderness areas, and preservation sites.

John Muir is forever regarded as the greatest advocate of the
wild, nurturing a national awareness of the continent's beauty
and stirring innate feelings of love and pride. Without his tireless
enthusiasm there is no doubt America would be far poorer than
it is today. The Sierra Club boasts over a million members and
John was its first president and figurehead. As Donald Worster, the
environmental historian and John Muir's biographer, wrote:

> Muir would henceforth be identified as the greatest founder of the
> conservation movement, even though others preceded him, others
> showed up at critical moments, and others contributed important

ideas. He was always a reluctant leader, diffident and inclined to head for the hills when he heard the call to arms. What he gave the movement was, nonetheless, indispensable: the compelling image and words of a prophet standing before unsullied nature in a posture of unabashed love. That love of nature was both rhapsodical and worldly, a love that knew no bounds but knew how to compromise. He inspired Americans to believe that nature deserved higher consideration. Plenty of others shared that belief, but no one articulated it better.[38]

At the time of his death he had written five books. *The Mountains of California* (1894), *Our National Parks* (1901), *My First Summer in Sierra* (1911), *The Yosemite* (1912) and *The Story of My Boyhood and Youth* (1912). Marion Parsons, a family friend and literary helper of John in his final months, finished collating his writings on Alaska which were published posthumously as *Travels in Alaska* (1915). William Badè assembled three more books, *A Thousand-Mile Walk to the Gulf* (1916), *The Cruise of the Corwin* (1917) and *Steep Trails* (1918). Muir is credited with developing a new genre in nature writing. James Bryce, the distinguished historian and professor of civil law at Oxford University, greatly admired his work:

> The very air of the granite peaks, the very fragrance of the deep solemn forest, seem to breathe around us and soothe our senses as we read the descriptions of his lonely wanderings in the Sierras when their majesty was first revealed…You of the Club will cherish the memory of a singularly pure and simple character, who was in his life all that a worshiper of nature ought to be.[39]

The Muir name is now used by many schools, businesses, and parklands, and the Muir Glacier, Mount Muir, Muir Inlet, and the Muir Woods National Monument forever enshrine his spirit. Even a minor planet whirling in space between Earth and Jupiter is named after him. Statues, quotes, and books for all tastes and ages pay him tribute. John Muir is still infused into the life of America and continues to inspire people to protect nature, grand and humble, through the Sierra Club and in Britain The John Muir Trust works to protect wild places.

Muir's legacy lives on in those who carry his spirit forward. Perhaps, however, it is best to end with John's own words, envisioning the time when he would be freed from the constraints of his body to go anywhere and everywhere with no ties or responsibilities, only called by instinct and a desire to get ever closer to the mind of God:

If my soul could get away from this so-called prison, be granted all the list of attributes generally bestowed on spirits, my first ramble on spirit-wings would not be among the volcanoes of the moon. Nor should I follow the sunbeams to their sources in the sun. I should hover about the beauty of our own good star. I should not go moping among the tombs, not around the artificial desolation of men. I should study Nature's laws in all their crossings and unions; I should follow magnetic streams to their source and follow the shores of our magnetic oceans. I should go among the rays of the aurora, and follow them to their beginnings, and study their dealings and communions with other powers and expressions of matter. And I should go to the very centre of our globe and read the whole splendid page from the beginning. But my first journeys would be into the inner substance of flowers, and among the folds and mazes of Yosemite's falls. How grand to move about in the very tissue of falling columns, and in the very birthplace of their heavenly harmonies, looking outward as from windows of ever-varying transparency and staining![40]

John Muir Today:
Some Thoughts on His Legacy

In some ways John Muir was a man of his time, but in others he stands aside from dates on a calendar and speaks to all generations. His legacy is intertwined with how we view wilderness and the role we see nature playing in our increasingly citified lives.

Today the battle for Hetch Hetchy continues in many different places around the world. Whether it is on the savannah of East Africa, where economic development is pitched against the needs of wildlife, or in the UK where the needs of songbirds to eat insects is hard to reconcile with the requirement to produce large amounts of cheap food, the bread versus beauty argument is alive and well. It is also played out in the ivory trade, in whaling, in the rapidly expanding palm oil industry and so on. There is barely any part of the earth where the needs and desires of people are not pitched full-square against nature. We still debate whether wild areas are luxuries today's crowded planet can no longer afford. Is it far better to use the resources of all parts of the earth for the health and development of humanity? Or are there some places that provide us with an inspiring manifestation of existence beyond our needs and we have a moral duty to protect them for ourselves and those yet to come? Or perhaps it is fair game and good commercial sense to make large profits quickly by stripping natural resources before anyone else? Behind it all though are 7 billion people with an innate desire for beauty. To lose wilderness to practicalities is to degrade our souls, or as Professor E O Wilson puts it, "Burning a rainforest for economic gain is like burning a Renaissance painting to cook a meal."[1]

Whether it is Pinchot's "wise use" or rampant commercialisation for short term gain or Muir's long-term commitment to nature, all positions are still present today. They may have different protagonists, but the battle seems to be eternal, as Muir knew it would be.

> The battle we have fought, and are still fighting, for the forests is a part of the eternal conflict between right and wrong, and we cannot expect to see the end of it… So we must count on watching and striving for these trees, and should always be glad to find anything so surely good and noble to strive for.[2]

Today the beauty argument is underlined by a more in-depth understanding of the role of intact ecosystems that keep the planet functioning in a way that suits our needs. Without wetlands, forests, mountains, grasslands, protected oceans and so on, we lose the ability to clean water, cleanse the air, fix soils and provide habitat for pollinators and other essential wildlife that provide for our health and well-being. Beauty now has a more practical, even a financial edge that was not considered in the nineteenth century. "Ecosystem services" and the market value of nature have entered the fray, an attempt to persuade economists that nature provides many valuable services that we don't account for in financial planning. It isn't enough to settle the debate yet though.

However for me John Muir provides more than one side of an argument, he allows me to relax in the face of so much debate and concern. When I think of John Muir I smile inside. His legacy is an outpouring of unsullied love for nature which is as relevant today as in the nineteenth century. He treasured the natural world truly, deeply, and sincerely. When in the presence of a flower or a mountain, he was lifted out of his own skin and was transported upwards and beyond, full of joy and respect. He saw fun and excitement, majesty and wonder everywhere. He saw creatures with characters and landscapes with moods. God was as present in the waving branches of a tree as in the devastating grinding of tectonic plates. He didn't pretend to have easy answers but was prepared to open himself to the unfolding story of the earth. He cared little for his own concerns when faced with the ineffable mystery of this living, vibrant world. That is refreshing in a world where humanity appears to be so weighed-down and inward-looking.

That is not to say he thought we could live on inspiration. He understood the practicalities of life and had no doubt that part of the earth should be use for our needs, but he had a strong and unerring conviction that there were some areas that were simply too special to be used for anything other than pleasure and prayer.

Of course the world is very different today from the time when John Muir walked the earth. In the last decades of the nineteenth century, when he was lost in love-filled wanderings throughout America and beyond, the total world population was around 1.3 billion people; today it is over 7 billion. Humanity is more crowded together, uses more resources, and has more opportunities than ever before, putting the earth under increasing strain. We can now add to that worrying list a further fact: the momentous changes being wrought by our warming climate. Can the thoughts of a man of the mountains, now dead for a century, impart anything meaningful today?

The beauty of John Muir is that he doesn't provide a handbook for modern environmentalists. What he offers is more timeless. He has left a mindset of love and respect for the natural world that penetrates down through the complex layers of "environmental issues" to the very bedrock of what it is to be human. His gift is to constantly remind us of who and what we are, no matter what our present circumstances.

The earth for Muir was not an "issue" to be dealt with or a set of problems to be solved. It glows with a divine presence and is a source of inspiration. His philosophy took God out of theological straitjackets and allowed every rock, as well as every living thing, to quiver with life. This sense of otherness and enthusiasm is infectious and helps us forge a way through problems with a light heart.

John Muir's spirituality was not confined to the earth. He gazed beyond our breathable atmosphere and saw a universe pulsating with energy through time and space. How it came into being and where it was destined to end he could not say: all he knew was that it was a privilege to be part of the mystery.

His battles to save forests and mountains from short-termism were based on his moral conviction that destruction is desecration. To destroy beauty is to destroy sacredness. Very little of that mindset is present in today's compartmentalized world. Few environmentalists talk of the earth as a spiritual mystery and few religions, Christian or otherwise, talk passionately about the destruction of the planet. This is a pity, because Muir's approach touches many people who instinctively understand his spiritual yearnings as well as his desire to save the earth from needless ruin. He provides a bridge between two worlds that have drifted further and further apart over the last one hundred years. Reading his words makes it seem extraordinary that there was ever a rift at all.

"We have broken the great conversation with the earth," said the twentieth-century environmental theologian Thomas Berry.[3] John Muir would have agreed. It is time once again to converse with the rocks and play among the pines to learn the news, as Muir did in the Sierras and beyond, teaching us that living on a singing, vibrant planet is not a one-way relationship.

Muir was also an advocate of the growing re-discovery of simplicity. He ate simple foods, advocated restraint and personal sacrifice, and agreed with Thoreau that richness is not defined by a bank balance but by an absence of commercial stuff. He knew how to party when the time was right, but as a baseline for daily living his default position was one of modest requirements. His writings on gluttony, excessive use of meat and milk, and obsession with food ring true in many environmental circles today.

Muir thought the best way to preserve wilderness form commercial interests was to protect areas within set boundaries and to be governed by the state – National Parks. Perhaps his greatest legacy for most is as one of the founding fathers of the national park system. The first was Yellowstone and the idea, once established in America, spread worldwide. They are not areas just for nature though, they are specifically for people to enjoy in perpetuity. The idea is so ingrained that it is hard to imagine a time when this was far from desired. How does the concept of a national park fit into today's world?

I grew up about half an hour's drive from the Peak District National Park in the centre of England, a beautiful area covering 555 square miles. The northern section, called the Dark Peak, is a wild, millstone-grit moorland rising to 2,000 feet. Its distinctive rounded crags are used by climbers and the rugged, heather-clad moor is home to short-eared owls, mountain hares, and red grouse. The southern end of the park is completely different. Called the White Peak because of the underlying limestone rock, it changes character to soft green hills, white drystone walls, steep gorges cloaked in woodland, and clear rivers. It is a miniature Dordogne. Over 10 million people visit the Peaks each year, coming mainly from the surrounding cities of Manchester, Sheffield, Stoke-on-Trent, and Derby. It is an island of beauty surrounded by the industrial heartland of England.

The Peak District is the oldest of Britain's national parks, established in 1951, three-quarters of a century after the world's first national park, Yellowstone. It is, however, nothing like Yellowstone or Yosemite or the Grand Canyon, or any of the other traditional parks in America, not just because it can't boast the spectacular scenery, but also because people live and work in it. The national park system in the UK was imposed on an already heavily used and managed countryside. Unlike in the States, where people were moved out and the landscape protected in its "natural" state to ensure that it could be enjoyed in perpetuity, in Great Britain the grand concept of a national park was overlaid on working land.

People travelling to a British national park probably only know they have entered it if they spot a roadside sign. There are no gates and no fees to pay. The area called "National Park" is seamlessly meshed with the surrounding land, forming a continuum where life goes on inside the boundary pretty much as it does outside, with some extra regulations. John Muir's vision of a land set aside for nature, visited only by people who wish to replenish their soul surrounded by divine beauty, cannot be applied to the Peak District or indeed any of the national parks in the UK. They are certainly beautiful but they are not wildernesses. John Muir would be bemused by the high numbers of sheep that dot the hills, the numerous extractive industries, the forestry plantations, the villages, and the extensive road network. National parks in Britain are not what he had in mind.

The national parks in the UK are part of a continuum of types of protected land around the world, many of which take the name "National Park" but differ widely from the original concept in the amount of human involvement within their boundaries. Brand National Park, however, has been very successful. There are 113,000 national parks, or areas with similar protection, worldwide, and together they cover 6 per cent of the surface of the earth, equalling 57 million square miles. Very few of them are like the traditional parks of America, which have the highest level of protection, but all aim to give nature a prominent place to varying degrees. Protecting unchanging nature for future generations to enjoy is a powerful concept that seems to speak to humanity's heart, even though in reality what that means varies enormously. The term "national park" is therefore more like a brand than a template to be followed. Lord Bryce, the British Ambassador to America at the beginning of the nineteenth century, called the national park "the best idea you (Americans) ever had". But it was an idea that could not possibly be reproduced worldwide in its original form.

National parks have a lot more to contend with in today's crowded world. Pollution, disease, invasive species, and human pressure affect what happens inside their boundaries; outside the parks our consumption of fossil fuels has led to a change in climate that affects the whole planet.

In Glacier Bay National Park the ice is melting fast and glaciers are in retreat. Winters continue to get warmer and the melt season is longer. Since 1941, the Muir Glacier has retreated seven miles and thinned by over 2,500 feet. The US Geological Survey estimates that, if warming continues, the glaciers will be gone by 2030.

At the other end of the heat scale, the Joshua Tree National Park in the Mojave Desert in south-eastern California now has such warm winters that the ubiquitous Joshua trees, which need a cold season to flower and set seed, are dying in large numbers. A USGS report in 2011 estimated that 90 per cent of them will be eradicated from their current range in sixty to ninety years' time.

Even the giant sequoias, which so inspired John Muir, are struggling to survive. Natural regeneration has fallen markedly owing to a change in fire regimes, which has allowed competitors to take over. As old trees die and new seedlings find it hard to grow, even this serene symbol of permanence is groaning under the strain of the modern world. The giant sequoia is now classified by the IUCN (the International Union for the Conservation of Nature) as an endangered species. There is no doubt that America's national parks are in flux, despite the desire for the opposite.

The first part of the original statute for John Muir's national parks, that they remain unchanged, is therefore not a reflection of reality. The second, that future generations will have the opportunity to enjoy them, does not seem to be panning out either. The population of America is now nearly 320 million, an eightfold increase since Yellowstone was established. Despite this rapid rise, visitor rates to national parks are not keeping trend with the population figures. In the Yosemite the numbers visiting the park have fluctuated by half a million or so, but have basically remained the same since 1987, when they first reached over 3 million visitors a year (3,152,275 in 1987 and 3,691,191 in 2013). Only once did they hit 4 million, in 1996. Increasing numbers of people are not flocking to American parks, despite very strong public support for them.

What is this telling us? Are fewer people able to afford a trip? Are the traditional visitors to national parks, namely white and affluent people, an increasing minority? Are the new populace of America less inclined to spend their leisure time in such highly regulated areas, preferring places where more activities are allowed? Are the younger generation simply not interested in nature? Whatever the reason, in such a vast country with such a large population, national parks are just not seen as a mainstream attraction by the majority. Bear in mind that Disney World Florida receives about 17 million visitors a year. Perhaps American national parks, as envisioned by John Muir, are like classic literature: admired and well respected, but increasingly rarely experienced first-hand by new generations.

In the UK our problems are perhaps more complicated. The intricate human landscape weaves nature into its fabric as much as possible, but the balance between wilderness and people is the subject of a constant and sometimes bitter debate. Any discussion about the future of national parks in Britain has to include stakeholders and partners, such as farmers, businesses, industry, tourism, local communities, and environmental organizations. Some say the result is a mish-mash, in which the natural world has to fight its corner alongside strong human interests if it is to survive in such a competitive arena.

All this is a world away from when John Muir wandered the soaring peaks of the Sierra Nevada and dreamed of defending them for ever. We cannot look to John Muir for a list of action points to be completed by park managers, and we cannot assume a nineteenth-century mindset is necessarily appropriate everywhere today, but we can, as already suggested, rediscover his mindset.

One story about John Muir helps put his attitude into focus. In the Appalachian Mountains, he was accompanying an upright Victorian dignitary. Tears streamed down John's face as they looked at the sublime scenery. The dignitary was disconcerted by this "unmanly" show of emotion and pointed out that he didn't wear his heart on his sleeve. "Ah, my dear mon," said Muir in his broad accent, "in the face of such a scene as this, it's no time to be thinkin' o' where to wear your heart."[4]

Such a strong, unabashed love of nature that sweeps away all social niceties and conventions was at the root of John Muir's approach to anything to do with the natural world. No one could ever be in any doubt where he stood. Whether it was encouraging people to share his passion or fighting for the protection of wild places, it was love of the planet and the various forms of life on it that empowered him. He spoke his mind no matter who he found himself talking to and no matter how many insults he had to absorb. His mind was always focused on nature.

Often today it is not so easy to say who has taken up that baton. Embroiled as the modern conservation world is in finding ways for so many of us to live with nature, environmental language is shrouded in compromise and dense terminology. The natural world is now described by management speak and open to wide interpretation. "Sustainable development", "ecosystem services", and "biodiversity" are controlled by "stakeholder partnerships", "directives", and "rural planning", leaving many wondering where insects, mammals, birds, or trees fit in. As Peter Marren, a writer on wildlife, put it in an article for *The Independent* (14 September 2011), "The result is that, at a time when green issues are at the forefront of everyone's lives, we have somehow managed to overlook the greenest issue of all – wildlife."[5] William Frederic Badè, John's literary executor, captured the unique role John Muir played in conservation in his eulogy to him after his death: "The shy creatures of forest and plain have lost in him an incomparable lover, biographer, and defender."[6]

John Muir never veiled his passion in opaque terminology. The words he chose to express his love were clear and beautiful, and he agonized over each one. Someone once said environmentalists should never use words that couldn't be found in a poem; Muir certainly did just that, which is why his love shines out of every page and inspires people as much today as in the past.

Passionate as he was, John was not opposed to progress. It was never a case of people versus nature. He saw us as intricately involved with the fate of the earth, travelling through space and time together with our "fellow mortals". He welcomed roads, railways, and machines in the right places, designed them even, and wanted to see the lot of humanity released from endless grind into freedom and dignity. As he famously said when battling for Hetch Hetchy, he did not support blind opposition to progress, but was only opposed to blind progress.

Standing up for nature for its own sake, not just because it might be useful, reminding us of the sacredness of the earth and being a passionate political activist for the wild are important legacies of John Muir. There is however another aspect of his outlook, one less talked about or even recognized.

During the long years of labour on his father's farm in Wisconsin, John learned that kindness to animals was a fundamental step towards a new environmental ethic. Acts of kindness towards those who cannot reciprocate creates a different feel to the universe, and this, believed John, was the foundation of a just and peaceful world. Recognizing the human traits and shared experiences of animal and human life led him on a lifelong journey of kindness. Kindness is fundamental to all religious faiths, and John's strong Christian approach recognized kindness as a divine gift freely available to all. Kindness differs from compassion in that it is not a response to plight but a lifelong, daily act of giving with a gentle heart. Kindness is derived from the word "kin", meaning descended from a common ancestor. To live kindly is a selfless way of life that treats all as direct relations, be they human or not. Acts of kindness can involve personal sacrifice to make the path easier for those we meet, and for John that meant being kind to stones, trees, and all sentient life. Indeed, Theodore Roosevelt described John as "brimming over with friendliness and kindliness".[7]

Gifford Pinchot, John Muir's adversary who finally triumphed in the battle over Hetch Hetchy, illustrated the difference between living a kind life and a life of principle. When the two men camped together, Pinchot was amazed and bemused that John would not allow him to kill a tarantula that crawled near their camp. John insisted it was doing no harm and had a right to life. This idea was not one that sat easily in Pinchot's ethic. If nature was not useful then it was not embraced and welcomed. A tarantula was certainly not loved and not kin. Yet John Muir's kindness to all things is something that was commented on by many who knew him, and it remains as a warm glow surrounding his persona. Through simple acts of kindness, Muir lived his beliefs in a way that inspired those who witnessed them, and they still live on in his writings, giving others the desire to act. Lao Tzu, the ancient Chinese philosopher, understood the role that kindness plays in life:

> Kindness in words creates confidence. Kindness in thinking creates profoundness. Kindness in giving creates love.[8]

John Muir was a kind man, a kindness that sprang from his recognition of the interconnectedness of life. It is never a word that is heard in environmental circles today, but it is one that we would do well to consider as the basis for our actions towards life on earth.

The legacies of John Muir are profound and as relevant as ever. If he were alive today, what he would think of the state of the earth and how we are approaching solutions to our many environmental problems? No doubt he would write eloquently and inspiringly, urging us all to care and act on behalf of the wild places and their creatures. His words, though, would be laced with spirituality and humour. He would appeal to our sense of fun and our innate desire to look above and beyond the everyday to a higher meaning. Under his pen the earth would be transformed from a problem to a sparkling jewel whirling through space and time, and, like a precious object, we would want to care for it.

He would also go against the grain of modern environmental thinking and welcome people as a blessing on the earth. Muir never sank into cynicism about the true heart of humanity; he always believed that people were innately good if given the chance to reflect inside the balancing effect of nature.

The wrongs done to trees, wrongs of every sort, are done in the darkness of ignorance and unbelief, for when the light comes, the heart of the people is always right.[9]

Despite the destruction he witnessed he believed that reconnection with nature was the cure for uncaring actions and that, once sunlight was allowed through to the hardest of hearts, goodness would result.

But I think after the writing was done, the meetings attended, and the politicians lobbied, he would smile kindly and ask us to go with him along a mountain track and climb to higher planes. Here he would point out the beauty of a small flower and the power of the glacier. He would delight in an ouzel and chat to the pines, revelling in their stories of their wild lives. Then, as the sun set, we would rest with him under a giant sequoia and quietly listen to the beat of nature's warm heart. Only then, he would say, can we begin to formulate the answers to our environmental woes:

Oh, these vast, calm, measureless mountain days, inciting at once to work and rest! Days in whose light everything seems equally divine, opening a thousand windows to show us God. Nevermore, however weary, should one faint by the way who gains the blessings of one mountain day; whatever his fate, long life, short life, stormy or calm, he is rich forever.[10]

Bibliography

The most commonly referenced books have been abbreviated as follows:

EWDB: *The Eight Wilderness Discovery Books*, Diadem Books, 1992. (This is a collection of John Muir's most famous works: *The Story of My Boyhood and Youth, A Thousand Mile Walk to the Gulf, My First Summer in the Sierra, The Mountains of California, Our National Parks, The Yosemite, Travels in Alaska, Steep Trails*.)

KRS: Quotes from all correspondence between John Muir and Mrs Jeanne Carr are in *Kindred and Related Spirits*, edited by Bonnie Johanna Gisel, The University of Utah Press, 2001.

LLOW: *John Muir, His Life Letters and Other Works*, edited by William Frederic Badè, Bâton Wicks Publications, 1996.

JOM: *John of the Mountains: The Unpublished Journals of John Muir*, edited by Linnie Marsh Wolfe, University of Wisconsin Press, 1979.

Other sources of interest:

A collection of quotes in chronological order can be found in *John Muir In His Own Words: A Book of Quotations*, Peter Browning, Great West Books, 1988.

A recent extensive biography is *A Passion for Nature: The Life of John Muir*, Donald Worster, Oxford University Press, 2008.

Notes

Introduction

1. "Mormon Lilies", *San Francisco Daily Evening Bulletin*, 19 July 1877
2. "The Yellowstone National Park", *The Atlantic Monthly*, Vol. LXXXI, No. 486, April 1898
3. EWDB, *The Mountains of California*, Chapter 13
4. *ibid.*
5. EWDB, *My First Summer in Sierra*, Chapter 6, 27 July 1869
6. *ibid.*, Chapter 10, 30 August 1869
7. JOM, June 1890, p. 299

Chapter 1

1. Linnie Marsh Wolfe, *Son of the Wilderness: The Life of John Muir*, A. A. Knopf, 1945, p. 14
2. Frederick Turner, *John Muir: From Scotland to the Sierra – A Biography*, Canongate, 2014, p. 16
3. EWDB, *The Story of My Boyhood and Youth*, Chapter 1, p. 36
4. *ibid.*, p. 39
5. Obituary, published in *Portage Record*, 12 October 1885
6. Letter to Robert Underwood Johnson, 28 June 1896, quoted in Donald Worster, *A Passion for Nature*, Oxford University Press, 2008, p. 350
7. EWDB, *The Story of My Boyhood and Youth*, Chapter 1, p. 27
8. *ibid.*, p. 32
9. *ibid.*, p. 41
10. *ibid.*, p. 36
11. EWDB, *My First Summer in the Sierra*, Chapter 3, p. 218
12. EWDB, *The Story of My Boyhood and Youth*, Chapter 1, p. 28
13. *ibid.*, p. 35
14. *ibid.*, p. 33
15. *ibid.*, p. 40
16. *ibid.*, Chapter 2, p. 41
17. Alexander Wilson, *American Ornithology*, Vol. 1, Collins & Co., 1818–1829
18. EWDB, *The Story of My Boyhood and Youth*, Chapter 2, p. 42
19. Alexander Wilson, "The Fisherman's Hymn", *An American Anthology*, Edmund Clarence Stedman (ed.), 1787–1900
20. John James Audubon, "The Passenger Pigeon", *Ornithological Biography*, 1831, written to accompany his seminal work *The Birds of America*
21. *ibid.*
22. Alexander von Humboldt, *Cosmos*, Vol. 1, Introduction, George Bell, 1845
23. EWDB, *The Story of My Boyhood and Youth*, Chapter 1, p. 41
24. *ibid.*, p. 27

Chapter 2

1. EWDB, *The Story of My Boyhood and Youth*, Chapter 2, p. 42
2. *ibid.*
3. *ibid.*, p. 43
4. Roger Daniels, *Coming to America: A History of Immigration and Ethnicity in American Life*, Harper Collins, 1991
5. United States Census 1850
6. EWDB, *The Story of My Boyhood and Youth*, Chapter 2, p. 44
7. "Land Use History of North America", *USGS LUHNA project*, Chapter 6 and Jeanine M. Rhemtulla, "Regional land-cover conversion in the US upper Midwest: magnitude of change and limited recovery (1850–1935–1993)", *Landscape Ecol*, 2007, Vol. 22, pp. 57–75
8. EWDB, *The Story of My Boyhood and Youth*, Chapter 2, p. 45
9. John James Audubon, "The Red-headed Woodpecker", *Ornithological Biography*, Vol. 1, 1831
10. EWDB, *The Story of My Boyhood and Youth*, Chapter 4, p. 67.
11. John Burroughs, "The Bluebird", *Bird Stories from Burroughs*, Houghton Mifflin, 1871, p. 13
12. John Burroughs, *The Art of Seeing Things: Essays*, Charlotte Zoe Walker (ed.), Syracuse University Press, 2001, p. 49
13. EWDB, *The Story of My Boyhood and Youth*, Chapter 2, p. 48
14. *ibid.*
15. *ibid.*, Chapter 6, p. 87
16. *ibid.*, Chapter 2, p. 47
17. *ibid.*, p. 51
18. *ibid.*, p. 49
19. *ibid.*, Chapter 3, p. 61
20. *ibid.*, p. 64
21. EWDB, *Steep Trails*, Chapter 2, p. 878
22. EWDB, *The Story of My Boyhood and Youth*, Chapter 3, p. 65
23. *ibid.*, Chapter 4, p. 73
24. *ibid.*, Chapter 5, p. 80
25. Basil Hall, *Travels in North America*, Cadell and Co., 1829, p. 135

Chapter 3

1. Paul Hatcher and Nick Battey, *Biological Diversity: Exploiters and Exploited*, Wiley-Backwell, 2011, p. 399
2. Patricia Ann Lynch and Jeremy Roberts, *Native American Mythology A–Z*, Chelsea House Publications, 2010 and S. K. Robisch, *Wolves and the Wolf Myth in American Literature*, University of Nevada Press, 2009
3. EWDB, *The Story of My Boyhood and Youth*, Chapter 6, p. 91
4. *ibid.*, p. 92
5. *ibid.*, p. 86

6. *ibid.*, Chapter 3, p. 86
7. *ibid.*, p. 92
8. *ibid.*, p. 91
9. *ibid.*, Chapter 6, p. 85
10. *ibid.*, p. 89
11. *ibid.*, p. 93
12. *ibid.*, p. 95
13. *ibid.*, Chapter 3, p. 53
14. *ibid.*, p. 54
15. *ibid.*, p. 59
16. *ibid.*, p. 53
17. *ibid.*, p. 59
18. Arthur Schopenhauer, *On the Basis of Morality*, Berghahn Books, 1840, p. 115
19. Darwin's Beagle Notebooks (1837), quoted in *The Environmental Handbook of Environmental Sociology*, Michael Redclift and Graham Woodgate (eds.), 2010, p. 199
20. EWDB, *The Story of My Boyhood and Youth*, Chapter 2
21. Francis Henry Allen and John Muir, *Stickeen: The Story of a Dog*, Ulan Press, 2012
22. KRS, Letter to Jeanne Carr, 7 October 1874
23. LLOW, Account of John Muir by Charles E. Vroman, a room-mate of Muir at Madison University, 1916, p. 57
24. EWDB, *The Story of My Boyhood and Youth*, Chapter 5, p. 81

Chapter 4

1. EWDB, *The Story of My Boyhood and Youth*, Chapter 6, p. 97
2. *ibid.*, Chapter 7, p. 98
3. *ibid.*, p. 99
4. KRS, Letter to Jeanne Carr, Autumn 1870
5. George Gilfillan and James Nichol, *The Poetical Works of Mark Akenside*, Aldine Poets Bell and Daldy, 1857, p. 200
6. William Stanley Braithwaite (ed.), *The Book of Georgian Verse*, Third Book, Brentano's, 1909
7. Charles W. Eliot (ed.), *The Poems and Songs of Robert Burns*, The Harvard Classics, P. F. Collier and Son, 1909–14, 144
8. John Muir, "Robert Burns", *Pasadena Evening Star*, 26 January 1907
9. "Lines Composed a Few Miles Above Tintern Abbey", 13 July 1798, William Wordsworth, *The Complete Poetical Works*, Macmillan and Co., 1888
10. *ibid.*
11. EWDB, *The Story of My Boyhood and Youth*, Chapter 7, p. 98
12. *ibid.*, p. 99
13. EWDB, *My First Summer in the Sierra*, Chapter 6, 27 July 1911

14. Widely attributed to Edison and appears in John L. Mason, *An Enemy Called Average*, Insight Publishing Group, 1990, p. 55
15. *The Collected Works of Ralph Waldo Emerson*, Vol. VII, Society and Solitude, Harvard University Press, 1871, p. 14
16. EWDB, *The Story of My Boyhood and Youth*, Chapter 7, p. 103
17. *ibid.*, Chapter 8, p. 104

Chapter 5
1. EWDB, *The Story of My Boyhood and Youth*, Chapter 8, p. 105
2. Joseph G. Baier, *John Muir's Timepieces*, Wisconsin Academy Review 45, Summer 1999:14
3. Linnie Marsh Wolfe, *Son of the Wilderness: The Life of John Muir*, A. A. Knopf, 1945, p. 60
4. Mrs D. H. Johnson, "Interesting Reminiscences of a Celebrated Naturalist", *Evening Wisconsin*, 18 February 1915
5. *ibid.*
6. Letter from John Muir to Mrs Pelton, *c.* 1861, University of the Pacific, John Muir Correspondence Collection
7. EWDB, *The Story of My Boyhood and Youth*, Chapter 8, p. 108
8. *ibid.*
9. *ibid.*, p. 110
10. LLOW, Account of John Muir by Charles E. Vroman, a room-mate of Muir at Madison University, 1916
11. Ezra Carr, "The Claims of the Natural Sciences, To Enlarged Consideration in Our Systems of Education", Calkins and Proudfit, 1856
12. KRS, Letter to Jeannie Carr, Trout Mills, 13 September 1865
13. KRS, Letter to Jeannie Carr, Yosemite, 3 April 1871
14. KRS, Letter from Jeannie Carr to John Muir, 1 May 1871
15. KRS, Letter to Jeanne Carr, 13 September 1865
16. Ralph Waldo Emerson, *From Nature*, James Munroe and Co., 1836, p. 74
17. EWDB, *The Story of My Boyhood and Youth*, Chapter 8, p. 109
18. *ibid.*, p. 111
19. "Libraries as Leven", *American Bibliopolist*, 1875
20. LLOW, Letter from John Muir to Emily Pelton, 27 February 1864

Chapter 6
1. C. S. Lewis, *Surprised By Joy: The Shape of My Early Life*, Geoffrey Bless, 1955
2. KRS, Letter to Jeanne Carr, 1866; published as "The Calypso Borealis, Botanical Enthusiasm" in *Boston Recorder*, 21 December 1866
3. KRS, Letter to Jeanne Carr, 13 September 1865
4. *ibid.*
5. KRS, Letter to Jeanne Carr, 21 January 1866

6. Statutes of the State of Illinois, Chapter CV, 1845
7. Sam F. Carman, *Indiana Forest Management History and Practices*, USDA Northern Research Station, Forestry Service, 2013
8. KRS, Letter from Jeanne Carr, 15 March 1867
9. KRS, Letter to Jeanne Carr, 3 April 1867
10. KRS, Letter from Jeanne Carr, 15 March 1867
11. KRS, Letter to Jeanne Carr, 3 April 1867
12. KRS, Letter from Jeanne Carr, 15 March 1867
13. KRS, Letter to Jeanne Carr, 6 April 1867
14. LLOW, Chapter 1, p. 155
15. KRS, Letter to Jeanne Carr, 30 August 1867
16. EWDB, *A Thousand Mile Walk to the Gulf*, Chapter 1, p. 119
17. David Henry Thoreau, *Walden,* Vol. 1, Houghton Mifflin, 1882, p. 15
18. *ibid.*, p. 129
19. "Arctic Coal Mines – The Diomede Bay Islands", *San Francisco Daily Evening Bulletin* (part 18 of 21-part series "Cruise of the Corwin"), dated 25 August 1881, published 25 October 1881
20. Lee A. Vedder, *John James Audubon and The Birds of America: A Visionary Achievement in Ornithological Illustration*, Huntington Library Press, 2006, p. 4
21. Stanley Clisby Arthur, *Audubon: An Intimate Life of The American Woodsman*, Pelican Publishing Company, 2000, p. 384
22. "The Wild Parks and Forest Reservations of the West", *The Atlantic Monthly*, Vol. 81, Issue 483, January 1898
23. EWDB, *A Thousand Mile Walk to the Gulf*, Chapter 1, 9 September
24. *ibid.*, 6 September
25. *ibid.*
26. David Henry Thoreau, *Walden, Or, Life in the Woods, Bold-faced Ideas for Living a Truly Transcendent Life*, Stirling Publishing Co., 2009, p. 328
27. JOM, Quote from 1875, p. 220
28. David Henry Thoreau, *Walden,* Vol. 1, Houghton Mifflin, 1882, p. 25
29. LLOW, p. 71
30. EWDB, *A Thousand Mile Walk to the Gulf*, Chapter 2, 12 September
31. *ibid.*, 10 September
32. *ibid.*, 11 September
33. *ibid.*, 18 September
34. *ibid.*, Chapter 3, 28 September
35. *ibid.*, 1 October

Chapter 7
1. EWDB, *A Thousand Mile Walk to the Gulf*, Chapter 5, 18 October
2. *ibid.*, Chapter 4, 9 October
3. William Wordsworth, *Preface to Lyrical Ballads*, 1800
4. EWDB, *A Thousand Mile Walk to the Gulf*, Chapter 4, 9 October

5. *ibid.*
6. KRS, Letter to Jeanne Carr, September–October 1867
7. EWDB, *A Thousand Mile Walk to the Gulf*, Chapter 5, 15 October
8. *ibid.*
9. *ibid.*
10. *ibid.*
11. U.S. Census Office, Eighth Census [1860], Population, Washington, D.C., 1864
12. EWDB, *A Thousand Mile Walk to the Gulf*, Chapter 5, 16 October
13. *ibid.*
14. *ibid.*, 18 October
15. *ibid.*, 19 October
16. *ibid.*, 16 October
17. *ibid.*, 22 October
18. Samuel Smiles, *Self-Help*, John Murray, 1868, p. 339
19. EWDB, *A Thousand Mile Walk to the Gulf*, Chapter 6, 23 October
20. Robert Burns, *Poems, Chiefly in the Scottish Dialect*, John Wilson, 1786, p. 138
21. EWDB, *A Thousand Mile Walk to the Gulf*, Chapter 6, 23 October
22. *ibid.*, Chapter 4, 9 October, p. 141
23. *ibid.*, Chapter 6, 23 October, p. 159
24. *ibid.*
25. KRS, Letter to Jeanne Carr, 18 November 1867
26. KRS, Letter from Jeanne Carr, 25 May 1868
27. EWDB, *A Thousand Mile Walk to the Gulf*, Chapter 6, 23 October
28. *ibid.*
29. *ibid.*
30. *ibid.*
31. *ibid.*, Chapter 7, p. 162
32. *ibid.*, p. 164
33. *ibid.*, 16 January
34. *ibid.*

Chapter 8
1. EWDB, *A Thousand Mile Walk to the Gulf*, Chapter 8, p. 170
2. *ibid.*, p. 173
3. *ibid.*, p. 172
4. *ibid.*
5. *ibid.*, p. 171
6. *ibid.*, p. 173
7. Forty-First Congress. Sess. III. Resolution 22, 1871
8. EWDB, *A Thousand Mile Walk to the Gulf*, Chapter 8, p. 173
9. *ibid.*, p. 174
10. *ibid.*, p. 175

11. *ibid.*
12. KRS, Letter to Jeanne Carr, 26 July 1868
13. Barry M. Pritzker, *A Native American Encyclopedia*, Oxford University Press, 2000
14. Rand Richards, *Historic San Francisco: A Concise History and Guide*, Heritage House Publishers, 1991
15. Reprinted in Steve Nicholls, *Paradise Found: Nature in America at the Time of Discovery*, University of Chicago Press, 1 August 2009
16. *California History*, Google ebook, p. 190
17. KRS, Letter from Jeanne Carr, 15 April 1867
18. EWDB, *A Thousand Mile Walk to the Gulf*, Chapter 8, p. 176
19. *ibid.*
20. *ibid.*
21. KRS, Letter to Jeanne Carr, 26 July 1868
22. EWDB, *A Thousand Mile Walk to the Gulf*, Chapter 9, p. 178
23. KRS, Letter from Jeanne Carr, 28 March 1869
24. EWDB, *A Thousand Mile Walk to the Gulf*, Chapter 9, p. 179
25. *ibid.*
26. KRS, Letter to Jeanne Carr, 24 February 1869
27. KRS, Letter to Jeanne Carr, 26 July 1868
28. EWDB, *A Thousand Mile Walk to the Gulf*, Chapter 9, p. 182
29. *ibid.*, p. 183
30. James Thurber, "The Shore and the Sea", *Further Fables for Our Time*, Hamish Hamilton, 1956

Chapter 9

1. EWDB, *The Yosemite*, Chapter 1, p. 614
2. KRS, Letter to Jeanne Carr, 7 October 1874
3. EWDB, *My First Summer in the Sierra*, Chapter 1, p. 191
4. *ibid.*, p. 194
5. *ibid.*, 6 June
6. Mary Dow Brine, "Wild Flowers", *From Gold to Grey*, Cassell, 1886
7. EWDB, *My First Summer in the Sierra*, Chapter 1, 6 June
8. *ibid.*, Chapter 10, 30 August
9. LLOW, Letter to Catherine Merrill, Yosemite Valley, 9 June 1872
10. EWDB, *My First Summer in the Sierra*, Chapter 2, 13 June
11. *ibid.*, 16 June
12. *ibid.*, Chapter 4, 14 July
13. *ibid.*, 10 July
14. *ibid.*, 9 July
15. Charles W. Eliot (ed.), *English Poetry II: From Collins to Fitzgerald*, The Harvard Classics, P. F. Collier and Son, 1909–14, p. 372

16. JOM, Excerpt from field notes written on 20 March 1869 at Smokey Jack's Sheep Camp, June 1890
17. EWDB, *My First Summer in the Sierra*, Chapter 4, 9 July
18. *ibid.*, Chapter 2, 16 June
19. *ibid.*, 18 June
20. *ibid.*, Chapter 5, 23 July
21. *ibid.*, Chapter 6, 27 July
22. KRS, Letter from Jeanne Carr, 30 July 1869
23. KRS, Letter to Jeanne Carr, 3 October 1869
24. KRS, Letter from Jeanne Carr, 30 July 1869
25. KRS, Letter to Jeanne Carr, 11 July 1869
26. KRS, Letter to Jeanne Carr, 11 July 1870
27. EWDB, *My First Summer in the Sierra*, Chapter 5, 15 July
28. *ibid.*, p. 234
29. KRS, Letter to Jeanne Carr, 6 December 1869
30. EWDB, *My First Summer in the Sierra*, Chapter 10, 31 August
31. Excerpt from "In the Heart of the Californian Alps", *Scribner's Monthly*, Vol. 20, No. 3, July 1880
32. "Among the Animals of the Yosemite", *Atlantic Monthly*, December 1898, 753
33. EWDB, *The Yosemite*, Chapter 3, p. 637
34. EWDB, *The Mountains of California*, Chapter 10, p. 399
35. EWDB, *The Yosemite*, Chapter 1, p. 628
36. KRS, Letter to Jeannie Carr, September or October 1871
37. EWDB, *The Mountains of California*, Chapter 4, p. 324
38. Stephen E. Whicher, *The Early Lectures of Ralph Waldo Emerson 1833–1836*, Harvard University Press, 1959
39. JOM, p. 436
40. EWDB, *Our National Parks*, Chapter 4, p. 513
41. *Journals of Ralph Waldo Emerson*, Vol. X, p. 385, June 1872, Digital Archives, www.perfectidius.com/Volume_10_1864-1876.pdf
42. William Frederic Badè, *The Life and Letters of John Muir*, Bâton Wicks Publications, 1996, p. 146
43. KRS, Letter to Jeanne Carr, 8 October 1872
44. *ibid.*
45. JOM, p. 86

Chapter 10

1. KRS, Letter to Dr and Mrs Carr, 3 November 1873
2. "The Hetch Hetchy Valley", *Boston Weekly Transcript*, 25 March 1973
3. "Explorations in the Great Tuolumne Cañon", *Overland Monthly*, August 1873

4. KRS, Letter to Jeanne Carr, 29 May 1870
5. United States Census of 1870
6. Data from US Census Bureau
7. Julie Husband and Jim O'Laughlin, *Daily Life in the Industrial United States, 1870–1900*, Greenwood Press, 2004, p. 2
8. Letter to Sarah Muir Galloway, 17 April 1876, reprinted in William Frederic Badè, *The Life and Letters of John Muir*, Bâton Wicks Publications, 1996, p. 221
9. EWDB, *Our National Parks*, Chapter 9, p. 579
10. EWDB, *My First Summer in the Sierra*, 24 July
11. Samuel Manning, *American Pictures Drawn with Pen and Pencil,* The Religious Tract Society, 1876, p.113
12. *Report on the Big Trees of California*, US Government Printing Office, 1900, p. 13
13. JOM, p. 191
14. "The Summer Flood of Tourists", *San Francisco Daily Evening Bulletin* (part 1 of the 11-part series "Summering in the Sierra"), dated 14 June 1875
15. "Snow-Storm on Mount Shasta", *Harper's New Monthly Magazine* , Vol. 55, No. 328, September 1877
16. JOM, p. 98
17. KRS, Letter to Jeanne Carr, 7 October 1874
18. KRS, Letter from John Muir to Daniel Muir Jr, 1 November 1871
19. Letter from Daniel Muir to John Muir, 19 March 1874, published in William Frederic Badè, *The Life and Letters of John Muir*, Houghton-Mifflin, 1924, 1:9
20. Charles Lyell, *Principles of Geology,* John Murray, Vol. 3, 1835, p. 305
21. KRS, Letter to Jeanne Carr, 11 December 1871
22. KRS, Letter from Jeanne Carr, 4 February 1872
23. KRS, Letter to Jeanne Carr, September 1874
24. KRS, Letter to Jeanne Carr, 31 July 1875
25. KRS, Letter from Jeanne Carr to Mrs Strenzel, May 1880

Chapter 11
1. EWDB, *Travels in Alaska*, Part 1, Chapter 1, p. 723
2. Letter to Dr and Mrs Strenzel, 28 January 1879, printed in William Frederic Badè, *The Life and Letters of John Muir*, Vol. 2, p. 118
3. EWDB, *Travels in Alaska*, Part 1, Chapter 1, p. 724
4. Samuel Hall Young, *Alaska Days with John Muir*, Fleming H. Revell Co., 1915, Chapter 1, p. 12
5. EWDB, *Travels in Alaska*, Chapter 2, p. 731
6. Samuel Hall Young, *Alaska Days with John Muir*, Fleming H. Revell Co., 1915, Chapter 3, p. 60
7. EWDB, *Travels in Alaska*, Chapter 2, p. 731
8. EWDB, Letter to Robert Underwood Johnson, 13 September 1889, p. 18
9. Samuel Hall Young, *Alaska Days with John Muir*, Fleming H. Revell Co.,

1915, Chapter 1, p. 24
10. EWDB, *Travels in Alaska*, Chapter 10, p. 792
11. *ibid.*, Chapter 5, p. 754
12. Louis Agassiz, *Geological Sketches,* Houghton Mifflin, 1875, p. 99
13. EWDB, *Travels in Alaska*, Chapter 11, p. 799
14. *ibid.*, Chapter 16, p. 839
15. *ibid.*, Chapter 13, p. 814
16. Francis Henry Allen and John Muir, *Stickeen: The Story of a Dog*, Ulan Press, 2012
17. William Frederic Badè (ed.), *The Cruise of the Corwin*, Houghton Mifflin, 1918, p. 155
18. LLOW, p. 798
19. William Frederic Badè (ed.), *The Cruise of the Corwin*, Houghton and Mifflin, 1917, p. 119
20. *Alaska as it was and is 1865–1895*, Annual Presidential Address delivered before the Philosophical Society of Washington, 6 December 1895

Chapter 12

1. Figures quoted and sourced in Donald Worster, *A Passion for Nature*, Oxford University Press, 2008, p. 281
2. Alhambra Creek Watershed Management Plan, April 2001
3. JOM, p. 67
4. Samuel Hall Young, *Alaska Days with John Muir*, Fleming H. Revell Co., 1915, p. 204
5. *ibid.*, p. 205
6. EWDB, *Our National Parks*, Chapter 2, p. 474
7. Daniel Muir obituary, published in *Portage Record*, 12 October 1885
8. Letter to Louie in Linnie Marsh Wolfe, *Son of the Wilderness*, A. A. Knopf, 1946, p. 240
9. EWDB, *Steep Trails*, Chapter 5, p. 909
10. John Muir, "Washington and Puget Sound", *Picturesque California*, J. Dewing Company, 1888–1890
11. Chauncey Mitchell Depew, *One Hundred Years of American Commerce 1795–1895*, D. O. Haynes and Co., 1895
12. EWDB, *Steep Trails*, Chapter 23, p. 998
13. *ibid.,* Chapter 22, p. 986
14. *ibid.*, Chapter 5, p. 900
15. "John Muir as I Knew Him", *Sierra Club Bulletin*, John Muir Memorial Number, January 1916
16. JOM, p. 282
17. LLOW, p. 588
18. *ibid.*, p. 614
19. EWDB, *Travels in Alaska*, Chapter 19, p. 862
20. JOM, p. 191

21. EWDB, *Our National Parks*, Chapter 1, p. 459
22. EWDB, *Steep Trails*, Chapter 22, p. 984
23. JOM, p. 317
24. EWDB, *Our National Parks*, Chapter 1, p. 465

Chapter 13

1. "The Hetch Hetchy Valley", *Sierra Club Bulletin*, January 1908, 211
2. Letter to J. B. McChesney, 19 September 1871, University of the Pacific Library, Holt-Atherton Special Collections
3. State of California, *Biennial Report of the Commissioners to Manage Yosemite Valley and the Mariposa Big Tree Grove for the Years 1889–90*, State Printing Office, 1890, p.15
4. John Burrough's Journal, 22 June 1896 reprinted in James Perrin Warren, *John Burroughs and the Place of Nature*, University of Georgia Press, 2010
5. EWDB, *Our National Parks*, Chapter 4, p. 513
6. *ibid.*
7. LLOW, p. 311
8. John Muir, "Robert Burns", *Pasadena Evening Star*, 26 January 1907
9. LLOW, Letter to Louie Strenzel, 13 June 1893, p. 311
10. http://vault.sierraclub.org/john_muir_exhibit/john_muir_newsletter/honegger_reminiscences.aspx
11. The National Parks and Forest Reservations address to Sierra Club meeting 1985, published in *Sierra Club Bulletin*, Vol. 1, No. 7
12. Speech to the Society of American Foresters, 1903, published in Thomas H. Russell, *Life and Work of Theodore Roosevelt*, L. H. Walter, 1919
13. EWDB, *Our National Parks*, Chapter 10, p. 604
14. *ibid.*
15. "Save the Redwoods", *Sierra Club Bulletin*, Vol. XI, No. 1, January 1920
16. EWDB, *Our National Parks*, Chapter 10, p. 601
17. Letter from President Theodore Roosevelt to John Muir, 14 March 1903, published by University of the Pacific Library Holt-Atherton Special Collections
18. Theodore Roosevelt, "John Muir – An Appreciation", *Outlook*, Vol. 109, pp. 27–28, 16 January 1915
19. LLOW, p. 375
20. Theodore Roosevelt Association Journal, 1982, Vol. 8–11, p. 156
21. Patricia O'Toole, *When Trumpets Call: Theodore Roosevelt After the White House*, Simon and Schuster, 2005, p. 205
22. KRS, Letter to John Muir from Elijah Melanthon Carr, 18 December 1903
23. JOM, p. 95
24. Charles Augustus Keeler, *San Francisco Through Earthquake and Fire*, Paul Elder and Company, 1906
25. EWDB, *The Yosemite*, Chapter 15, p. 716

26. Char Millar, *Gifford Pinchot and the Making of Modern Environmentalism*, Island Press, 2004, p. 140

27. John Muir Centre for Environmental Ethics, University of the Pacific, *John Muir Newsletter* Vol. 1, No. 2, Spring 1992

28. Quoted in Stephen R. Fox, *The American Conservation Movement*, Little Brown, 1981, p. 144

29. Letter from Marsden Manson to G. Woodruff, 6 April 1910, Bancroft Library, University of California

30. Quoted in House, Committee on the Public Lands, Granting Hetch Hetchy, p. 16

31. Letter to Helen Funk (nee Muir), May 1911 in John Muir papers, 20: 11347, www.pacific.edu/Library/Find/Holt-Atherton-Special-Collections/John-Muir-Papers.html

32. *ibid.*, 21 August 1908

33. LLOW, Letter to Mrs J. D. Hooker, 15 September 1910, p. 353

34. *San Francisco Chronicle*, Vol. 105, No. 196, 28 December 1914, p. 9

35. "John Muir as I Knew Him", *Sierra Club Bulletin*, John Muir Memorial Number, January 1916

36. *ibid.*, "To Higher Sierras"

37. Samuel Hall Young, *Alaska Days with John Muir*, Fleming H. Revell Co., 1915, p. 246

38. Donald Worster, *A Passion for Nature*, Oxford University Press, 2008, p. 331

39. "A Message of Appreciation", *Sierra Club Bulletin*, John Muir Memorial Number, January 1916

40. LLOW, p. 43

Epilogue

1. Quoted in R. Z. Sheppard, "Nature: Splendor in The Grass", *Time*, 3 September 1990

2. "The National Parks and Forest Reservations", *Sierra Club Bulletin*, 1896

3. Thomas Berry, "The Dream of the Earth: Our Way Into the Future", *Dream of the Earth*, Sierra Club Books, 1988, pp. 205–216

4. "John Muir as I Knew Him", *Sierra Club Bulletin*, John Muir Memorial Number, January 1916

5. "Our Wildlife Needs a Voice", *The Independent*, 14 September 2011

6. "John Muir as I Knew Him", *Sierra Club Bulletin*, John Muir Memorial Number, January 1916

7. "A Message of Appreciation", *Sierra Club Bulletin*, John Muir Memorial Number, January 1916

8. Lao-Tzu, Chinese philosopher, 604–531 BC

9. "Save the Redwoods", *Sierra Club Bulletin*, Vol. XI, No. 1, January 1920

10. EWDB, *My First Summer in Sierra*, Chapter 2, 23 June 1869

Index